Dreamweaver™ For Dummies®

Cheat Sheet

P9-DZO-883

Keyboard Shortcuts

Action	On Windows	On Macintosh
Align Center	Ctrl+Alt+C	⌘+Option+C
Align Left	Ctrl+Alt+L	⌘+Option+L
Align Right	Ctrl+Alt+R	⌘+Option+R
Bold	Ctrl+B	⌘+B
Check Links in Current Document	Ctrl+F7	⌘+F7
Check Links in Entire Site	Ctrl+F8	⌘+F8
Check Spelling	Shift+F7	Shift+F7
Close	Ctrl+W	⌘+W
Copy	Ctrl+C	⌘+C
Cut	Ctrl+X	⌘+X
Edit Style Sheet	Ctrl+Shift+E	⌘+Shift+E
Exit	Ctrl+Q	⌘+Q
Find	Ctrl+F	⌘+F
Heading 1	Ctrl+1	⌘+1
Heading 2	Ctrl+2	⌘+2
Heading 3	Ctrl+3	⌘+3
Heading 4	Ctrl+4	⌘+4
Indent	Ctrl+]	⌘+]
Insert Line Break	Shift+Enter	Shift+Enter
Insert Nonbreaking Space	Shift+Ctrl+Space	Option+Space
Italic	Ctrl+I	⌘+I
Launch External Editor	Ctrl+E	⌘+E
New Page	Ctrl+Shift+N	⌘+N
New Paragraph	Enter	Enter
New Window	Ctrl+N	n/a
No Formatting	Ctrl+0 (zero)	⌘+0 (zero)
Open and Close the Property Inspector	Ctrl+Shift+J	⌘+Shift+J
Open	Ctrl+O	⌘+O
Outdent	Ctrl+[	⌘+[
Paragraph	Ctrl+T	⌘+T
Paste	Ctrl+V	⌘+V
Preview in Alternate Browser	Shift+F12	Shift+F12
Preview in Primary Browser	F12	F12
Redo	Ctrl+Y	⌘+Y
Replace	Ctrl+H	⌘+H
Save All	Ctrl+Shift+S	⌘+Shift+S
Save	Ctrl+S	⌘+S
Select All	Ctrl+A	⌘+A
Switch between Document Window and HTML Inspector	Ctrl+Tab	⌘+Tab
Undo	Ctrl+Z	⌘+Z

...For Dummies®*: Bestselling Book Series for Beginners*

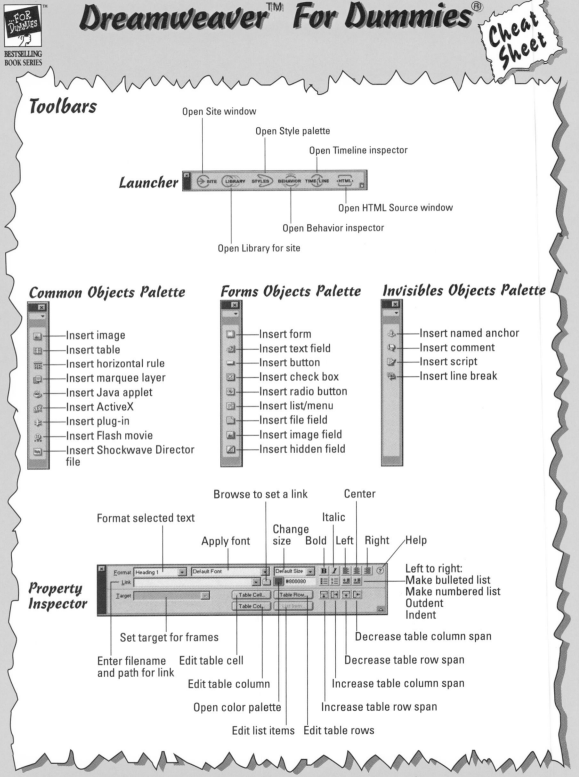

Dreamweaver™ For Dummies® Cheat Sheet

Toolbars

Launcher

- Open Site window
- Open Style palette
- Open Timeline inspector
- Open HTML Source window
- Open Behavior inspector
- Open Library for site

Common Objects Palette

- Insert image
- Insert table
- Insert horizontal rule
- Insert marquee layer
- Insert Java applet
- Insert ActiveX
- Insert plug-in
- Insert Flash movie
- Insert Shockwave Director file

Forms Objects Palette

- Insert form
- Insert text field
- Insert button
- Insert check box
- Insert radio button
- Insert list/menu
- Insert file field
- Insert image field
- Insert hidden field

Invisibles Objects Palette

- Insert named anchor
- Insert comment
- Insert script
- Insert line break

Property Inspector

- Format selected text
- Apply font
- Browse to set a link
- Change size
- Bold
- Italic
- Left
- Center
- Right
- Help
- Left to right:
  Make bulleted list
  Make numbered list
  Outdent
  Indent
- Set target for frames
- Enter filename and path for link
- Edit table cell
- Edit table column
- Open color palette
- Edit list items
- Edit table rows
- Decrease table column span
- Decrease table row span
- Increase table column span
- Increase table row span

DREAMWEAVER™
FOR
DUMMIES®

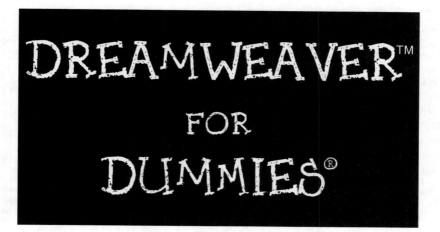

DREAMWEAVER™ FOR DUMMIES®

by Janine Warner

IDG Books Worldwide, Inc.
An International Data Group Company

Foster City, CA ♦ Chicago, IL ♦ Indianapolis, IN ♦ New York, NY

Dreamweaver™ For Dummies®

Published by
IDG Books Worldwide, Inc.
An International Data Group Company
919 E. Hillsdale Blvd.
Suite 400
Foster City, CA 94404
www.idgbooks.com (IDG Books Worldwide Web site)
www.dummies.com (Dummies Press Web site)

Library of Congress Catalog Card No.: 98-85676

ISBN: 0-7645-0407-X

Printed in the United States of America

10 9 8 7 6 5 4

1B/QR/RR/ZZ/IN

Distributed in the United States by IDG Books Worldwide, Inc.

Distributed by CDG Books Canada Inc. for Canada; by Transworld Publishers Limited in the United Kingdom; by IDG Norge Books for Norway; by IDG Sweden Books for Sweden; by IDG Books Australia Publishing Corporation Pty. Ltd. for Australia and New Zealand; by TransQuest Publishers Pte Ltd. for Singapore, Malaysia, Thailand, Indonesia, and Hong Kong; by Gotop Information Inc. for Taiwan; by ICG Muse, Inc. for Japan; by Intersoft for South Africa; by Eyrolles for France; by International Thomson Publishing for Germany, Austria and Switzerland; by Distribuidora Cuspide for Argentina; by LR International for Brazil; by Galileo Libros for Chile; by Ediciones ZETA S.C.R. Ltda. for Peru; by WS Computer Publishing Corporation, Inc., for the Philippines; by Contemporanea de Ediciones for Venezuela; by Express Computer Distributors for the Caribbean and West Indies; by Micronesia Media Distributor, Inc. for Micronesia; by Chips Computadoras S.A. de C.V. for Mexico; by Editorial Norma de Panama S.A. for Panama; by American Bookshops for Finland.

For general information on IDG Books Worldwide's books in the U.S., please call our Consumer Customer Service department at 800-762-2974. For reseller information, including discounts and premium sales, please call our Reseller Customer Service department at 800-434-3422.

For information on where to purchase IDG Books Worldwide's books outside the U.S., please contact our International Sales department at 317-596-5530 or fax 317-596-5692.

For consumer information on foreign language translations, please contact our Customer Service department at 1-800-434-3422, fax 317-596-5692, or e-mail rights@idgbooks.com.

For information on licensing foreign or domestic rights, please phone +1-650-655-3109.

For sales inquiries and special prices for bulk quantities, please contact our Sales department at 650-655-3200 or write to the address above.

For information on using IDG Books Worldwide's books in the classroom or for ordering examination copies, please contact our Educational Sales department at 800-434-2086 or fax 317-596-5499.

For press review copies, author interviews, or other publicity information, please contact our Public Relations department at 650-655-3000 or fax 650-655-3299.

For authorization to photocopy items for corporate, personal, or educational use, please contact Copyright Clearance Center, 222 Rosewood Drive, Danvers, MA 01923, or fax 978-750-4470.

is a registered trademark or trademark under exclusive license to IDG Books Worldwide, Inc. from International Data Group, Inc. in the United States and/or other countries.

About the Author

Janine Warner is an author, speaker, and Web designer. Since 1994, her company, Visiontec Communications, has designed Web sites for such diverse clients as Levi Strauss & Co., AirTouch International, Thai Farmers Bank, and the Pulitzer Prize-winning *Point Reyes Light* newspaper.

She has written six books about Web design, including *Small Business Web Strategies For Dummies* (IDG Books Worldwide, Inc.), *The Flash 2 Web Animation Book* (Ventana Press), *Conversion Techniques for Web Publishing* and *Hybrid HTML Design* (both published by New Riders, a division of Macmillan Computer Publishing). She is also a freelance magazine writer who specializes in reviewing Web design programs and contributes regularly to *Publish* magazine.

An award-winning former reporter, she earned a degree in journalism and Spanish at the University of Massachusetts and has worked for several California newspapers. She speaks fluent Spanish and was a founder and editor of *Vision Latina,* a bilingual Spanish-English newspaper serving Marin and Sonoma counties. She believes in the power of information to transform people's lives and is inspired by the potential of the Internet.

To learn more about Janine, her books, and her company, visit www.visiontec.com.

Acknowledgments

First, I want to thank Kim Ladin and Jessica Burdman for their contributions to this book. As promised, a virtual foot-kissing goes out to Kim Ladin and her wonderful Cockatiels at Riotbrrd Productions for her excellent chapter and tips on using BBEdit for the Macintosh.

Big hugs to Jessica Burdman, her puppy, and her husband for her great chapter on HomeSite for Windows, and for Jessica's technical review of the book. I always love working with you, Jess! I also want to thank Kevin Spencer for his technical review on the HomeSite and BBEdit chapters.

To Francisco Rivera, thanks for creating the images used in the DHTML samples in Chapter 13 and for all your help and support in running my Web design business while I worked on this book.

To Sheila Castelli, thanks for your wonderful friendship and for your great tips for using BBEdit and Dreamweaver on the Macintosh.

Thanks to my editors, Clark Scheffy and Ted Cains, for all the ways they found to make this a stronger and more informative book. Thanks to my agent, Margot Maley, and my acquisitions editor, Jill Pisoni, for making this happen in the first place, and thanks to everyone else at IDG Books who contributed to this project. A special thank you to the brilliant and talented Andrea Burnett, and everyone else in IDG public relations, for all the fun in New York and all your help in publicizing this book.

Love and thanks for all the support from my family. Thanks to my talented mother, Malinda McCain, for all her help as an editor on my books and articles (even though she couldn't work on this one); thanks to my father, Robin Warner, for calling me his "famous daughter," and to their wonderful partners (my "other moms") Helen Welford and Janice Webster. Thanks also to my cool big brothers, Kevin and Brian Warner, for putting my books on their bookshelves, even if they don't want to read them.

Thanks to a long list of teachers and mentors, including professors Karen List and Norm Simms from the University of Massachusetts and editor/publisher David Mitchell of the Pulitzer Prize-winning *Point Reyes Light* newspaper.

Thanks to so many supportive friends for reminding me to take breaks and long walks, and for wonderful gatherings: Ken Milburn, Adriene Josephs, Bob Cowart, Robin Cowart, Kare Anderson, Linda Langford (and all of the PINEHEADS), Victor Reyes, Angie Sanchez, Brett Phaneuf, Owen Lampe, Terry Parker, Yolanda Burrell, Yuki (the queen of my abode), and so many more.

Publisher's Acknowledgments

We're proud of this book; please register your comments through our IDG Books Worldwide Online Registration Form located at http://my2cents.dummies.com.

Some of the people who helped bring this book to market include the following:

Acquisitions, Editorial, and Media Development

Project Editors: Ted Cains, Clark Scheffy

Acquisitions Editor: Jill Pisoni

Media Development Manager: Heather Heath Dismore

Associate Permissions Editor: Carmen Krikorian

Copy Editor: Gwenette Gaddis

Technical Editors: Jessica Burdman, Kevin Spencer

Media Development Editor: Marita Ellixson

Editorial Managers: Mary C. Corder, Colleen Rainsberger

Editorial Assistant: Darren Meiss

Production

Associate Project Coordinator: Tom Missler

Layout and Graphics: Lou Boudreau, Maridee V. Ennis, Angela F. Hunckler, Todd Klemme, Drew R. Moore, Heather Pearson, Brent Savage, Janet Seib, Rashell Smith

Proofreaders: Kelli Botta, Christine Berman, Michelle Croninger, Rachel Garvey, Brian Massey, Jennifer K. Overmyer, Rebecca Senninger, Janet M. Withers

Indexer: Liz Cunningham

Special Help

Kelly Ewing, Wendy Hatch, Michelle Vukas, Publications Services

---

General and Administrative

IDG Books Worldwide, Inc.: John Kilcullen, CEO; Steven Berkowitz, President and Publisher

IDG Books Technology Publishing Group: Richard Swadley, Senior Vice President and Publisher; Walter Bruce III, Vice President and Associate Publisher; Joseph Wikert, Associate Publisher; Mary Bednarek, Branded Product Development Director; Mary Corder, Editorial Director; Barry Pruett, Publishing Manager; Michelle Baxter, Publishing Manager

IDG Books Consumer Publishing Group: Roland Elgey, Senior Vice President and Publisher; Kathleen A. Welton, Vice President and Publisher; Kevin Thornton, Acquisitions Manager; Kristin A. Cocks, Editorial Director

IDG Books Internet Publishing Group: Brenda McLaughlin, Senior Vice President and Publisher; Diane Graves Steele, Vice President and Associate Publisher; Sofia Marchant, Online Marketing Manager

IDG Books Production for Dummies Press: Debbie Stailey, Associate Director of Production; Cindy L. Phipps, Manager of Project Coordination, Production Proofreading, and Indexing; Tony Augsburger, Manager of Prepress, Reprints, and Systems; Laura Carpenter, Production Control Manager; Shelley Lea, Supervisor of Graphics and Design; Debbie J. Gates, Production Systems Specialist; Robert Springer, Supervisor of Proofreading; Kathie Schutte, Production Supervisor

Dummies Packaging and Book Design: Patty Page, Manager, Promotions Marketing

◆

The publisher would like to give special thanks to Patrick J. McGovern, without whom this book would not have been possible.

◆

Contents at a Glance

Cartoons at a Glance

By Rich Tennant

"Finally - a Web publishing program with enough patterns and colors to handle our line of clothing on the Web."

page 281

"Hold your horses. It takes time to build a home page for someone your size."

page 163

page 7

" It says, 'Seth - Please see us about your idea to wrap newsletter text around company logo.' It's signed, 'Webmaster.'"

page 103

"No, Thomas Jefferson never did 'the Grind;' however, this does show how animation can be used to illustrate American history on the Web."

page 221

"You know, I've asked you a dozen times not to animate the torches on our Web page!"

page 53

Fax: 978-546-7747 • E-mail: the5wave@tiac.net

Table of Contents

● ●

Part V: Making It Cool **221**

Chapter 13: Adding Interactivity with Dynamic HTML 223

Chapter 14: Showing Off with Multimedia 249

Introduction

*I*f the other Web design tools on the market frustrate you because they don't have all the latest features you want or they don't create clean HTML code, you're going to be delighted when you discover that Macromedia's Dreamweaver offers high-end features while still respecting your HTML code.

Dreamweaver is a relatively new player in the Web world. Macromedia kept the development under wraps for more than a year and ended up creating a tool that outshines competing programs, such as Microsoft FrontPage and Adobe PageMill. Dreamweaver has already won a slew of awards, including Best of Show at Internet World and New Media Magazine's Hyper Award for Visual Web Authoring.

I've been reviewing Web design programs since the first ones hit the market a few years ago and I can assure you that this is the best one I've ever worked with. What distinguishes Dreamweaver from other Web design programs is its sophisticated support for the latest HTML features, such as Dynamic HTML and Cascading Style Sheets, as well as its clean HTML code. Macromedia has also integrated two powerful HTML text editors — BBEdit, the most popular HTML editor for the Macintosh, and HomeSite, the powerful text editor for Windows — with the easy-to-use WYSIWYG design environment of Dreamweaver. That makes switching back and forth between Dreamweaver and a text editor a breeze and provides a best-of-both-worlds solution for developers who still like to work in the raw HTML code at least part of the time.

Dreamweaver For Dummies is for anyone who wants to build sophisticated Web pages that are easy to create and maintain. Professional or novice, this book can get you up and running quickly with the best Web design program on the market today.

About This Book

I designed *Dreamweaver For Dummies* to make your life easier as you work with this new Web program. You don't have to read this book cover to cover and memorize it. Instead, each section of the book stands alone, giving you easy answers to particular questions and step-by-step instructions for specific tasks.

Want to find out how to change the background color on a page, create a nested table, build HTML frames, or get into the really cool stuff like style sheets and layers? Then jump right in and go directly to the section that most interests you. Oh, and don't worry about keeping all those new HTML tags in your head. You don't have to memorize anything. The next time you need to do one of these tasks, just go back to that section. Feel free to dog-ear the pages, too — I promise, they won't mind!

Conventions Used in This Book

Keeping things consistent makes them easier to understand; in this book, those consistent elements are *conventions*. Notice how the word *conventions* is in italics? That's a convention I use frequently. I put new terms in italics and then define them so you know what they mean. When you have to type something in, I put it in **bold** type.

When I type URLs (Web addresses) or e-mail addresses in a block of text, they look like this: `www.visiontec.com`. Sometimes, I set URLs off on their own lines:

```
www.visiontec.com
```

That's so you can easily spot them on a page if you want to type them into your browser to visit a site. I also assume that your Web browser doesn't require the introductory `http://` for Web addresses. If you use an older browser, remember to include this before the address.

Even though Dreamweaver makes knowing HTML code virtually unnecessary, you may have to occasionally wade into HTML waters. So I set off HTML code in the same monospaced type as URLs:

```
<A HREF="http://www.visiontec.com">Visiontec</A>
```

When I introduce you to a set of features, like options in a dialog box, I set off these items with bullets so that you can tell that they're all related. When I want you to follow instructions, I use numbered steps to walk you through the process.

What You're Not to Read

Don't read anything in this book that doesn't interest you. Some of the material here is for people just starting out in Web design. If you've been at this for a while, this material may be too basic for you. For example, experienced designers may want to skip Chapter 10, unless you want a quick refresher course on the Hypertext Markup Language. If you've never worked with HTML before, Chapter 10 may be a good place to start because it can give you a foundation that can help you as you read other parts of the book.

If you're already a pro with BBEdit or HomeSite (the text editors that come bundled with Dreamweaver), then skip the chapters on these programs. If you're a graphics guru or you don't care about design issues, skip over the chapters on design and image creation.

Just pick and choose the information that you want to work with. Don't feel that you have to read everything to get the most out of it. Use this book as the reference that I intended it to be. Your time is more important than reading stuff that you don't need to know about!

Foolish Assumptions

When Macromedia developed Dreamweaver, they set out to make a professional Web development program and identified their target audience as anyone who spends more than 20 hours a week doing Web design. Fortunately for the rest of us, they also created a powerful program that's intuitive and easy to use.

Macromedia assumes that you're a *professional* developer; I don't. Even if you're new to Web design, this program can work for you and this book can make Dreamweaver easy to use. In keeping with the philosophy behind the *...For Dummies* series, this book is an easy-to-use guide designed for readers with a wide range of experience. It helps if you're interested in Web design and want to create a Web site, but that desire is all I expect from you. I show you all the steps you need to create Web pages in the chapters of the book and all the vocabulary you could need in the glossary.

If you're an experienced Web designer, *Dreamweaver For Dummies* can make a good reference for you. This book can get you up and running with this new program in a day or a weekend.

How This Book Is Organized

To ease you through the learning curve associated with any new program, I organized *Dreamweaver For Dummies* to be a complete reference. You can read it cover to cover (if you want), but you may find it more helpful to jump to the section most relevant to what you want to do at that particular moment. Each chapter walks you through the features of Dreamweaver step-by-step, providing tips and helping you understand the vocabulary of Web design.

Here's a breakdown of the parts and what you'll find in each one:

Part I: Fulfilling Your Dreams

This part introduces you to Dreamweaver and covers getting started with the basics. Chapter 1 gives you a handy reference to toolbars and menu options. Chapter 2 starts you on the road to creating your first Web site, including creating new Web pages, applying basic formatting to text, and even placing images and setting links on your pages.

Chapter 3 helps you make the transition from other Web design programs to Dreamweaver. If you started your Web site with another popular HTML authoring tool or if you're editing files that someone else created with another tool, this chapter provides tips and guidance in resolving common problems when moving from other programs to Dreamweaver. I also give you tips for using Dreamweaver with other Web design tools.

Part II: Looking Like a Million (Even on a Budget)

Planning your Web site is perhaps the most important part of Web site development — it can save you plenty of reorganizing time later. Chapter 4 starts you out on the right foot with tips on Web site management and strategies that can save you countless hours later. Chapter 5 introduces you to design concepts and the rules of Web design that can make your site look good, load fast, and keep your viewers coming back for more. Chapter 6 takes you a step farther, showing you how to add graphics to your pages. I also suggest tools and strategies that can help you create the best Web graphics for your pages.

Part III: Advancing Your Site

Part III introduces you to using Dreamweaver to create more advanced HTML features. Chapter 7 covers HTML tables, which you can use to create complex page layouts that work in the most common Web browsers. Chapter 8 tells you all you need to know about designing a site with HTML frames. This chapter helps you decide when you should and shouldn't use frames and gives you plenty of step-by-step instructions to creating HTML frames in Dreamweaver.

Chapter 9 gives you an overview of Cascading Style Sheets — how they work and how they can save you time. I describe all the style definition options available in Dreamweaver and show you how to create and apply your first styles.

Part IV: Writing It Out: The Dreamweaver Text Editors

But wait a minute, you say. I thought I wouldn't have to write HTML code if I use Dreamweaver! Well, most of the time, you don't. But for those rare times when you have to do some HTML tweaking, this part gives you the skinny on HTML and shows you the basics of using the HTML text editors that come bundled with Dreamweaver.

Chapter 10 is your HTML primer — whether you're new to HTML or a pro in need of a refresher course. Chapters 11 and 12 cover the text editors themselves, BBEdit (for the Mac) and HomeSite (for Windows). If you prefer to work in HTML code, these programs make it a breeze while still giving you all the control you desire.

Part V: Making It Cool

Now for the really fun stuff. In this part, you go for a walk on the wild side of HTML. Chapter 13 gets into Dynamic HTML's features, such as behaviors, timelines, and layers, which you can use to create animations and other interactive features. Chapter 14 helps you use Dreamweaver to show off your multimedia talents — I tell you how to link a variety of file types, from Shockwave to Java to RealAudio, to your Web pages. Chapter 15 addresses HTML forms and how you can use Dreamweaver to add interactive CGI elements — such as search engines, online discussion areas, and commerce systems — to your Web pages.

Part VI: The Part of Tens

In the Part of Tens, I tell you about ten great Web sites that were created with Dreamweaver, give you ten great Web design ideas, and highlight ten timesaving tips when using Dreamweaver.

Other stuff

Sometimes the most essential info is in the appendixes — it figures that they put it at the back of the book! Appendix A is a glossary of all the terms that you need to know when using Dreamweaver, and then some. I give you a bunch of useful Web resources in Appendix B, and don't forget about Appendix C — a guide to the CD that accompanies this book.

Icons Used in This Book

 This icon signals technical stuff that you may find informative and interesting, but isn't essential for using Dreamweaver. Feel free to skip over this stuff.

 This icon indicates a tips or technique that can save you time and money — and a headache — later.

 This icon points you toward valuable resources on the World Wide Web.

 Danger, Will Robinson! This icon warns you of any potential pitfalls — and gives you the all-important information on how to avoid them.

 When I want to point you toward something on the CD that accompanies this book, I use this icon.

 This icon tunes you into information elsewhere in the book that you may find useful.

Part I
Fulfilling Your Dreams

In this part . . .

Dreamweaver is aptly named, and Part I shows you that you're not dreaming as I introduce you to the basics of this great Web design program. You find a quick reference that outlines the features, toolbars, and menus of Dreamweaver, and then you dive right in to creating your first Web page. I also give you tips for adapting pages created in other Web design programs, such as Adobe PageMill and Microsoft FrontPage.

Chapter 1
Introducing Your New Best Friend

In This Chapter

▶ Getting started

▶ Taking it all in

▶ Introducing the features

▶ Finding the real goodies

*W*elcome to the wonderful world of Dreamweaver. If you're an experienced Web designer, you're going to love the power and sophistication of this HTML editor. If you're new to Web design, you may appreciate the simplicity and intuitive interface. Either way, this chapter starts you on your way to making the most of Dreamweaver by introducing you to the menus and palettes that make this program so useful.

Dreamweaver can help you with every aspect of Web development, from designing simple pages, to fixing links, to publishing your pages on the World Wide Web. Dreamweaver can handle the simplest HTML, as well as some of the most complex, advanced features possible on the Web, such as Cascading Style Sheets and Dynamic HTML (see Chapters 9 and 13, respectively). It also integrates a powerful HTML text editor into its easy-to-use WYSIWYG design environment. (Don't know what WYSIWYG means? Then check out the glossary in Appendix A, which defines this term and many others for you.)

If you already work in another Web design program, don't worry — you can use Dreamweaver to modify existing Web pages and can continue to develop your Web site without losing all the time you've already invested. In Chapter 3, I show you the best ways to work with files created in other common HTML editors. In this chapter, I give you an overview of Dreamweaver, introducing you to the features that make it such a powerful Web design program.

So, what's the big deal with Dreamweaver?

Dreamweaver has gotten great reviews and attracted considerable attention because it solves common problems found in other Web programs. Many Web designers complain that WYSIWYG design tools create sloppy HTML code, alter the code in existing pages, and make manually customizing pages difficult. Most of these problems stem from the fact that people who know how to write HTML code manually are used to having total control over their HTML pages. Unfortunately, many Web design programs force you to give up that control in order to have the convenience and ease of a WYSIWYG tool.

Dreamweaver gives you both by packaging an easy-to-use WYSIWYG tool with a powerful HTML text editor that you can use to work on your page. Then Dreamweaver goes a step farther with what Macromedia calls Roundtrip HTML — Dreamweaver respects your HTML and promises never to alter any work you do outside the program. A big problem with many other WYSIWYG editors is that they can dramatically change HTML code if it doesn't conform to their rules. Unfortunately, the rules on the Web constantly change, so many designers like to break the rules or at least add their own variations to the theme. If you

create a page with custom HTML code in a text editor and then open it in a program such as Adobe PageMill, you run the risk that PageMill may change your design when it tries to make your code fit the limited rules of PageMill.

Dreamweaver promises never to alter your code. That's one of the reasons it's becoming the best friend of so many professional designers. Designers can enjoy the ease of the WYSIWYG design program and add their custom HTML touches whenever they want, without having to worry about what Dreamweaver may do to their work. This wasn't easy for Macromedia — they dedicated the attention of three engineers for more than a year to this problem.

The challenge was figuring out how to display in the WYSIWYG side of the program the HTML code that was created in a text editor without ever changing it, even if Dreamweaver has never seen your unique HTML code before. Macromedia's success in solving this problem is much of the reason why Dreamweaver has gotten so much attention, won so many awards, and attracted the loyalty of even the most die-hard HTML coders.

Setting Up a Site

Before you launch into building Web pages, take some time to plan your site and think about its structure and organization. Start by thinking about the goals and objectives of your Web site. (I've included many tips and suggestions about planning your site in Chapter 4.)

This stage should also involve deciding how you want to organize the files in your site, where you're going to store images, how many directories you want, and how you can track development and accommodate growth. You also want to think about the navigation system of your site — that is, how to make it easy for visitors to move from one area of your Web site to another. In Chapter 2, I cover the site-management features of Dreamweaver before getting into the specifics of creating Web pages.

Introducing the Many Components of Dreamweaver

Dreamweaver can seem a bit overwhelming at first. It has so many features that you find lots of palettes, toolbars, and dialog boxes when you start poking around. In the next few sections, I introduce you to the basic functions and some of the terminology of Dreamweaver. I also show you where to find various features and explain, in general terms, the function of the buttons and menu options. I cover all of these features in more detail later in the book.

The Workspace

Creating a basic Web page in Dreamweaver is remarkably easy. When you launch Dreamweaver, a blank page — called the *Workspace* — appears automatically, much like when you open a program such as Microsoft Word. You can type text directly on the page and apply basic formatting, such as bold and italics, simply by selecting Text➪Style➪Bold or Text➪Style➪Italics.

You build your Web pages in the Workspace, which consists of a main window that shows the HTML page that you're working on and a number of floating palettes and windows that provide tools you can use to design and develop your pages. The following four basic components make up the Workspace.

The Document window

The largest part of the Workspace, the Document window, is where you edit and design your Web page. The Document window displays images, text, and other elements in much the same way that a Web browser displays them.

Pages viewed on the World Wide Web may not always look exactly the way they do in the Document window in Dreamweaver, because not all browsers support the same HTML features or display them equally. For best results, you should always test your work in a variety of Web browsers and design your pages to work best in the browsers that your audience most likely uses. Fortunately, Dreamweaver includes features that help you target your page designs to specific browsers. For more information on browser differences, check out Chapters 5 and 13.

The floating palettes

The floating palettes in Dreamweaver provide easy access to many of the program's features. You can move the palettes around the screen by selecting them and using drag-and-drop to reposition them. If you find that having all of these palettes open distracts you from your ability to focus on your design, you can close any or all of them, as shown in Figure 1-1. You can access all the palettes via the Window menu. If you want to open a palette, for example the Launcher, simply choose Window➪Launcher and it reappears on your screen.

The palettes are integral parts of this program, so I've included lots more information about them throughout the book. Check out the Cheat Sheet at the front of this book for a handy reference to what all these buttons do. In Chapter 2, I cover some of the most common features, such as inserting images, that you find in the Common Buttons palette. The chapter also covers linking and the anchor button that you find in the Invisibles palette. In Chapter 7, I explain how to use the table feature, and in Chapter 14, I get into using plug-in files. Chapter 15 goes over all the HTML form options available in the Forms palette.

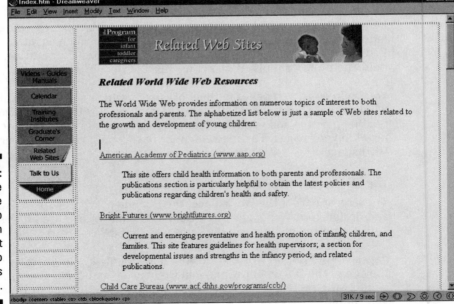

Figure 1-1:
The Workspace with a Web page in development and no palettes open.

The Object palette

This floating palette contains buttons for creating HTML elements, such as tables and layers, and for inserting images, plug-in files, and other objects. The Object palette has three sets of buttons, and you can switch from one to another by selecting the small arrow at the top-right of the palette. Figure 1-2 shows the three different palette options.

Figure 1-2: The Object palette with (left to right) the Common Buttons, the Forms Buttons, and the Invisible Buttons.

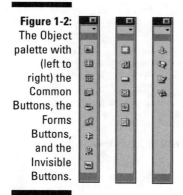

The Property inspector

This floating palette displays properties. *Properties* are usually HTML attributes used to set such object features as the alignment of an image or the size of a table cell. You can keep the Property inspector open at all times. When you select an element on a page, such as a table or an image, the inspector reveals the properties that you can change for that element. For example, Figure 1-3 shows the Property inspector as it appears when you select an image — in this case, the image located at the top of the navigation bar on the left side of the page — and reveals the attributes for that image, such as its height and width, its alignment, and the URL (*Uniform Resource Locator* or, more simply, Web address) to which it links.

At the bottom-right of the Property inspector, you'll find a small arrow. Click on it to reveal additional attributes that enable you to control more advanced features.

Figure 1-4 shows the Property inspector with a table selected. Notice that the fields in the inspector have changed to reflect the attributes for an HTML table, such as the number of columns and rows. If you want to know more about HMTL tables, check out Chapter 7.

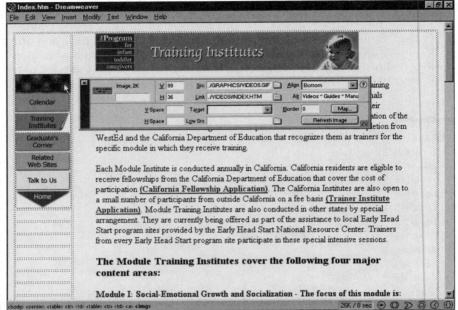

Figure 1-3:
The
Property
inspector
as it
appears
when you
select an
image.

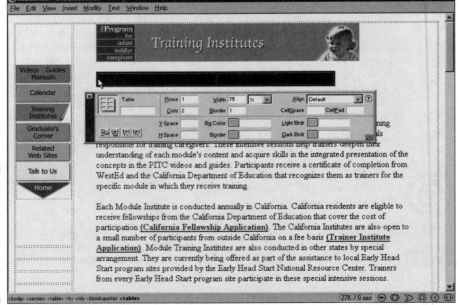

Figure 1-4:
The
Property
inspector
as it
appears
with table
selected.

The Launcher (Your way to the best goodies)

The Launcher, as shown in Figure 1-5, is another floating palette that contains a list of shortcuts that open dialog boxes for more Dreamweaver features, such as the Library, timeline, and HTML text window, all of which I cover in more detail later in this book. If you're interested in the DHTML features, such as timelines, behaviors, and styles, make sure to read Chapters 9 and 13. The following are some general descriptions of each of these elements and what they offer.

Figure 1-5:
The
Launcher.

The Site dialog box lists all the folders and files in a Web site and helps you manage the structure and organization of the site. The best way to create a site is to design it on your hard drive first, and then send all the files to a server. When you do that, you must maintain the same *relative file structure* on your hard drive as on your server. HTML links are based on the location of one file to another; if you use the same relative structure, your links function on both your hard drive and the server. The Site dialog box helps you organize your site and ensure that you don't break links when you publish your site online. The Site dialog box is also where you find FTP *(file transfer protocol)* capabilities.

By using the Connect button at the top-left of the Site dialog box, you can conveniently dial into your server. The Get and Put buttons enable you to transfer your pages back and forth between your computer and the server. The Site dialog box also provides information about the files in your site. In Chapter 2, I cover the Site dialog box features in greater detail, but for now, Figure 1-6 shows that dialog box, and Table 1-1 explains the heading above the file and folder names.

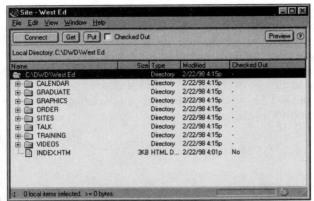

Figure 1-6:
The Site
dialog box.

Table 1-1	The Site Dialog Box
This Heading	*. . . Does This*
Name	Shows the name of the file or folder
Size	Displays the size of individual files (doesn't show a size for folders)
Type	Displays the file format (HTML, GIF, or other format type)
Modified	Shows the date the file was last altered
Checked Out	Indicates whether a file has been accessed from the server by someone else. This is especially valuable when multiple people work on a site because it can help prevent one person from overwriting someone else's work.

The Library dialog box enables you to store items in a central place so that you can easily add them to multiple pages. In Figure 1-7, you see that I moved one of the buttons from the navigation row on a Web site into the Library dialog box. I can now open other pages and drag that button from the Library onto those pages. The Library is ideal for elements that are used throughout a Web site, as well as those that you must update frequently.

The Library feature only works in conjunction with the Site feature. If youfind the Library options not available to you, make sure you follow the steps in Chapter 2 to set up a site.

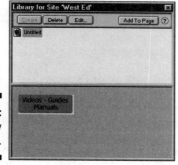

Figure 1-7:
The Library
dialog box.

The Style dialog box enables you to define styles using Cascading Style Sheets (CSS). CSS styles are similar to style sheets used in desktop publishing programs, such as QuarkXPress and Adobe PageMaker. You define a style and name it, as you see being done with "head1" in Figure 1-8. Dreamweaver provides an intuitive dialog box where you can specify the type, size, and formatting of the style. After you define a style, you can apply it to text or other elements on a page.

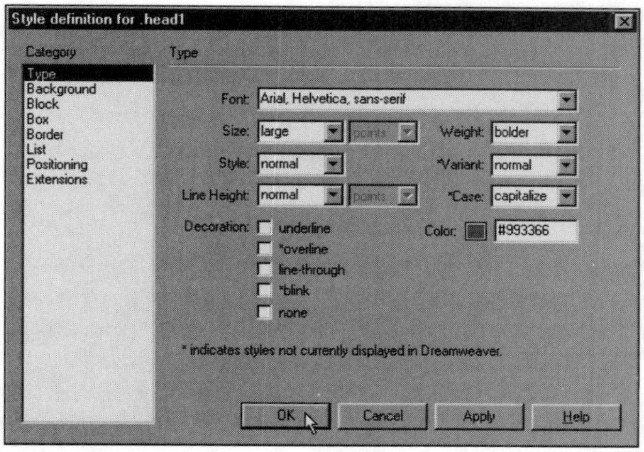

Figure 1-8:
The Style
dialog box.

Style sheets are a big timesaver because they enable you to set several attributes simultaneously by applying a defined style. They're even more useful if you decide to change a style, because all you have to do is change the definition of your style and those changes are automatically applied to every element to which you applied that particular style. Because this is such a valuable feature in Dreamweaver, I dedicate all of Chapter 9 to style sheets.

The Behaviors dialog box. Behaviors in Dreamweaver are scripts (usually written in JavaScript) that you can apply to objects to add interactivity. Essentially, a *behavior* is made up of a specified *event* that, when triggered, causes an *action*. For example, an event may be a visitor clicking on an image and the resulting action may be that the image turns into an animation and does a little dance. Another common behavior is to swap images when a visitor moves a cursor over a link. You can apply behaviors to almost any element on an HTML page, including links, images, form elements, layers, and even the entire page.

Figure 1-9 shows the Behaviors dialog box: The left pane displays events; the right pane displays the actions triggered by those events. You can find more information on creating and applying behaviors in Chapter 13.

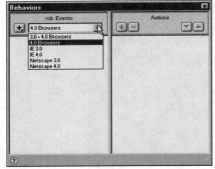

Figure 1-9:
The
Behaviors
dialog box.

The timeline. One of the more advanced features of Dreamweaver is the *timeline* (see Figure 1-10), which enables you to create animations to make page elements change over time using Dynamic HTML. For example, you can specify that an image should start in one place on a page and, as time progresses, move to another part of the page. If you have ever used a multimedia development program, such as Macromedia Director, you're probably already familiar with how timelines are used to control elements. You can even use the timeline with behaviors to make them happen in a particular sequence and time frame. I offer more information on timelines in Chapter 13.

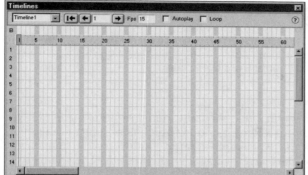

Figure 1-10:
The
timeline.

The HTML window. Dreamweaver features the best-integrated HTML text editor of any Web design program. Notice in Figure 1-11 that the highlighted text in the WYSIWYG area is also highlighted in the HTML text editor window. Changes made in one immediately appear in the other. This integration makes moving back and forth between writing HTML code manually and creating it in the graphical editing environment nearly seamless. If you want to work with a more sophisticated HTML text editor, Dreamweaver comes with BBEdit for the Macintosh and HomeSite for the PC. These programs don't provide as seamless an experience as the built-in text editor, but changes made in either of these text editors are also made in the Dreamweaver file. I cover these sophisticated HTML text editors in Chapters 11 and 12, respectively.

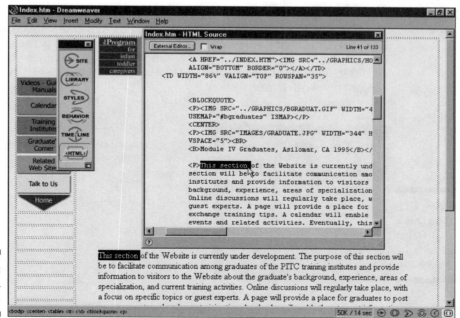

Figure 1-11:
The HTML
window.

The menu bar

At the top of the screen, the Dreamweaver menu bar provides easy access to all the features that you find in the floating palettes, as well as a few others that are available only from the menu.

The File menu

Under the File menu, you find many familiar options, such as New, Open, and Save. You also find a Revert option, which is similar to the Revert feature in Adobe Photoshop. This sophisticated "undo" feature enables you to return your page to its last-saved version if you don't like the changes you've made.

You can also find a few unique features under the File menu that are useful for checking your work in Web browsers. Most Web design programs include some way of previewing your work in a browser. Dreamweaver takes this two steps farther by enabling you to check your work in a number of browsers and even test the compatibility of your pages in different versions of different browsers.

Figure 1-12 shows the Check Target Browser(s) dialog box where you can specify a browser and version, such as Netscape 2.0 (still a widely used browser on the Web) or Internet Explorer 4.0 (which provides some of the most advanced support for DHTML features). When you do a browser check, Dreamweaver generates a report listing any HTML features you have used that the chosen browser doesn't support (see Figure 1-13).

The Edit menu

The Edit menu contains many features that you may find familiar, such as Cut, Copy, and Paste. One feature that may be new to you is the second to the last option — Launch External Editor. This feature enables you to open an HTML text editor, such as BBEdit or HomeSite, that you can use in conjunction with Dreamweaver.

Figure 1-12:
The Check
Target
Browser(s)
dialog box.

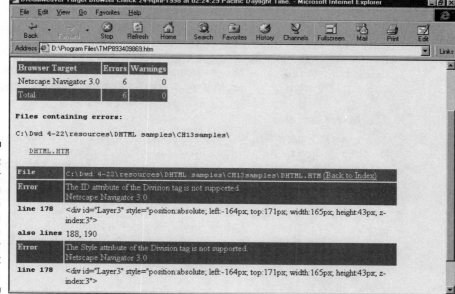

Figure 1-13:
Dreamweaver
tells you
which
elements an
alternate
browser
doesn't
support.

You can also find the preferences settings under the Edit menu. Before you start working with a new program, it's always a good idea to go through all of the preferences options to ensure that the program is set up the best way possible for you.

The View menu

The View menu provides access to some helpful design features, such as grids and rulers, shown in Figure 1-14. The View menu also gives you the option of turning on or off the borders of your HTML tables, frames, and layers. This is useful because you often want to set the border attribute of these HTML tags to zero so that they're not visible when the page displays in a browser. However, while you work on the design of your page in Dreamweaver, seeing where elements, such as tables and layers, start and stop can be very useful. Checking the frame options in the View menu enables you to see the borders in Dreamweaver even if you don't want them to be visible to your site's visitors.

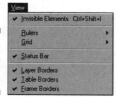

Figure 1-14:
The View
menu.

Another useful feature available from the View menu is the status bar, which is visible at the very bottom of the screen. The status bar provides short-cuts to all the features available in the Launcher palette at the far-right of the status bar. On the left-hand side, you find HTML codes that indicate the formatting applied to elements on your page. If you run your cursor over text that is bold, for example, the status bar displays <B>. This makes double-checking the kind of formatting applied to any element on your page easy.

The Insert menu

As shown in Figure 1-15, the Insert menu offers access to a number of features unique to Web design. From this menu, you can insert elements, such as a horizontal rule, a Java applet, or a form. Inserting plug-in files, such as sound files created with RealAudio, is also easy.

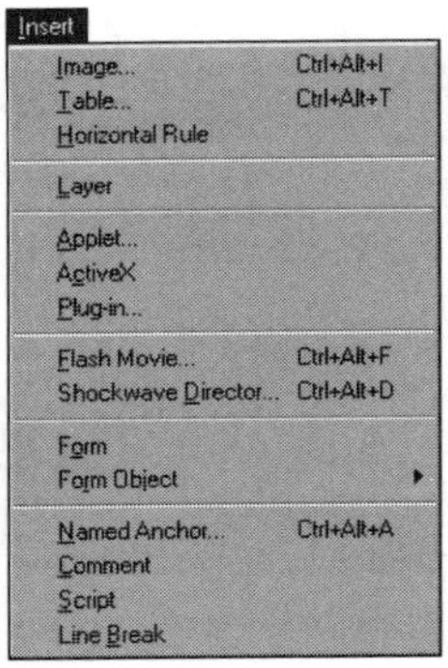

Figure 1-15:
The Insert
menu.

Insert	
Image...	Ctrl+Alt+I
Table...	Ctrl+Alt+T
Horizontal Rule	
Layer	
Applet...	
ActiveX	
Plug-in...	
Flash Movie...	Ctrl+Alt+F
Shockwave Director...	Ctrl+Alt+D
Form	
Form Object	▶
Named Anchor...	Ctrl+Alt+A
Comment	
Script	
Line Break	

Dreamweaver offers extra support for inserting Flash or Shockwave Director files (both of which are products from Macromedia). Dreamweaver enables you to place Flash movies and Director files on a Web page in a way that provides ideal support for different Web browsers. This feature helps you insert plug-in files using a combination of HTML tags that takes best advantage of the different features found in Netscape Navigator and Internet Explorer. I give lots of attention to using multimedia files, such as Shockwave and RealAudio, in Chapter 14.

The Modify menu

The Modify menu is another way to view and change object properties, such as the table attributes shown in Figure 1-16. The properties (usually called attributes in HTML) enable you to define elements on a page, setting alignment, height, width, and other specifications.

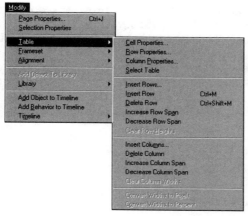

Figure 1-16:
The Modify
menu
provides
access to
table
properties.

Note that you can also set nearly all these properties, or attributes, using the Property inspector. One exception to this is the Page Properties option under the Modify menu. Changing page properties (see Figure 1-17) enables you to set link and text colors for the entire page and to specify the background color or image.

The Text menu

You can easily format text with the Text menu, using simple options, such as bold and italic, as well as more complex features, such as font styles and custom style sheets. Text formatting options have evolved dramatically on the Web. Just a couple of years ago, you didn't even have the option of specifying a particular font style or controlling leading and spacing. Today, although these options aren't yet universally supported, you have more control over the look of your Web pages than ever.

For example, if you choose a particular font for your text, that font must be available on the user's computer for the text to display properly. Because of this, HTML enables you to specify a few font possibilities to improve your

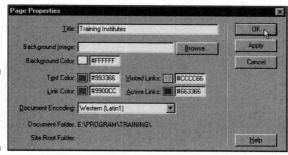

Figure 1-17:
The Page
Properties
dialog box.

odds that the font you want displays. Then the browser searches the user's computer for one of these fonts in the order you list them. Dreamweaver recognizes the importance of specifying more than one font and the safety of using the more popular fonts. In Figure 1-18, you can see the options Dreamweaver includes so that you can easily set your font to a common font and specify alternatives if your first choice isn't on your user's computer.

Figure 1-18: The Text menu makes setting multiple font options easy.

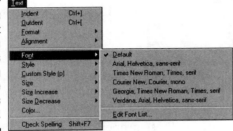

The Window menu

The Window menu enables you to control the display of palettes and dialog boxes. The menu in Figure 1-19 indicates that the three primary palettes (Objects, Properties, and the Launcher) are visible by showing check marks next to their names. To turn these features on or off, select the palette name to place (turn the feature on) or remove (turn the feature off) the check mark next to the name of the palette in the menu.

The Help menu

The Help menu provides easy access to help options, which can assist you in figuring out many features of Dreamweaver. This is also where you find access to the Dreamweaver template and example files. Templates and examples provide visual samples of common HTML designs, such as tables and frames, providing design ideas and great shortcuts to creating complex layouts.

Figure 1-19: The Window menu.

Chapter 2

Creating Your First Web Site with Dreamweaver

*I*f you're ready to dive in and start building your Web site, you've come to the right place. In this chapter, I show you how to create new Web pages or an entirely new site, and how to open an existing site so that you can add to or edit your previous work.

Before you work on individual pages, you need to set up your site by using the site-management features in Dreamweaver. Whether you're creating a new site or working on an existing site, follow the steps in the next section to get Dreamweaver set up to manage the site for you. You can use Dreamweaver without doing the initial site setup, but some of the features — such as the Library, which enables you to store elements for easy use throughout your site — won't work.

Creating a New Site

To set up a site in Dreamweaver, you simply create a folder on your hard drive in which you can keep your Web pages and then tell Dreamweaver where that folder is so that the site-management features work. If you're working on an existing site, use the same steps that follow, but instead of creating a new folder, simply direct Dreamweaver to a folder that contains the existing site. (You can find more about importing a site, as well as tips about working with sites created in other programs, in Chapter 3.) The site setup process is important because when you finish your site and upload it to your Web server, the individual pages must remain in the same relative location to each other on the Web server as on your hard drive. The site-management features in Dreamweaver can help ensure that things work properly on the server by making certain that you set links and other features correctly when you create them. That way Dreamweaver won't break links between pages when you upload your site to your Web server.

Figure 2-1 shows the Site Information dialog box that you use to locate a new or existing site. The following steps walk you through the process of using this dialog box.

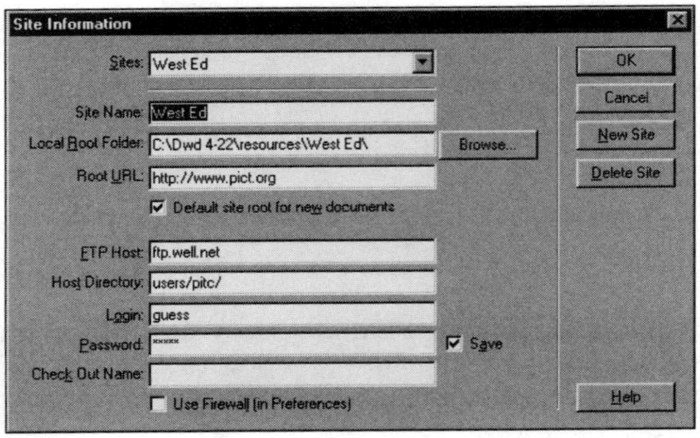

Figure 2-1:
Creating a
new site.

1. **In Windows Explorer or the Macintosh Finder, depending on the system you use, create a new folder for housing your Web site.**

   In Windows Explorer, the command is File⇨New⇨Folder.

   In the Macintosh Finder, the command is File⇨New Folder.

   You can call this folder anything you like; it's just a container that represents the server space where your Web site will reside later. All the files, subfolders, and images for your Web site should go in this folder.

2. **Choose File⇨Open Site⇨Edit Sites.**

   The Site Information dialog box appears with grayed-out boxes.

3. **Select the New Site button.**

   The Site Information dialog box changes so that you can fill in the various text box options.

4. **In the Site Name text box, enter a name for your site.**

You can call your site whatever you like. This name appears in the Sites pull-down list (the first text box in the Site Information dialog box). You use this name to select the site you want to work on when you open Dreamweaver.

5. Use the Browse button next to the Local Root Folder text box to locate the folder on your hard drive that you created in Step 1 to hold your Web site.

If you're working on an existing site, follow the same step to locate the folder that holds the site you want to work on.

6. Click to place a check mark in the box next to Default Site Root for New Documents if you want Dreamweaver to automatically save all the new pages you create to this folder.

In order for links to pages to work, you must save the pages. Selecting the Default Site Root for New Documents option avoids some hassle by ensuring that your pages are always saved in the appropriate folder. However, if you want to save your pages in subfolders or you're working on multiple Web sites, you probably want to leave this box unchecked.

7. Click OK to finish.

The rest of the options in the Site Information dialog box are only necessary if you plan to use Dreamweaver to publish your site on a remote server, such as an Internet service provider or a server in your company or your university. Most people build a site on their hard drive and then use FTP features, such as those in Dreamweaver, to transfer the site to a server when complete.

If you don't have a server yet, you can leave these fields blank and skip over the following steps. (You can always go back and fill this in later.) If you already have a server lined up for your site, ask your Internet service provider or system administrator for the access information needed to fill in this dialog box. The following steps show you what to do:

1. Next to FTP Host, enter the name of your server, such as
`ftp.att.net`.

2. Next to Host Directory, enter the path to your Web site.

The *path* represents the location of the directory where you store your site on the host server and usually looks something like this:

```
users/www/public/yourdirectoryname
```

3. Next to Login, enter your user name for your server.

4. Next to Password, enter your password.

Your password appears in the box as asterisks (*) to help protect your privacy from people looking over your shoulder.

5. **Check the Save box if you want Dreamweaver to remember your name and password so that you don't have to enter them every time you log on to your server.**

Beware that if you do this, anyone using your computer can gain access to your site.

6. **Click OK to finish.**

For more information on the FTP capabilities of Dreamweaver and on uploading your site, jump to "Putting Your Web Site Online" later in this chapter.

Creating New Pages

Every Web site begins with one page. The front page — or *home page* — of your site is a good place to start building. Dreamweaver makes it easy: When the program opens, it automatically creates a new page. If you want to create another page, simply choose Edit⇨New.

Creating a new page to start a Web site may seem obvious, but consider this: You may want to create a bunch of new pages before you get too far in your development. This enables you to organize your pages before you start setting links. After all, you can't set a link to a page that doesn't exist. So if you plan to have five links on your front page to other pages in your site, you should go ahead and create those other pages, even if you don't put anything on them.

When I first start building a Web site, I often create a bunch of pages with nothing but a simple text headline across the top of each (see Figure 2-2). I make a page like this for each of the areas of my site and often place them in subdirectories. For example, if I were creating a site for my department at a big company, I might have a page about my staff, another about what we do, and a third with information about the resources that we provide. At this initial stage, I'd create four pages — one for the front page of the site and three others for each of the subsections. With these initial pages in place, I benefit from an early idea of how I can organize the site, and I can start setting links among the main pages right away. This saves me having to go back and set those links later. (In Chapter 4, you can find many more tips about Web site planning and organization.)

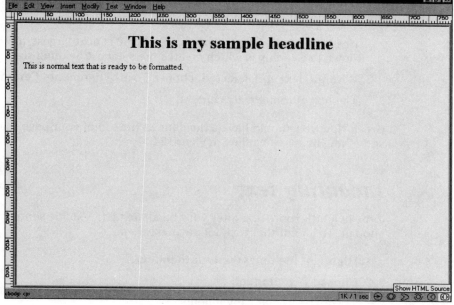

Figure 2-2:
A headline
centered
and
formatted at
the largest
headline
size, H1.

Designing your first page

Before you start throwing text, images, or other elements on your Web page, you should spend time planning how to organize your site. See Chapter 4 for more on organizing a site, and check out Chapter 5 for the rules of good Web design.

For now, I'm not going to worry too much about design or organization. Here, I want to give you a general idea about how to do basic tasks in Dreamweaver, such as formatting text and setting links. If you're ready to plunge right in, click to insert your cursor at the top of the blank page and type a little text. Type anything you like; you just need something that you can format. If you have text in a word processor or another program, you can copy and paste that text from the other program into your Dreamweaver page. After you enter the text on your page, dive into the following sections in which I show you how to play around with formatting your text.

Creating a headline

If you want to make a line of text look like the headline in Figure 2-2 by centering it and applying a heading tag to make it larger and bold, follow these steps:

1. **Highlight the text you want to format.**

2. **Choose Text➪Format➪Heading 1.**

   Heading 1 is the largest option, Heading 2 is next largest, all the way down to Heading 6, which creates the smallest heading size.

3. **With the text still selected, choose Text➪Alignment➪Center.**

   The text automatically centers.

Great! Now you should have a headline at the top of your page that looks something like the headline in Figure 2-2.

Indenting text

Type in a little more text after your headline text. A single sentence is enough. To indent that text, follow these steps:

1. **Highlight the text you want to indent.**

2. **Choose Text➪Indent.**

   The text automatically indents.

If you just want to indent a line or two, the Indent option in the Text menu is ideal. If, however, you want to create the effect of a narrower column of text on a page, an HTML table is a better option. You can find information about creating HTML tables in Chapter 7.

Adding images

Adding an image to your Web page is simple with Dreamweaver. The challenge is to create a good-looking image that loads quickly in your viewer's browser. For more information on finding and creating images, as well as keeping file sizes small, see Chapters 5 and 6. For now, I assume that you have a GIF or JPEG image file ready, and I walk you through the steps to link your image to your page. (Don't know what a GIF or JPEG is? Check out the glossary in Appendix A.)

If you don't have an image handy, you can find a few GIF and JPEG files in the Chaptr13 folder on the *Dreamweaver For Dummies* CD-ROM at the back of this book. You can use any image, as long as it's in GIF or JPEG format.

You need to do two important things before inserting an image on a Web page. First, save your page in your Web site's folder on your hard drive. Dreamweaver can't properly set the path to your image until it can identify the relative location of the page.

For the same reason, you need to save the image file in the same relative folder location as where you want it to reside in your Web site. If you move the page or image to another folder after you establish the link, you end up breaking the link. (If for some reason you do end up breaking a link, simply delete the broken image icon that appears in its place and insert the image again.)

Follow these steps to link an image to your Web page:

1. **Choose Insert⇨Image.**

   The Image dialog box opens.

2. **Click Browse.**

   A dialog box opens, displaying files and folders on your hard drive.

3. **Navigate to the folder that has the image you want to insert.**

4. **Click to select the image you want and click the Select button.**

5. **Click OK.**

   The image automatically appears on your Web page.

6. **Double-click the image on your Web page to open the Image Property inspector, as shown in Figure 2-3.**

   Use the Image Property inspector to specify image attributes, such as alignment, horizontal and vertical spacing, and alternative text.

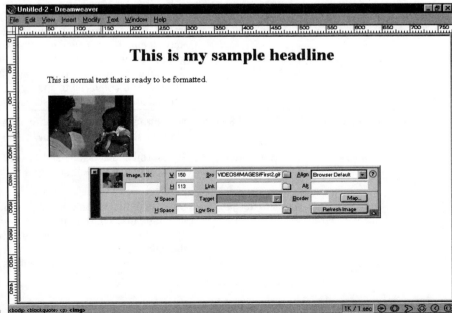

Figure 2-3: The Image Property inspector enables you to specify image attributes.

The Image Property inspector dialog box enables you to specify many attributes for images that you use in your Web site. Table 2-1 describes those attributes. If you don't see all the attributes listed in the table, click the down-pointing triangle in the bottom-right corner of the Image Property inspector.

Table 2-1		Image Attributes
Abbreviation	*Attribute*	*Function*
W	Width	Dreamweaver automatically specifies the width of the image based on the actual size of the image file.
H	Height	Dreamweaver automatically specifies the height of the image based on the actual size of the image file.
Src	Source	The source is the link or the filename and path to the image. Dreamweaver automatically sets this when you insert the image.
Link	Hyperlink	This field shows the address or path if the image links to another page. (For more about linking, see "Setting Links" later in the chapter.)
Align	Alignment	This option enables you to align the image. Text automatically wraps around images that are aligned to the right or left.
Alt	Alternate Text	The words you enter here display if the image doesn't appear on your viewer's screen because the viewer either has images turned off or can't view images. Special browsers for the blind also use this text and convert it to speech with special programs, such as *screen reader*.
V Space	Vertical Space	Measured in pixels, this setting inserts blank space above and below the image.
H Space	Horizontal Space	Measured in pixels, this setting inserts blank space to the left and right of the image.
Target	Link Target	Use this option when the image appears in a page that's part of an HTML frameset. The Target specifies the frame into which the linked page should open. I cover creating frames and how to set links in frames in Chapter 9.

Abbreviation	Attribute	Function
Low Src	Low Source	This option enables you to link two images to the same place on a page. The Low Source image loads first and is then replaced by the primary image. You may find this option especially useful when you have a large image size because you can set a smaller image (such as a black-and-white version) as the Low Source, which displays while the main image downloads. The combination of two images in this way can also create the illusion of a simple animation.
Border	Image Border	Measured in pixels, this attribute enables you to put a border around an image. I nearly always set the image border to 0 (zero) when linking an image to get rid of the colored border that automatically appears around a linked image.
Map	Image Map	The Map button enables you to turn any image into an image map with different portions linked to different Web page URLs.
Refresh Image	Refresh Image	This button resizes the image. Use this feature if your image size changes after you link it to the page and you need to reset the size so that it displays properly.

Image maps are a cool way to use graphics in your Web site. Dreamweaver provides you with the Image Map Editor dialog box, shown in Figure 2-4, as a great tool for creating an image map.

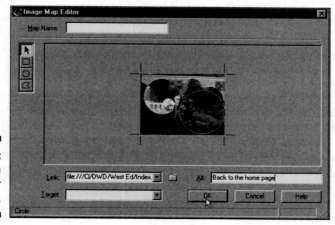

Figure 2-4:
The Image
Map Editor
dialog box.

Setting Links

Dreamweaver is truly a dream when it comes to setting your links. The most important thing to keep in mind is that a link is essentially an address (URL) that tells a viewer's browser what page to go to when the viewer selects the text or image with the link.

If that page is within your Web site, then you want to create a *relative link* that includes the path that describes how to get from the current page to the linked page. A relative link doesn't include the domain name of the server. Here's an example:

```
<A HREF="staff/boss.html">The boss</A>
```

If you link to a page on a different Web site, then you want to create an *absolute link* that includes the full Internet address of the other site. An absolute link can look like this:

```
<A HREF="http://www.visiontec.com/books">Janine's Books</A>
```

Linking pages within your Web site

Linking from one page in your Web site to another — which I call an *internal link* — is easy. The most important thing to remember is to save your pages in the folders that you want to keep them in before you start setting links. If you set a link and then move the page that you linked to a new location, you break the link.

Here's how you create an internal link:

1. **In Dreamweaver, open the page from which you want to link.**

2. **Select the text or image that you want to act as a link.**

3. **Choose <u>W</u>indow⇨<u>P</u>roperties to open the Property inspector, if it's not open already.**

4. **Click the folder icon next to the Link text field (see Figure 2-5).**

5. **Select the page to which you want your image or text to link, and then click Select.**

   The link is automatically set and the window closes. If you haven't already saved your page, a dialog box opens, explaining that you can only create a relative link after you save the page. You should always save the page you're working on before you insert images.

Figure 2-5:
Linking to
another
page.

If the page is part of a frameset, use the Target field in the Property inspector to specify which frame the linked page should open into. (You find more on setting links in frames in Chapter 8.)

Setting links to named anchors within a page

Named anchor links, often called *jump links,* enable you to set a link to a specific part of a Web page. You can use named anchors to link from one page to another place on the same page, or to link from one page to a specific part of another page. To create a named anchor link, you must firsty insert a Named Anchor in the place that you wnt to link to, and then you can use that anchor to direct the browser to display a specific part of a page when it follows a link.

For example, if you want to set a link from the word *Convertible* at the top of a page to a section lower on the page that starts with the headline, "Convertible Sports Cars," you first insert a Named Anchor and then link the word *Convertible* from the top of the page to that anchor. The followin steps show you how to insert a Named Anchor and then set a link to it:

1. **Open the page in which you want to insert the Named Anchor.**

2. **Click to inset your cursor next to a word or image that you want to link to.**

   You don't need to select the word or image; you just need a reference point that displays when the link is selected. In my example, I'd place the cursor to the left of the headline "Convertible Sports Cars."

3. **Choose Insert⇨ Named Anchor.**

   The Insert Named Anchor dialog box appears.

4. **Enter a name for the anchor.**

   You can name anchors anything you want: just make sure you use a different named for each anchor on the same page. Then make sure you remember what you call the anchor because you need to type in the anchor name to set the link (Unlike many other Web design programs, Dreamweaver doesn't automatically enter anchor names). In my example, I would choose convertible as the anchor name.

5. Click OK.

The dialog box closes and a small anchor icon appears on the page where you inserted the anchor name. You can move an anchor name by clicking on the anchor icon and dragging it to another location on the page.

If you're curious about what this Named Anchor looks like in HTML, here's the code that would appear before the headline in my example:

```
<A NAME=convertible></A>
```

6. To set a link to the Named Anchor location, click to select the text or image that you wan to link from.

You can link to a Named Anchor from anywhere else on the same page or from another page. In my example, I link from the word *Convertible* that appears at the top of the page to the anchor I made next to th e headline.

7. In the Property inspector, enter the pound sign (#) followed by the anchor name to the link to the anchor.

In my example, I would enter **#convertible** in the Link text box. The HTML code for this line would look like this:

```
<A HREF="#convertible">Convertible</A>
```

If you wanted to link to an anchor named convertible on another page with the filename coolcars.html, you would enter coolcars.html#convertible in the link text box.

Linking to pages outside your Web site

Linking to a page on another Web site — a link I call an *external link* — is even easier than linking to an internal link. All you need is the URL (the Web address) of the page to which you want to link, and you're most of the way there. Here's how to create the link:

1. In Dreamweaver, open the page from which you want to link.

2. Select the text or image that you want to act as a link.

3. Choose Window⇨Properties to open the Property inspector, if it's not open already.

4. Enter the URL of the page to which you want your text or image to link in the Link text field, as shown in Figure 2-6.

The link is automatically set.

Figure 2-6:
Linking to
another
Web site.

Figure 2-6:
Linking to
another
Web site.

Linking to e-mail addresses

Another common link option goes to an e-mail address. E-mail links make it easy for visitors to send you messages. I always recommend that you invite visitors to contact you because they can point out mistakes in your site and give you valuable feedback about how you can further develop your site.

Setting a link to an e-mail address is almost as easy as setting a link to another Web page. Before you start, you need to know the e-mail address to which you want to link. The only other thing you need to know is that e-mail links must begin with the code `mailto:`. Here's an example of the full line of code behind an e-mail link:

```
<A HREF="mailto:webmaster@anysite.com">Send a message to
         the boss</A>
```

To create an e-mail link in Dreamweaver, follow these steps:

1. **In Dreamweaver, open the page from which you want to link.**

2. **Select an image or highlight the text that you want to act as a link.**

3. **Choose <u>W</u>indow⇨<u>P</u>roperties to open the Property inspector, if it's not already open.**

4. **Type** mailto:, **followed by the e-mail address in the Link text field, as shown in Figure 2-7.**

   The link is automatically set. Even if the page is part of a frameset, you don't need to specify a Target for an e-mail link. When a visitor clicks an e-mail link, the browser automatically opens an e-mail message window where the user can type a subject and message before sending it.

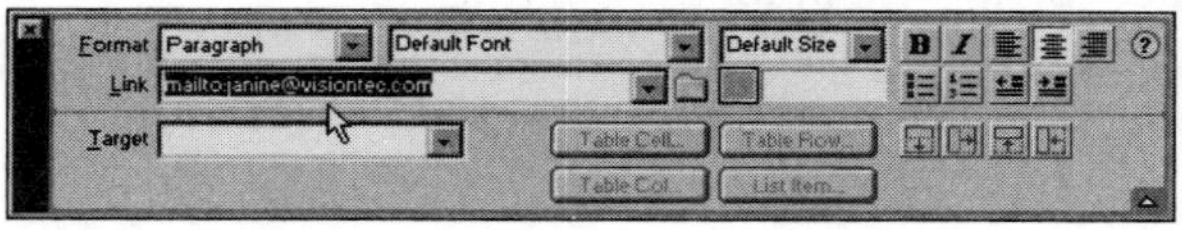

Figure 2-7:
Creating an
e-mail link.

Putting Your Web Site Online

In "Creating a New Site" earlier in this chapter, I tell you how to set up a site and enter the address, login name, and password for your server. In this section, I show you how to put pages on your server, as well as retrieve them, using the built-in FTP capabilities of Dreamweaver.

To transfer files between your hard drive and a remote server, follow these steps:

1. **Choose File⇨Open Sites.**

   The Site dialog box appears.

2. **Select the name of the site that you want to upload from the Remote Sites list.**

3. **Click the Connect button.**

   If you're not already connected to the Internet, the Connect button should start your dial-up connection. If you have trouble connecting this way, try establishing your Internet connection as you usually do to check e-mail or surf the Web, and then return to Dreamweaver and choose Connect again. After you're online, Dreamweaver should have no trouble establishing an FTP connection with your host server.

   After you establish the connection, the directories on your server appear in the left pane of the Site dialog box (see Figure 2-8). If the files on your local hard drive don't appear in the right pane of the dialog box, use the small arrow at the bottom-left of the dialog box to open the right pane.

4. **To *upload* a file (that is, transfer a file from your hard drive to your Web server), drag the file or folder from the right pane (which shows the files on your hard drive) to the left pane (which shows the files and folders on the server).**

5. **To *download* a file (that is, transfer a file from your Web server to your hard drive), drag files or folders from the left pane to the right pane.**

   The files are automatically copied when you transfer them. When the transfer is complete, you can open the files on your hard drive or use a Web browser to view them on the server.

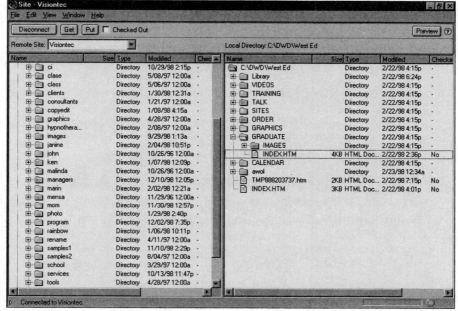

Figure 2-8:
The Site
dialog box
with an FTP
connection
established.

When you download files, Dreamweaver copies them from the remote server to your hard drive. However, you can't alter downloaded files unless you disable the write protection in Dreamweaver. To do this, turn off the Enable File Check In and Check Out options in the Site FTP Preferences available by choosing Edit➪Preferences and then selecting Site FTP from the left pane of the Preferences dialog box.

More FTP Programs

If you're not happy with the FTP capabilities in Dreamweaver, you may want to get a dedicated FTP program, such as Fetch for the Macintosh or WS_FTP for Windows. You can download either of these shareware programs from www.shareware.com.

Chapter 3

Working with Files Created in Other Visual Editors

● ●

In This Chapter

▶ Comparing Web design programs

▶ Importing files and Web sites

▶ Working with files created in other programs

▶ Editing files from FrontPage 98, PageMill, Fusion, and more

● ●

*M*oving from one computer program to another when the programs aren't compatible is a frustrating and all-too-common experience in the world of technology. Many people start a project in one program and then learn that another product is better, but they are afraid to change because doing so often requires redoing all their work in the new program. Macromedia has worked hard to minimize this problem in Dreamweaver with a feature they call Roundtrip HTML.

Roundtrip HTML means that you can create HTML pages in any program and then open them in Dreamweaver without your original HTML code being altered. This feature is important because not all Web design programs use the same rules to create HTML code, and opening a page in some Web programs can dramatically alter the design of a page. Roundtrip HTML solves this problem and makes converting and using files from other HTML editors in Dreamweaver easy.

In this chapter, I show you some of the differences among Web design programs and provide tips on how best to leverage work you've started in another HTML program when you move to Dreamweaver.

Corralling Your HTML Files

Theoretically, compatibility among Web design programs should never be a problem because HTML files are, at their heart, just ASCII (or plain-text) files. You can open an HTML file in any text editor, from Macintosh SimpleText to Windows Notepad to Microsoft Word.

However, some HTML editors take a radically different approach to Web design. NetObjects Fusion, for example, creates pages in a special format and then generates HTML pages when you publish your site. Fusion also creates very complex HTML code that can be difficult to work with in other editors. Similarly, Adobe PageMill includes special codes that aren't part of the HTML standard and are used just by PageMill to track images. PageMill also changes HTML code when it doesn't adhere to PageMill's stringent, and limited, rules.

Moving files from the Mac to the PC

HTML files are easy to transfer from one platform to another because they are simple text files. You should be able to open an HTML file created on a Macintosh computer in a text editor or Web program on a PC, and vice versa. The HTML code itself doesn't change between platforms.

However, you may have problems with links getting broken when you move an entire site to a different platform because filenames may change from lowercase to uppercase. This isn't a problem if you use a Mac or Windows NT server, but if you use a UNIX server, your link references and filenames must be the same case. Another problem that arises when moving files across platforms is that line breaks may not convert. This becomes painfully evident if you open a page in Notepad or another simple text editor that can't adjust line breaks, because all the text

on your page appears as one long line that extends off the page, making it nearly impossible to read.

A great solution to both of these problems is a shareware program called HTML Rename! You can use this handy utility to change filenames and automatically alter all corresponding link references at the same time. You can use HTML Rename! to globally change all of the filenames in a Web site, making them all uppercase or lowercase, and forcing them to conform to the filename restrictions (such as the 8.3 rule for DOS). HTML Rename! also changes line breaks to match your target operating system.

To learn more about HTML Rename!, point your browser to www.visiontec.com and download a trial version.

The Diverging "Standard"

Understanding the differences among HTML programs can get complicated, but you don't have to know much HTML to appreciate the concept. The incompatibilities among Web design programs stem from the fact that HTML isn't a clear standard that's universally supported by browsers and design programs. Instead, the Hypertext Markup Language is a rapidly changing and evolving language that suffers from too many cooks taking the recipe off in their own directions.

Efforts have been made to prevent this problem. The World Wide Web Consortium (W3C) is charged with the task of setting HTML standards. However, the W3C has moved slowly to agree on changes and early versions of the HTML standard were extremely limited. As the Web became more commercial, Netscape and, later, Microsoft pushed the standard by adding new HTML tags that only their browsers could understand. The result is that many of the HTML features in use on the Web today aren't "official" HTML, and the creators of Web design programs have had a hard time keeping up and deciding which tags to include. As a result, programs such as Adobe PageMill and Claris HomePage may feature different sets of HTML tags.

Given that no clear HTML standard exists, each company has come up with its own list of HTML tags in its program — and so the various programs often don't agree. As a result, when you open a page created in one Web design program, you may find that it includes tags that another program doesn't understand. Often the second program alters the code of the page in an effort to make it work in the new program.

Importing Web Sites

The first thing you have to do when you move a Web site from another program into Dreamweaver is to import the site by using the Site Information dialog box (see Figure 3-1). You have two options for importing: from your hard drive where you store a site under development, or from the Web server where your site resides.

Importing a site from your hard drive

Follow these steps to bring any existing site into Dreamweaver:

1. **Choose File⇨Open Site⇨Edit Sites.**

   The Site Information dialog box appears.

Figure 3-1:
You can
import an
existing site
using the
New Site
button in
the Site
Information
dialog box.

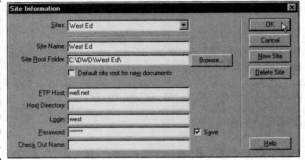

2. **Click the New Site button.**

3. **Enter a name for the site that you're importing in the text box next to Site Name.**

   Call your site whatever you like. This name is only used in the pull-down list to identify it for you. This is handy when you work on multiple sites in Dreamweaver.

4. **Use the Browse button next to the Site Root Folder text box to locate the folder on your hard drive that contains your existing Web site.**

   You can also manually enter the path to the folder by typing it into the text box.

5. **Check the box next to Default Site Root for New Documents if you want new pages you create in Dreamweaver to be saved in this folder.**

   This is a useful step because you always need to save your pages before you set links or add images to a page. If you want to save your pages in subfolders, you probably want to leave this box unchecked. Just make sure that you save your pages before you start working on them.

6. **In the text box next to FTP Host, enter the name of your server, such as** ftp.well.net.

7. **In the text box next to Host Directory, enter the path to your Web site.**

   This path represents the location of your site on the host server and usually looks something like this:

   ```
   users/www/public/yourdirectoryname
   ```

8. **In the text box next to Login, enter the login name you use to access the Web server where you store your site.**

9. **In the text box next to Password, enter your password.**

   Your password appears as asterisks (*) to help protect your privacy.

10. **Check the Save box if you want Dreamweaver to record your name and password so that you don't have to enter it every time you log on to your server.**

11. **Click OK to finish.**

Downloading a site from a Web server

If you don't already have a copy of an existing Web site on your computer's hard drive, you can use Dreamweaver to download any Web site to which you have access.

To do so, follow these steps to download the site from the server to your hard drive, and then follow the steps for importing a new site into Dreamweaver that I describe in the preceding section:

1. **Choose File⇨Open Site.**

   The Site dialog box appears.

2. **Click the Connect button to log on to your server.**

   Your computer connects to your Web site. To find out how to set up Dreamweaver to connect to your site, see Chapter 2.

3. **Click in the left pane of the Site dialog box to select the files and folders that you want to retrieve from the server.**

4. **With the files and folders that you want selected, click the Get button to copy the site from your server to your hard drive.**

   You can also drag and drop the folders and files from the left pane to the right pane.

5. **After the preceding files download to your computer, use the steps in the preceding section to set up the site in Dreamweaver.**

Working on Sites Created in Other Editors

Many Web design programs promise to make working in HTML fast and easy. If you've fallen for that promise with other programs and then found that they weren't quite as good as you originally thought, you're not alone. Fortunately, Dreamweaver is much better than other programs on the market, and to help you, Dreamweaver makes the transition from other programs easy. The following sections describe the most popular HTML editors and what you need to know if you're moving files from one of these programs to Dreamweaver.

Microsoft FrontPage 98

Microsoft FrontPage 98 offers powerful features, as well as an attractive bundle of programs. In addition to an HTML editor, shown in Figure 3-2, FrontPage 98 ships with Image Composer, a graphics program designed for creating images for the Web. FrontPage also includes *Web components,* CGI (Common Gateway Interface) scripts that can add interactive features, such as a search engine or a simple discussion area. Web components work only if their corresponding programs reside on the Web server you use, but many commercial service providers now offer FrontPage Web components. Another attractive feature in FrontPage is its site-management capabilities, shown in Figure 3-3, which make managing links and organizing files and folders easy.

However, FrontPage has some shortcomings and has frustrated many Web designers with its complexity. Because this product has so many features, many users get lost using it. If you just want to edit a single HTML file, for example, FrontPage can be very confusing because it wants to keep everything in tidy "webs" so that it can track and manage links. Dreamweaver is proving much more appealing to professional Web site developers, in part because it's more flexible whether you want to edit a single page or an entire site. FrontPage also lacks the sophistication of an integrated text editor, like HomeSite. FrontPage does include a built-in text editor, but it's a simple text editor, about as sophisticated as NotePad in Windows.

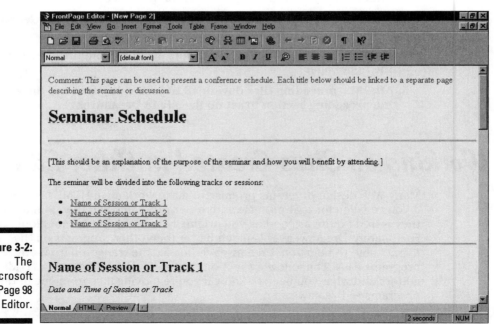

Figure 3-2: The Microsoft FrontPage 98 Editor.

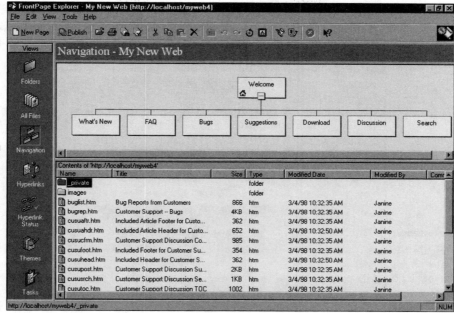

Figure 3-3:
FrontPage 98
provides
several
ways to
view and
organize
your site's
structure
and links.

If you want to move from FrontPage to Dreamweaver, make note of any FrontPage Web components you've used, such as search engines or forms. Dreamweaver doesn't offer these features. You don't have to worry about your pages being changed, so they will continue to work as they have, but you won't be able to further develop Web components in Dreamweaver.

If you've used the Dynamic HTML features in FrontPage, you need to pay special attention to them as you convert your site. Microsoft FrontPage isn't as good as Dreamweaver at creating DHTML features that work in both Netscape Navigator and Microsoft Internet Explorer, so you probably want to improve your DHTML code if you expect viewers to use any browser other than Internet Explorer 4.0. DHTML is much more complex than HTML, so you probably don't want to edit this code manually. Instead, you may find that the simplest thing to do is delete the DHTML features that you created in FrontPage and re-create them in Dreamweaver. For more on DHTML, check out Chapters 9 and 13.

Adobe PageMill 2.0

PageMill, shown in Figure 3-4, creates enough strange characters in its HTML code that the text editor BBEdit has a special "Clean Up PageMill" feature. BBEdit comes with Dreamweaver for the Macintosh; you can easily "fix" these pages before bringing them into Dreamweaver.

Figure 3-4:
The Adobe
PageMill 2.0
editor.

If you're using Dreamweaver on a PC, you get HomeSite in place of BBEdit. Unfortunately, HomeSite doesn't offer a "Clean Up PageMill" feature. However, working on PageMill files is still easy.

Despite complaints about the HTML generated by PageMill being hard to read, this program does create basic HTML pages, and the pages will open and display in Dreamweaver without any special conversion.

What you really have to be careful of with PageMill is that you don't open pages created in Dreamweaver, or in another program, in PageMill. The biggest problem with PageMill is that it alters the code of pages created in other programs if the pages don't conform to PageMill's stringent and limited rules about how HTML code should appear. For example, PageMill provides an option in its preferences that enables you to choose either the <CENTER> or the <DIV> tags for alignment. However, you can't use both in a PageMill document (even though you can do that in other programs and doing so is perfectly legitimate under the rules of HTML). I strongly recommend that you never open a page that uses DHTML in PageMill because DHTML features use the <DIV> tag in a way that PageMill doesn't recognize and the changes PageMill makes can be a real mess to clean up.

At the very least, you probably want to get rid of one tag that's unique to PageMill. The image attribute, NATURALSIZEFLAG="3", isn't part of any HTML specification. Adobe created this attribute to help PageMill track images, enabling the program to resize an image if the original changes. If you don't plan to use PageMill to do any more editing on your pages, you can search out all the instances of NATURALSIZEFLAG="3" and delete them because the attribute isn't used by any other Web design program or Web browser.

Claris HomePage 3.0

Claris HomePage, shown in Figure 3-5, is similar to Adobe PageMill (except that it creates much cleaner HTML code). A basic HTML editor, HomePage creates relatively simple HTML code with no Dynamic HTML features, no special tags, and no CGI references. Any page you create in HomePage on the Macintosh or the PC should open easily in Dreamweaver and require little or no tailoring — you can just open it and start editing in Dreamweaver.

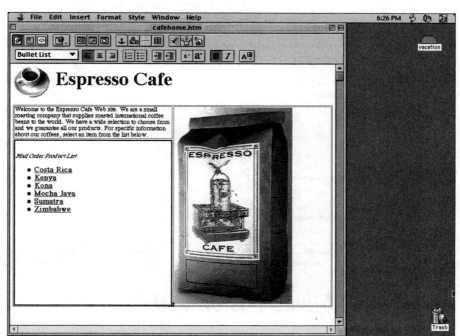

Figure 3-5:
The Claris HomePage 3.0 editor.

Symantec Visual Page 1.1

Symantec Visual Page, shown in Figure 3-6, is a simple HTML editor that provides basic editing features. Like Claris HomePage, Symantec Visual Page creates relatively simple, clean HTML code. Because Visual Page offers no CGI scripts or Dynamic HTML features, you don't have much to worry about when you use Dreamweaver to edit a Web page created in Visual Page.

Visual Page creates the simplest code possible, but it does enable you to embellish your code by working in the built-in text editor or using the Property inspector. Overall, compared to programs such as NetObjects Fusion or FrontPage, pages created in this program are easy to convert to Dreamweaver.

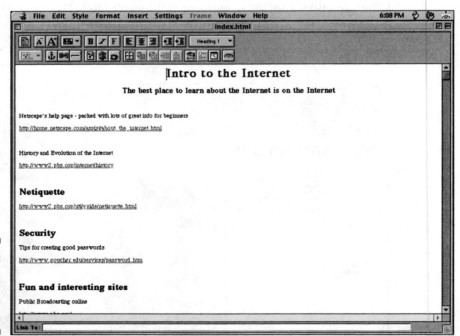

Figure 3-6:
The "Symantec" Visual Page 1.1 editor.

NetObjects Fusion 2.0.1

If you've been working in NetObjects Fusion 2.0.1, shown in Figure 3-7, you face a more dramatic transition to Dreamweaver than you would coming from any of the other HTML editors on the market. That's because Fusion takes a unique approach to Web design.

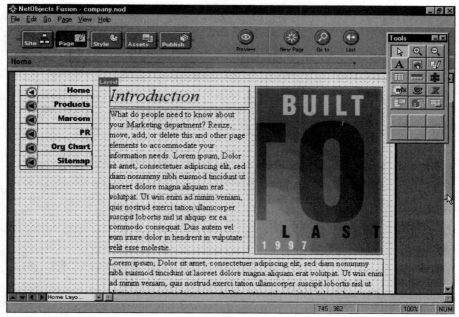

Figure 3-7:
The
NetObjects
Fusion 2.0.1
editor.

Using complex HTML tables and a transparent graphic to control spacing, Fusion provides down-to-the-pixel design control. This is an enticing feature to many graphic designers because they can create complex layouts with much less effort in Fusion. The problem is that Fusion generates very complex code to achieve this control, and that code doesn't convert well to other editors.

Unfortunately, if you want the cleanest HTML code possible, which speeds up download time and makes editing pages easier as they change and evolve, your best bet is dumping the code that Fusion creates and re-creating your designs from scratch. I'm sorry to break this to you, but if you've been using Fusion, you should probably start over with Dreamweaver. Move all your images into image directories and then start over with your design work.

GoLive CyberStudio 2.0

Available only for the Macintosh, files created in GoLive CyberStudio 2.0, shown in Figure 3-8, bring many of the same problems as those created in NetObjects Fusion 2.0.1. CyberStudio uses a grid to provide down-to-the-pixel layout control in much the same way that Fusion does.

Figure 3-8:
The GoLive
CyberStudio
2.0 editor.

Because you can see the alignment grid, you are more aware of the complex table that CyberStudio creates in the background. CyberStudio gives you the option not to use the grid, and if you've avoided using it, converting your pages to Dreamweaver should be an easier task. If, however, you've used the grid to create your Web pages, you may find that re-creating your pages from scratch in Dreamweaver is your best option. The code used to create the complex HTML tables that CyberStudio uses in its grids is difficult to edit and slows download time of your pages.

Other HTML editors

A wide range of Web design programs crowd this evolving market. I cover the most popular programs in this chapter, but you may use another program. As you consider how best to convert your work into Dreamweaver, look for unusual code combinations, stringent rules about HTML tags, and sophisticated features, such as Dynamic HTML and CGI scripts. These are the elements of an HTML page that are most likely to cause problems when you import them into Dreamweaver.

For the most part, you can open any HTML page with Dreamweaver and continue developing it with little concern. If you run into problems, remember that you always have the option of re-creating the page in Dreamweaver — a sure way to get rid of any unwanted code.

Part II
Looking Like a Million (Even on a Budget)

The 5th Wave   By Rich Tennant

"You know, I've asked you a dozen times not to animate the torches on our Web page!"

In this part . . .

No matter how great the content is on your Web site, the first thing viewers always notice is the design. This part helps you get organized and introduces you to the design rules of the Information Superhighway so that you can make your pages look great.

Chapter 4

Planning for Your Site

· ·

· ·

*B*efore you dive headfirst into developing your Web site, know this: You can save yourself tons of grief by planning ahead. You also stand a much better chance of creating an attractive Web site that's easy to maintain and update.

One of the most common mistakes new Web designers make is to plunge into developing a site without thinking through their goals, priorities, budget, and design options. In this chapter, I cover many of the common planning issues of Web design and help you start developing your site before you even start using Dreamweaver.

Preparing for Development

One of the first things I recommend is that you hold a brainstorming session with a few people who understand the goals you have for your Web site. The purpose of this session is to come up with all the possible features and elements for your Web site. A good brainstorming session is a nonjudgmental free-for-all — a chance for everyone involved to make all the suggestions that they can think of, whether realistic or not.

Not discrediting ideas at the brainstorming stage is important. Often an unrealistic idea can lead to a great idea that no one may have otherwise thought of. And if you stifle one person's creative ideas too quickly, that person may never feel inclined to come up with another.

Web site planning questionnaire

The following questions can help you assess your goals for your Web site. Your answers to these questions should shape your planning process and become an important reference anytime you're faced with a decision about your Web site.

1. Who is your target audience?

You should base all your design and navigation decisions on this answer. If you're creating a game site for school children, you need to make very different decisions than if you're creating a site for a bunch of busy CEOs. Keep your audience in mind and make sure that they can find what they want quickly. Whenever possible, gather together a group of people from your target audience to test your work as you develop your site.

2. Why do you want a Web site?

Before you even run Dreamweaver, you should spend some serious time thinking through the answer to this question. Then, you probably need to mentally prepare yourself for the fact that your answer may change and evolve over time. The important thing is to realize that the answer to this question should drive all the decisions you make about your site.

If you want a Web site because you think it may be fun, then keep that in mind as your goal and don't get too serious about it. If you want your site to generate money, then you should base your decisions on financial issues, and you need to spend time projecting costs and revenues. As you answer this question, consider what you can realistically expect to gain from your Web site. Will your Web site become a vehicle for attracting new customers, to better serve the ones you have, or both?

3. What are your three main objectives?

Do yourself a favor and define your three main objectives by writing them down on a piece of paper. Then put the list someplace where you're forced to look at it on a regular basis (tape it to the refrigerator or pin it up on the bulletin board next to your desk). Then, every time you're faced with a decision about your Web site, refer to this list and make sure that your choice fulfills your objectives.

4. What do you want people to do when they visit your site?

Build your site with clear goals in mind for your users. Do you want them to learn more about your product? Do you want them to have fun? Do you want them to purchase your product online? Keep your desired result in mind as you start on the early planning.

5. How much do you want to spend?

Web sites can become a black hole for money and time, so setting a budget is an important part of the planning process. Nobody wants to waste money developing a Web site, but sometimes if you don't spend the money required to create something valuable, you're just wasting the tight budget you *were* willing to invest. Make sure that you give your Web project the resources it deserves and then stick to your plans and budget. Remember, you can always start small and add more later if further site development proves cost-effective.

After the brainstorming session, you should have a long list of possible features to develop into your site. Now the challenge is to edit that list down to the best and most realistic ideas. Read the sidebar "Web site planning questionnaire" (earlier in this chapter) for help in defining the objectives for your Web site.

Storyboarding your site

An important part of planning for your Web site is *storyboarding*. Think of storyboarding as drawing a map or writing an outline that describes what your Web site may look like.

Storyboarding comes from the film and video industry as a way to show what appears on the movie screen as a story progresses — the storyboard is used to set up the shots. However, most storyboards are linear, so you have to adapt the storyboard model a bit to fit the Web. The challenge with storyboarding a Web site is that you don't have a clear beginning, middle, and end as with a movie. Instead, you need to allow for a wide range of approaches to make sure that you give visitors many ways to move through and find the information on your site.

You can do this kind of planning in many different ways. You can use a piece of paper and a pen, get a program that was designed for developing flow charts, such as MacFlow or Visio, or even use a program such as Adobe PageMaker or QuarkXPress to draw boxes and arrows that represent your pages. Many people create a rough draft of their page designs in Photoshop or another graphic program as part of this process. You can start by creating a simple flowchart of all the pages in the site. This chart is also called a *site architecture* by many Web developers. Then you can sketch out each individual page so that you can identify which elements will appear on each page, such as a header graphic or logo, before you actually begin creating the page.

As you develop your storyboard or outline, create a list of all of the elements you plan to include in the site. The list should be made up of the images, text, animations, sound files, or any other elements you want to include. Consider all the sections that you anticipate and divide the list of elements into sections, such as a staff section, an order section, or other logical divisions in the information you plan to present. Make sure to include the images that you already have and any other content that you have already developed, as well as the graphics and text that you may still need to create. Distinguish between these elements as well so that you can clearly identify the scope of the work that has to be done.

Paper stick 'em notes (the silly little yellow slips of sticky paper that often litter my desk) are a great tool for Web site planning because you can easily move them around on your desk or wall. Each stick 'em note can represent a page or section of the site. As you plan the structure and flow of the site, rearrange the stick 'em notes to accommodate new ideas. You may even want to use string to connect the pages and show how they're linked. Whatever works for you is fine — just make sure you take the time to think about your Web site structure and how and in what direction it'll grow *before* you start building.

Starting small and building sensibly

One way to make sure that your Web site is cost-effective is to start small and build sensibly. Fortunately, Dreamweaver makes this easier because you can so easily add new material at any time. This is another place where I appreciate Dreamweaver for being so respectful of HTML code created in other programs. If you have already started on your project in another HTML authoring tool, you'll be glad to know that you can further develop any existing site in Dreamweaver without having to completely redo your work. You'll find more information about working on sites developed in other Web design programs in Chapter 3.

Similarly, if for some reason you ever choose to work on your site in another program after developing it in Dreamweaver, you'll find that Dreamweaver creates nice clean code that you can import into any other Web design program.

With that in mind, you shouldn't feel that you need to build everything all at once for your site. Instead, I recommend what I call *phased development*. The benefit of phased development is that you build the first phase with the potential for future growth in mind, but you start relatively conservatively.

Build a small site, test and get feedback, and then grow from there. This kind of plan can make a big difference in the effectiveness of your site — and in your bottom line, because you don't blow all your budget up-front and then find out that one section works well and the other was a waste of half your budget. To implement phased growth effectively, you have to plan ahead, making sure that you start with a structure that can accommodate further growth wherever needed.

Tracking visitors to guide your site development

One of the greatest advantages of the Web, and one of the most compelling reasons for phased development, is that you can track your users and shape the development of your site based on where your customers go, what they explore most thoroughly, and what they come back to. Using records created on the server, you can see exactly how many visitors view each page in your Web site. This becomes exceptionally valuable data as you consider where to invest in further development of the site.

Most Web servers are set up to track download requests, commonly known as *hits*. Each hit represents an action by a user viewing a page, graphic, or other element in your Web site. If you study the report of hits to your site, you can see which pages are most frequently requested and how visitors move through your site. Your system administrator or Internet service provider can provide you with hit statistics. If you run your own server, you may want to use one of the reporting systems on the market. Programs to consider are Log Analyzer (Webtrends Corporation), WebTracker (Cambridge Quality Management), or SiteServer (Microsoft Corporation).

Because you get this kind of feedback right away, I usually recommend that businesses start with a general site that covers all the information that they think is most relevant but doesn't necessarily go into all the detail or complexity they want right away. Then I set a schedule that leaves some time for real users to come to the site and demonstrate, through their actions recorded by Web-tracking software, what works and what doesn't. Finally, I make time to study the data and develop a plan of action that draws on it. If one section of the site attracts only a few visitors, I may recommend eliminating that section entirely. If another section seems to get lots of attention, I know that section is probably a good place to expand.

In fact, a site that feels *incomplete* may actually be a good thing. If you're constantly adding new content, your site stays fresh and people return regularly to your Web site to see what's new. Macromedia's site is a good example of this theory put into practice. Visit their site at www.macromedia.com and find regular updates on software developments, such as upgrades for Dreamweaver, as well as tips and tricks about all their programs.

Getting direct feedback from visitors

You can also ask your visitors for direct feedback. Provide a form (such as a guest book or a survey) and, even better, an incentive for them to fill out the form. Offer a free sample or a chance to win a great prize if they take a few minutes to tell you what they think. Then ask visitors what they want to see in your site in the future, what works, and what would get them to visit your site more often. One of the most wonderful aspects of the Internet is that it's interactive. To build your Web site sensibly, take advantage of that interactivity and adapt your Web site accordingly.

Moving from Planning to Development

Up to this point, I cover the bigger site-planning issues — deciding what features to include in your site, how much it costs, and so on. From here on, I get a bit more hands-on: What does it actually mean to "build" a Web site and how can Dreamweaver help you as you move from planning to development?

In a nutshell, building a Web site involves creating separate pages and linking them to other pages. You should have a *home page* (often called the *front page*) that links to pages representing different sections of the site. Those pages, in turn, link to subsections that can then lead to additional subsections. A big part of Web site planning is determining how to divide your site into sections and deciding how pages link to one another. Dreamweaver makes it easy to create pages and set links, but how you organize your pages is up to you.

If you're still new to this, you may think that you don't need to worry much about expandability in your Web site. Think again. All good Web sites grow, and the bigger they get, the harder they are to manage. Planning the path of growth for your Web site when you get started makes a tremendous difference later. This is probably one of the most common mistakes among new designers — they jump right into the home page, add a few other pages, add a few more, throw them all in one directory, and before they know it, they're working in chaos.

Unfortunately, Dreamweaver 1.2 doesn't include any features that enable you to rearrange pages in your site, even though it does add link checking. If you just start creating new folders and moving files around, you'll break links. Dreamweaver 1.2 does help you fix links, but it can still be a messy, time-consuming process because you have to fix them one at a time. To find out more about the link-checking features in Dreamweaver, see "Finding and Fixing Broken Links" later in this chapter.

Managing your site's structure

Managing the structure of a Web site has two sides: the side that users see, which depends on how you set up links, and the behind-the-scenes side that depends on how you organize files and folders.

What the user sees

The side that the user sees is all about navigation. When users arrive at your home page, where do you direct them from there? How do they move around your site? A good Web site is designed so that users can navigate easily and intuitively and create their own path to find the information most relevant to them. As you plan, make sure that users can access key information easily from more than one place in the site. Make sure that they can move back and forth between pages and sections, and return to main pages and indexes in one step. Setting links is easy in Dreamweaver; the challenge is to make sure that they're easy for visitors to follow.

One of the most common navigational techniques for Web sites is the *menu bar,* also called a *navigation bar,* such as the one shown in Figure 4-1. Simply create a graphic or text listing with links to all the main pages, such as home, contact, products, and orders. Adding that menu bar to every page in the site provides a useful navigational tool for users because it makes getting to the main sections from any page easy.

Another technique that's especially useful for really big sites is to create a table of contents or Web site map so that users can go to one page that has links to every other page on the site.

What you see

The second side to managing your Web site structure happens behind the scenes (where your users can't see the information, but you want some kind of organizational system to remember what's what). Before you get too far into building your site with Dreamweaver, spend some time thinking about the management issues involved in keeping track of all the files you create

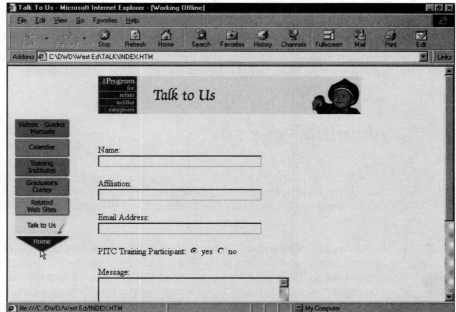

Figure 4-1:
The navigation bar on the left of this page makes it easy for visitors to move from one part of the site to another.

for your site. By files, I mean all the images, HTML pages, animations, and anything else you put in your Web site. As you create pages for your Web site, you want to keep them in folders or directories.

I've seen many Web developers get 20 or 30 pages into a growing Web site and then realize that having all their files in one folder was a mistake. In fact, it's more than a mistake; it's a mess. And to make matters worse, if you start moving things into new folders after the site grows, you have to change all the links. Not realizing this, some people start moving files around and then find that they have broken links and don't remember where things are supposed to go. Studying the site, coming up with an organizational plan, fixing all the links, and creating the structure and organization that you should have had when you started your site can take hours or even days.

So, before you build those first few pages, think about where you're likely to add content in the future. If you've been through the earlier sections in this chapter, you should have a list of all the key elements that you want to put into your site, and you should have drawn up a storyboard or outline. Use the list and storyboard to create logical sections of a site that anticipate growth. For example, you may start with one page that lists all your staff; however, after they see how cool it is, staff members may want to develop their own pages. If you're providing information for your sales team, you may find that you want a separate section for each product.

Make sure that you ask the right questions in the planning process: What will you do when you have more content? Where will you put it? And how will you find those pages again when someone wants to change some bit of information? If you work on an online magazine, for example, you want to have a plan for building in new issues, linking in new stories, and archiving old information. Whatever you do, make sure that users never get stuck on a page that goes nowhere because the link is broken or says "Under Construction."

Naming your site

You're more limited in your choices for filenames on your Web site than you are when you name most other files on your computer. Web site filenames can't have spaces or special characters, so coming up with names that you (and everyone else on your site development team) can remember can be difficult.

Dreamweaver lets you call your files any name that works on your operating system, but be aware that your Web server may use a different operating system that's more restrictive. Many of the servers on the Web are run on UNIX machines, which don't allow any special characters. UNIX systems are also case-sensitive.

Under Construction? No hard hats here!

All good Web sites are always under construction — it's just the nature of the Web. But you should build your site in such a way that you can add pages when they're ready, instead of putting up placeholders. Don't greet your viewers with a guy in a yellow hat saying "You clicked this link for no good reason. Come back another day, and maybe we'll have something for you to see." Don't use "Under Construction" signs; many people get so frustrated that they never come back.

Instead of creating "Under Construction" placeholders, create directory structures that make adding new pages later easy. You can let readers know that new things are coming by putting notices on pages that already have content — a "Come here next Thursday for a link to something even cooler" sign. But never make the user click on a link and wait for a page to load, only to find that the information isn't there yet but may be there someday.

Keeping track of the information on the pages in your Web site is much easier if you develop a naming structure that makes sense to everyone working on the project. For example, say your Web site is a newsletter that includes articles about the happenings in your town. Simple names such as fire.html and truck.html may make sense to you this week because you're familiar with the top stories. But, six months from now, if you're looking for that article on the big car accident, you may not remember that you called it fire.html. Adding dates to the end of filenames can help you identify the files that you need months — or even years — down the road. For example, fire8_12.html and truck8_19.html tell you that these articles were added in August.

Another option is to create a folder for each new update and name it with a date. For example, a folder named stories8_12 could contain all the stories from the August 12 issue. Then you can put truck.html and any other stories from that issue in the stories8_12 folder, and you can find them by date as well as by filename. Talk to other people who may work on the site and make sure that you create a system that makes sense to everyone and is easy to explain if a new person joins the team. Whatever you do, don't name files randomly and throw them all in one directory. You should also consider documenting your naming system. Printing out a list of all the filenames in your site can provide a handy reference if you're looking for a particular file. I give you more information about defining your naming system in "Creating a style guide" later in this chapter.

Organizing images

Before I go on, I want to make a few points about organizing images in a Web site. I've heard many HTML teachers and consultants suggest that you place all your images in a single folder at the top level of the directory structure and call it images or graphics. You may also find that many HTML authoring tools that provide Web site management features require you to keep all your images in one folder.

The advantage of having all your images in one folder is that the link to all your images can be the same and you have to go to only one place to look for them. However, the problem with using just one folder is that if all your images are in one place, you're likely to end up with a long list of image files, and you're likely to lose track of which image is which.

A good alternative is to store your images in a folder called images _within_ the folder that holds all the HTML files corresponding to those images. For example, keep all your staff photos for your staff pages in a folder called images within a folder called staff. If you have images that link throughout the site — a menu bar, for example — you may want to create an images folder at the top level of your directory structure for those images.

Dreamweaver makes no distinction between a folder called images and a folder by any other name, so you can call these folders whatever you like. Dreamweaver also makes it easy to set links to images, so having multiple folders for images won't make it harder to place them on your pages.

Creating a style guide

As you determine the styles and organizational system you want to use for your Web site, creating a style guide is a good idea. A _style guide_ is a reference that anyone on the project can use when a question about how something should be done comes up, such as how files should be named and organized, or the size to which image files should be limited. The bigger your Web site, the more formal your style guide should be. But, at a minimum, it needs to explain the overall structure of the Web site, common style conventions, and the file-naming system.

If you have an online discussion area, you may want to dedicate an entire section of the style guide to explaining how to manage discussions and what the rules are for contributing to a discussion. If you have a shopping area, you may need information on how new products should be added. Developing a good style guide can save you hours of cleanup time later.

Creating a test Web site

Many things can go wrong between the time you build pages on your computer and the time you put them on a server. Creating a test site enables you to check your work online before putting it at your public URL (Web address) for everyone to see.

The best way to create a test site is to put a copy of your entire site in a special folder on your Web server so that you can add new elements in relation to the entire site. After you have tested them and confirmed that your links all work and that all your files are in the right place in relation to each other, you can move the new pages into your usual Web site location on the server. If you have a big enough site and budget, you may want to have a second server to use as a test machine. This is especially useful at large companies where many people may work on the site at once. If you have a separate server where developers can build and test their work before they put it on the live server, you dramatically reduce the chance that someone will overwrite a file that isn't backed up or will cause a problem that affects the public site.

Using a test site to check server-side functions

An online test site or server is particularly useful when you're working on elements that require server-side functions, such as an online shopping system or a discussion area. With a test site, you can make sure that your server-side functions all work online as they're supposed to. It's a simple thing to set up, but many people overlook this option and run the risk of causing major problems to the site in the middle of a busy day, thereby losing visitors and their business.

When you're sure that your server-side functions work flawlessly, send your Web pages up to the directory for your main site URL.

Using a test site to encourage collaboration

Test sites are also great when you work with a remote team of developers or for clients in distant places. Even when I work with clients and coworkers that live nearby, I often load a "page in progress" into a test location and then send them the private URL to look at. Then, because my clients and colleagues all have more than one phone line these days, we can review the pages online while we talk on the phone, or trade e-mail about changes or additions without having to meet in person to review it. This is great for all kinds of remote collaboration.

Another thing that you need to keep track of when more than one person is working on a Web site is what techies call *version control*. Essentially, you don't want two people working on the same file only to find that one has inadvertently deleted the changes made by the other. This becomes even more difficult to manage when people are in remote locations and are pulling files off a server to work on them.

Although the version-control features are very limited, Dreamweaver does feature a check-in and check-out system that's managed by the FTP software built into the program. If everyone on your team uses the FTP system, you can use the check-in and check-out feature to track pages that someone else is working on. You can find more information about using this feature in Chapter 2.

One good solution to this problem is to assign just one person to manage the final revisions and the building of new pieces into the site. Then anyone else working on the project sends their work to the manager, who can assure that everything is okay before putting it online.

Creating structure out of chaos

If you started on a Web site project without realizing the potential problems I describe in this chapter, you may already be lost in dozens of HTML files, graphics, and broken links all in one or two folders. In this section, I help you get out of this mess and create some structure before you go any further with development. If you've just started using Dreamweaver to further develop your site, this is a good opportunity to clean everything up as you get to know Dreamweaver.

The first thing that you should do is sketch out a map or storyboard of your site on paper or in some graphics program so that you can get a sense of what you've created and what pages link to one another (see the section "Storyboarding your site" earlier in this chapter for the specifics). Even though you're obviously well into the process of developing your site, going through the earlier parts of this chapter still helps.

Next, make a list of all the elements — graphics, HTML pages, and other files — so that you can look at the overall picture and start to move these elements into a more organized structure. Consider the front page elements and where they link. Look at secondary pages. Then, move down the hierarchy of links. Your goal should be to turn your long list of elements into sections grouped by what they have in common.

You can then set up directories to store all the files at one hierarchical level in the links structure into the same directory. For example, if you have a page for each of five staff members that link from the main staff page, create a folder called staff and store all the staff pages in that folder.

You can also create subfolders to help you organize further. Look for logical divisions, such as issue updates, and distinguishable sections, such as product listings. Then, in a wise effort not to get back into this mess in another couple of months, consider where there may be future growth, leave room for it, and create a new folder every time you add a new section. Remember that Dreamweaver makes it easy to set links, so that you don't have to worry about making it more complex to specify the path between files when they're in multiple directories.

If you work on a Web site that you created, you have a distinct advantage in that you should have a pretty good idea of what's on every page and what the pages are called. If someone else created the site, you first face the difficult task of studying each page, checking where the links go, and then figuring out how to anticipate future growth.

Finding and Fixing Broken Links

If you're trying to rein in a chaotic Web site, or just want to check over a site because you fear that a few broken links may exist, you'll be pleased to discover the Check Links feature that Macromedia added with the release of Dreamweaver 1.2. You can use Check Links to verify the links in a single file or an entire Web site, and you can use it to automatically fix all the referring links at once.

Here's an example of what Check Links can do. Assume that you want to change the name of a page. Changing the filename isn't a problem, but what about all the links on other pages that refer to that filename. If you don't change those links when you rename the file, you break them. If only one page links to the filename you changed, then fixing it isn't such a big deal. As long as you remember what file the page links from, you can simply open the page and use the Property inspector to reset the link the same way you created the link in the first place. (I give you all the basics of link creation in Chapter 2.)

But many times, a single page in a Web site is referred to by links on many other pages. When that's the case, fixing all the link references can be time consuming, and it's all too easy to forget some of them. That's why Check Links is so helpful. First, it serves as a diagnostic tool that identifies broken links throughout the site. Then it serves as a sort of "global fix-it" tool. You can use the Check Links dialog box to identify the page a broken link should go to and then choose to have Dreamweaver automatically fix all referring links to that page.

Checking for broken links

Follow these steps to check a site for broken links:

1. **Choose File➪Open Sites.**

   The Site dialog box opens. You can also use choose Window➪Sites to open the Site dialog box.

   Link checking only works for sites listed in the Dreamweaver Site dialog box. For more information about the Site dialog box and how to create a new site, see Chapter 2. For information on how to import an existing site, see Chapter 3.

2. **From the Remote Site pull-down menu, choose the site you want to check for broken links.**

   The Site dialog box can display local sites, remote sites, or both. If you don't see the local sites in the dialog box, choose View➪Show Local to open the pane that displays the files and folders on your local hard drive. To make both panes visible in the Site dialog box, choose View➪Show Both.

3. **To check for broken links, right-click if you're working in Windows (Ctrl-click if using a Macintosh).**

   The shortcut menu, shown in Figure 4-2, appears.

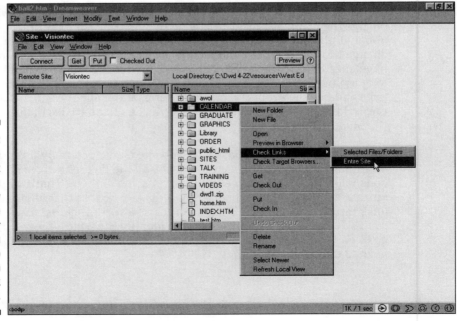

Figure 4-2: The Site dialog box enables you to identify the site and/or folders you want to check with the Link Checker.

4. Choose Check Links⇨Entire Site.

The Link Checker dialog box opens, as shown in Figure 4-3, displaying a list of filenames with broken links. This is a quick process, even on a site with hundreds of pages — Dreamweaver usually takes less than a minute to check all the links.

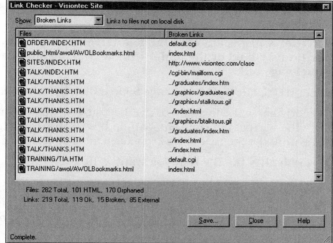

Figure 4-3:
The Link
Checker
dialog box
displays a
list of pages
with broken
links.

If you find broken links, the next section, "Fixing broken links," shows you how Dreamweaver automatically updates multiple link references.

To check the links in just one or more folders within a site, highlight the folders that you want to check in the Site dialog box and then follow Steps 3 and 4.

Fixing broken links

Broken links are one of the most embarrassing problems in Web design. After you identify a broken link in your site, you should feel compelled to fix it immediately. Nothing can turn your users off faster than clicking on a link and getting a "File Not Found" page instead. Fortunately, Dreamweaver makes fixing broken links simple by providing quick access to files with broken links and automating the process of fixing multiple links to the same file.

If you want to test your site for broken links, read "Checking for broken links" earlier in this chapter and then use the following steps to fix any broken links you find. If you discover a broken link on your own, you can always just open the page and reset the link to fix it the same way you created it. You can find information on how to create links in Chapter 2.

After using the Link Checker to identify broken links, follow these steps to use the Link Checker dialog box to fix them:

1. **Double-click a filename in the Link Checker dialog box.**

   The page and its corresponding Property inspector open, as shown in Figure 4-4.

2. **In the Property inspector, click the folder icon to the right of the Link text box (to fix a link) or the folder icon next to the Src text box to fix a broken image link.**

   The Select HTML File or Select Image Source dialog box appears.

   If you already know the location of the file that you want to link to, you can enter the correct filename and path in the Link text box to fix a link to a page, or in the Src text box to replace a missing image.

3. **Browse to identify the file that you want to link to.**

4. **Click the filename and choose the Select button. Then click OK.**

   The link automatically changes to reflect the new filename and location. If you're replacing an image, the image file reappears on the page.

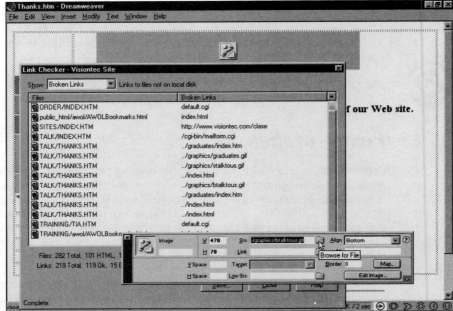

Figure 4-4:
Double-click any filename in the Link Checker to open the file and its corresponding Property inspector.

If the link that you correct appears in multiple pages, Dreamweaver prompts you with a dialog box (see Figure 4-5) asking if you want to fix the remaining broken link references to the file. Click Yes to automatically correct all other references. Click No to leave other files unchanged.

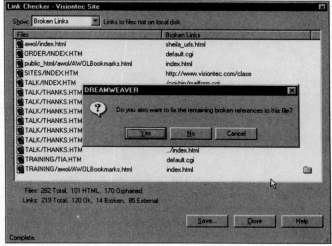

Figure 4-5:
Dream-
weaver can
automatically
fix all
references
to a broken
link.

Chapter 5
Designing for the Web

In This Chapter

▶ Taking advantage of a visual editor

▶ Setting the tone for your site

▶ Designing with Dynamic HTML (DHTML)

*I*f you're one of those code warriors who's been holding out because you could write code faster than a silly WYSIWYG editor, you're in for a treat now that you use Dreamweaver. Not only does Dreamweaver make Web design easier, it enables you to focus on design instead of type, and it makes Web design more intuitive.

In this chapter, I examine the rules of design that are best applied to the Web and show you how to create an overall look for your Web site. I also cover the kinds of features that go into good Web design. But before you get into the rules of good Web design, take a few minutes to look at a couple of Web sites that provide good examples of Web design.

Examining a Couple of Nifty Web Sites

Critiquing a Web site design and showing what's wrong with it is easy; the hard part is recognizing what features make a Web site work and incorporating those features into your own site. Here are a couple of my favorite Web sites that also happen to use good design principles.

Reefbound — MSN Australia

`reefbound.ninemsn.com.au`

Exploration Reefbound, shown in Figure 5-1, is an Australian Web site created by Massive Interactive for Microsoft Network. I love this site for its full-page images and powerful visual effects. Macromedia Flash technology makes it possible for developers to create a graphics-rich site such as this one and still enjoy short download times.

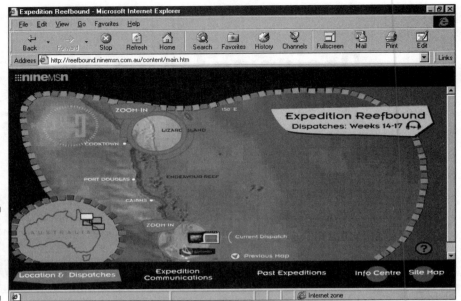

Figure 5-1:
The MSN
Australia
Reefbound
section.

Study this site to discover some great ways to take advantage of new technologies. Dreamweaver makes linking Flash files to your Web site or creating similar designs with DHTML easy. One of the features I like about this site is the *onmouseover* events (the text that pops up when you glide the mouse cursor over an element on the page) that bring up additional information about links. I also like the zoom maps that enable viewers to get more information about a specific section of a page, without leaving the page. Figure 5-5, later in this chapter, provides an excellent example of a fast-loading, zoom-image feature.

The Monterey Bay Aquarium

`www.mbayaq.org`

I like the Monterey Bay Aquarium site because the front page of this site, shown in Figure 5-2, is an excellent example of a page that combines many elements of good Web design.

Figure 5-2:
The
Monterey
Bay
Aquarium
home page.

First, notice the use of *white space* — that is, space that isn't taken up by images or text. The designers kept the front page clean and easy on the eyes by not overcrowding it with too many links. If you give users too many choices, you risk overwhelming them and then they don't make *any* choice, choosing instead to go somewhere else. The aquarium has done an excellent job of limiting its front-page links to the six main sections of the site, with a special link for new users that leads to instructions on how to use the site. As the designers added new features, such as a special section about El Niño, they created a new button style and placed those links below the main page design. I applaud these developers for such self-restraint.

The Monterey Bay Aquarium site uses another navigational feature that I recommend: text links. Notice that, at the very bottom of the front page, the links represented with graphics in the main part of the page repeat as text links. Text links not only load more quickly than graphic links, enabling experienced visitors to immediately follow a link, but they also provide an alternative for users who view Web pages with images turned off, use older browsers that don't support image maps, or are visually impaired and rely on a screen-reading device.

Applying the Rules of Web Design

Before you start designing your Web site, you should examine some of the
basic rules of good Web design. I don't mean that you should never try your
own thing, break out of the mold, and make your mark. But most artists
agree that, before you try breaking the rules, you should have a solid
understanding of what the rules are and why they work.

Create a consistent design theme

The Monterey Bay Aquarium maintains a consistent design theme throughout the site by using the same fonts and sets of colors on every page. In the
At the Core section, shown in Figure 5-3, you can see how the front page
design theme carries over to the subsequent pages. The same image that
represents the At the Core section on the front page repeats at the top of the
At the Core page, making it easy to follow your steps as you move through
the Web site.

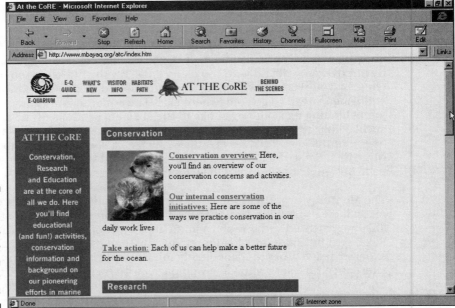

Figure 5-3:
The
Monterey
Bay
Aquarium
At the Core
page.

Develop an intuitive navigation system

An intuitive navigation system is one that's easy to use and follow. The Monterey Bay Aquarium succeeds by placing a row of navigation buttons across the top of each page in the site, making it easy for viewers find their way to any of the site's main sections. Notice also that the row of navigation buttons changes, as shown in Figures 5-3 and 5-4, to indicate the page you're viewing. This valuable technique helps viewers see where they are and quickly decide if they want to visit another section of the site.

Figure 5-4: The Monterey Bay Aquarium Visitor Information page.

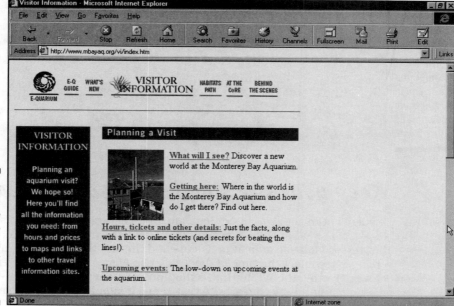

Make sure that your site loads quickly

No matter how fabulous your design, if it takes too long to download, no one will wait around to see it. Exploration Reefbound (see Figure 5-5) overcame this problem by using Macromedia Flash technology. Flash enables you to create vector-based animations, which load much faster than bitmapped images, such as GIF and JPEGs. I cover Flash and other animation programs in Chapter 14.

If you use GIF or JPEG images, reduce file sizes as much as possible. Programs such as Adobe Photoshop and Equilibrium Debabelizer can help reduce file sizes as you convert images for the Web. I include descriptions of these and other graphics programs in Chapter 6.

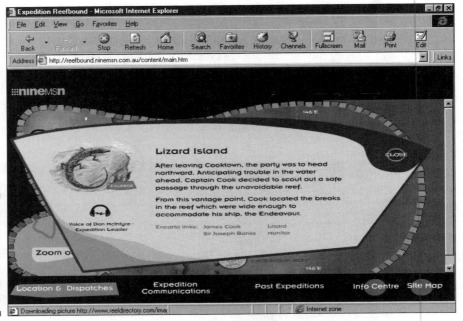

Keep your site simple and easy to read

If you want to see your tax dollars at work, visit the White House site at www.whitehouse.gov. I can't say that I'm overly impressed with the design, but the waving flag animation is cute and the fact that the front page changes to reflect the time of day (notice in Figure 5-6 that it's evening) is clever. Overall, the White House shouldn't win any fancy design awards, but it's a clear and easy-to-read site that keeps it simple — a rule too many Web designers forget.

Use lots of white space

White space isn't wasted space — it's just space with no text or images, and it doesn't even have to be white. With Web pages, which are even harder to read than print, your eyes need to rest more often. White space gives viewers a visual break and can draw the eye to particular elements on the page. The clean, crisp design created by Visiontec Communications, shown in Figure 5-7, works because the designers put lots of white space around the letters and design.

Figure 5-6:
The White House site features a simple and easy-to-read front page.

Figure 5-7:
The Visiontec Communications Web site.

Strive for original designs

Above all else, I've always admired originality. Red Sky Interactive (see Figure 5-8) has won many awards for its innovative designs and powerful compositions. This is one of the few Web design companies that consistently pushes the limit of what's possible on the Web and produces effective results. Examples of Red Sky's award-winning work include the Beyond Lands' End Web site, as shown in Figure 5-9, where visitors can track an Antarctic Expedition, watch a dog race in the Iditarod, and compare notes with one another; and Nike's Andre Agassi Web site, where you can play a challenging online game created in Shockwave. Visit Red Sky's Web site at www.redsky.com to see these and other inspirational Web design examples.

Figure 5-8:
Red Sky
Interactive
consistently
creates
original,
innovative
designs.

Test out your site

Probably the most important rule of Web design is to test, test, test. When you test your designs, you're not just making sure that you don't have broken links or missing images; you need to make sure that viewers understand your message and can easily find their way around your navigation system. The best way to ensure that you've achieved these goals is to invite

Figure 5-9: The Beyond Lands' End Web site is an example of Red Sky Interactive's award-winning designs.

people from your target audience to visit your Web site. Try to get a good cross section of potential viewers and then watch them as they move around your site. Be careful not to provide any guidance or suggestions; your goal is to see where they go on their own to make sure that they can find what they're looking for. This is a powerful exercise that can be instrumental in developing a clear and intuitive design and navigation system for your Web site.

Setting the Tone for Your Site

As you consider the look and feel of your Web site, think about what mood you want to set. Do you want a scary *X-Files* kind of look, as shown in Figure 5-10, or do you want the credibility of a respected news source, like *The New York Times,* as shown in Figure 5-11? Studying the designs of such Web sites can help you create your own compelling Web site. Notice, for example, that *The New York Times* site has a light background, making the text clean and easy to read, while the *X-Files* site has a black background, giving it a dark and mysterious feel.

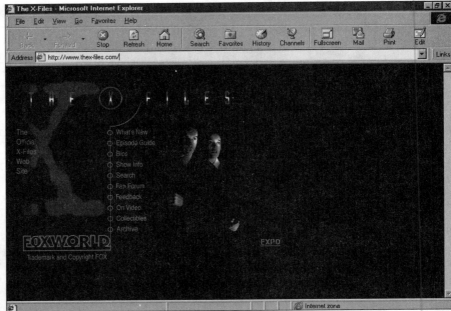

Figure 5-10:
The *X-Files*
Web site.

Figure 5-11:
*The New
York Times*
Web site.

After you determine the kind of look you want, stick with it. Choose a few colors and use them throughout your site. Pick a couple of fonts and use them consistently. The *X-Files* site uses lots of green, while *The New York Times* site uses touches of red, and both use consistent fonts. Creating a theme for your site helps you develop a clear identity and makes your site feel more familiar as visitors move through your pages.

Making the Most of the Design Features in Dreamweaver

Dreamweaver makes Web design easy by enabling you to create complex HTML features without working in HTML code. By working in the graphical design environment, you can apply interactive features and create animations using the Dreamweaver timeline feature without knowing JavaScript and manually coding sophisticated HTML features, such as Cascading Style Sheets and Dynamic HTML. These powerful design features can save you time and help you create beautiful, interactive designs.

Designing with Cascading Style Sheets

Cascading Style Sheets are a welcome addition to HTML. Microsoft introduced this feature, and Netscape quickly adopted it. Now Dreamweaver makes this timesaving HTML feature easy to use.

Cascading Style Sheets are a lot like style sheets in desktop publishing programs such as QuarkXPress and PageMaker or those found in sophisticated word-processing software. The idea is that you define a style, which can contain a variety of formatting options, and then apply that style to elements on the page.

For example, you could define a style for all your headlines, making them italic, centered, and header 1 size, and call it *headline*. Then, every time you apply the headline style to text, that text automatically appears with all three of the formatting options that you defined for the style.

You can define style sheets on a page-by-page basis or for an entire site. The latter option makes global changes possible. So, if one day you decide you want all your headlines aligned to the left instead of centered, you simply change the definition of the style, and all your headlines change automatically.

For more information on using Dreamweaver to create style sheets, check out Chapter 9.

Bringing your pages to life with DHTML

Dreamweaver makes it easy to create interactive pages by applying JavaScript to page elements in order to create *onmouseover* effects and other features that are triggered by your users. The timeline feature enables you to change the position and display of elements, such as layers, over time — a great way to create animations. Layers are part of the CSS-P (Cascading Style Sheets with Positioning) standard. Using these new HTML features, Dreamweaver provides precise positioning of elements on an HTML page and then enables you to move them over time. DHTML makes many new features possible so that your Web pages can look more like CD-ROM designs.

For lots more about what you can do with DHTML, see Chapters 9 and 13.

Chapter 6
Adding Graphics

● ●

In This Chapter

▶ Choosing a graphics program

▶ Creating images

▶ Using clip art

▶ Keeping file sizes small

▶ Linking images

● ●

*N*o matter how great the writing may be on your Web site, the graphics always get people's attention. And the key to making a good first impression is to use images that download quickly, look good, and are appropriate to your Web site.

In this chapter, I include information about choosing image programs, creating graphics, working with clip art, and keeping image file sizes small. I also show you how to link images to your pages and set a background image using Dreamweaver.

Getting Great Graphics

You want your Web graphics to look good, but where do you get them? If you have any design talent at all, you can create your own images with one of the image programs that I describe in "Creating your own images" later in this chapter. If you're not an artist, you may be better off gathering images from *clip art collections* (libraries of ready-to-use image files) and Web sites, as I describe in this section.

Unfortunately, Dreamweaver doesn't have any image creation or editing capabilities, so you have to use a different program if you want to create or edit images. The image placement features that I describe later in this chapter are all you can expect from Dreamweaver.

Buying clip art

If you don't want to hassle with creating your own images (or you lack the artistic talent like I do), you may be happy to find many sources of clip art. Clip art images, often called *royalty-free images,* are generally sold for a one-time fee that grants you all or most of the rights to use the image. (Read the agreement that comes with any art you purchase to make sure that you don't miss any exclusions or exceptions.) You can find a wide range of CD-ROMs and Web sites full of clip art, and even animations, that you can use on your Web site. Many professional designers buy clip art images and then alter them in an image program, such as Adobe Photoshop, to tailor them for a specific project or to make an image more distinct.

Some clip art suppliers include

- ✔ **Adobe Image Club Graphics (www.imageclub.com):** One of the world's largest sources of clip art, Image Club Graphics includes illustrations as well as photographs.

- ✔ **Artville (www.artville.com):** Artville (see Figure 6-1) is an excellent source of quality illustrations, and a great place to find collections of artistic drawings and computer-generated images that can provide a theme for your entire Web site.

- ✔ **Digital Stock (www.digitalstock.com):** Digital stock is another great source for royalty-free stock photographs.

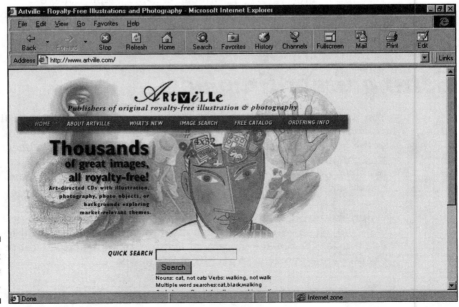

Figure 6-1:
The Artville
Web site.

✓ **PhotoDisc, Inc. (**www.photodisc.com**):** PhotoDisc, shown in Figure 6-2, is one of the leading suppliers of royalty-free digital imagery, specializing in photographs of a wide variety of subjects.

✓ **Stockbyte (**www.stockbyte.com**):** Stockbyte is a great source for international royalty-free photos.

Figure 6-2:
The
PhotoDisc
Web site.

Creating your own images

The best way to get original images is to create your own. If you're not graphically talented or inclined, consider hiring a contractor who can create images for you. If you want to create your own images but don't know where to start, the following list of image-editing programs shows you what's out there. Unless otherwise indicated, all of these programs are available for both Mac and Windows:

✓ **Adobe Photoshop 4.0 (**www.adobe.com**):** Adobe calls Photoshop the "camera of the mind." This is unquestionably the most popular image-editing program on the market. With Photoshop, you can create original artwork, correct color in photographs, retouch photographs and scanned images, and much more. Photoshop has a wealth of powerful painting and selection tools in addition to special effects and filters to create images that go beyond what you can capture on film or with classic illustration programs.

- ✔ **Adobe Illustrator 7.0** (www.adobe.com): Illustrator is the industry standard for creating illustrations. You can drag and drop illustrations that you create in Illustrator right into other Adobe programs, such as Photoshop or PageMaker. Illustrator also comes with an export feature that enables you to export your illustrations in GIF or JPEG format with a browser-friendly palette of colors so that your illustrations look great on the Web.

- ✔ **Adobe PhotoDeluxe 2.0** (www.adobe.com): Though not nearly as powerful as Photoshop, PhotoDeluxe (basically a limited and cheaper version of Photoshop) makes many tasks easier by automating common features. The program is designed to retouch photos (removing red-eye and improving color balance and contrast) and has the ability to crop and resize. You also find a collection of clip art included, as well as templates and wizards to help you create greeting cards, calendars, and more.

- ✔ **Equilibrium Debabelizer** (www.equilibrium.com): Debabelizer, by Equilibrium Technologies, is a graphics-processing system capable of handling almost every image format ever used on a computer. One of the best features of Debabelizer is its ability to convert images from just about any format to just about any other. If you have a bunch of images to convert, you can use Debabelizer's *batch convert* feature, which enables you to automatically convert hundreds of photographs into JPEGs or convert many graphics into GIFs all at once without having to open each file separately.

- ✔ **Jasc Paint Shop Pro 4.14** (www.jasc.com): Paint Shop Pro, by Jasc Software, is a fully featured painting and image-manipulation program. Paint Shop Pro is very similar to Photoshop, but on a more limited scale because it doesn't offer the same range of effects, tools, and filters. However, it costs less than Photoshop and may be a good starter program for novice image-makers.

- ✔ **Macromedia Freehand 8.0** (www.macromedia.com): Macromedia Freehand is an illustration program used widely both on the Web and in print. Freehand has many excellent Web features, such as support for Web file formats like GIF89a, PNG, and JPEG, and vector formats like Flash (.SWF) and Shockwave FreeHand (.FHC).

- ✔ **MicroFrontier Color It!** (www.microfrontier.com): This low-cost, easy-to-use graphics program is available only for the Macintosh and is a great tool for beginners, as well as those on a tight budget. Although it's much more limited than many of the other programs in this list, it provides enough features to create basic banners and buttons for a small business Web site.

- ✔ **Microsoft Image Composer** (www.microsoft.com): Image Composer was designed for creating Web graphics, so it's an ideal tool for the novice Web designer. Unfortunately, it's available only for Windows as part of the Microsoft FrontPage 98 Web design software.

When it comes to graphics, Adobe Systems, Inc., dominates the market, producing some of the most popular and sophisticated image programs available to consumers. Every graphic designer and illustrator I know owns a copy of Adobe Photoshop, despite its $600 price tag and steep learning curve. If you're looking for a serious graphics program, Photoshop is the clear choice.

However, if you don't have the budget, or the time to learn such a complex program, you may be better off with Adobe's more limited photo-editing program, PhotoDeluxe. For creating buttons, banners, and other Web graphics on a budget, consider Jasc Paint Shop Pro, MicroFrontier Color It!, or Microsoft Image Composer.

Understanding the Basics of Web Graphics

Because Dreamweaver doesn't include any graphics features, I don't spend much time talking about creating graphics in this book. However, it's so important to have a basic understanding of graphics formats and how they work on the Web that I include the following sections to give you an overview of what you need to know about graphics as you create them or place them on your pages.

The most important thing to keep in mind when placing images on a Web page is that you want to keep them small. That doesn't necessarily mean that the dimensions of an image are small, but that does mean that the *file size* is small.

Achieving small file sizes requires using compression techniques and color reduction. These are complex concepts that are well beyond the scope of this book. However, what you should understand is that image sizes can be reduced, and that the challenge is to find the best balance between small file size and image quality. If you really want to find out the best ways to create graphics for the Web, read *Web Graphics For Dummies* by Linda Richards (published by IDG Books Worldwide, Inc.).

One of the most common questions about images for the Web is when do you use GIF, and when do you use JPEG. The simple answer is that you use GIF for line art, such as one- or two-color logos, simple drawings, and so on, and you use JPEG for colorful, complex images, such as photographs. You can find lots more information about design and graphics in Chapter 4.

Inserting Images on Your Pages

Dreamweaver makes placing images on your Web pages easy. All you have to do is click the appropriate icon on the Object toolbar. Here's how:

1. **Choose File➪New to start a new page.**

   Remember to save your page before you start inserting images so that Dreamweaver can determine the correct location of your page when it creates the link to the image.

2. **Choose File➪Save to name and save the new HTML file.**

3. **If the Objects toolbar and Property inspector aren't already visible, choose Window➪Objects and Window➪Properties to open them.**

4. **Click the Insert Image icon in the Objects toolbar (the first icon).**

   The Insert Image dialog box appears, as shown in Figure 6-3.

5. **In the Insert Image dialog box, click Browse.**

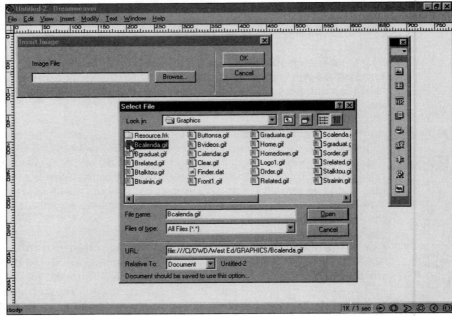

Figure 6-3: When you click Browse in the Insert Image dialog box, you open the Select File dialog box that lets you locate the image you want to link.

How an image appears on a Web page

The HTML tag that you use to place images on a Web page is similar to the link tag that you use to create hyperlinks between pages. Both tags instruct the browser where to find something. In the case of the link tag, the *path* to the linked page instructs the browser where to find another URL. In the case of an image tag, the path in the tag instructs the browser to find a GIF or JPEG image file. The path describes the location of the image in relation to the page on which it appears. For example, /images/baby.gif is a path that would instruct a browser to look for an image file called baby.gif in the images directory.

Trying to determine the path can get a little complicated. Fortunately, Dreamweaver sets the path for you, but you need to take care of two important steps before Dreamweaver can do this properly:

1. **Save your page.**

   When you save a page, Dreamweaver automatically remembers the exact location of the page in relation to the image.

2. **Make sure that your image and page stay in the same relative locations when you're ready to go public with your site and move all your pages and images to a server.**

6. **Navigate around your hard drive to the image that you want to insert.**

   Make sure that it's in the same location relative to your page that it will reside in on your server. See the sidebar "How an image appears on a Web page" for the details.

7. **When you find the image you want, double-click it and then click OK.**

   The image automatically appears on your page.

Aligning Images on a Page

After you've placed an image on your Web page, you probably want to center or align it so that text can wrap around it. In the following two sections, I show you the steps to accomplish both of these goals.

Centering an image

To center an image on a page, follow these steps:

1. **Click to insert your cursor just to the left of the image that you want to center.**

   This step is a bit counter-intuitive, but *don't* select the image if you want to center it. When you select an image, the Property inspector changes to image properties, which doesn't offer center as an alignment option.

2. **In the alignment options in the Property inspector, shown in Figure 6-4, click the Center Alignment icon.**

   The image automatically moves to the center of the page.

Aligning an image to the right with text wrapping around it on the left

To align an image to the right of a page and wrap text around it on the left, follow these steps:

1. **Place the image immediately to the left of the first line of the text, as shown in Figure 6-5.**

   Don't put spaces or line breaks between the image and the text.

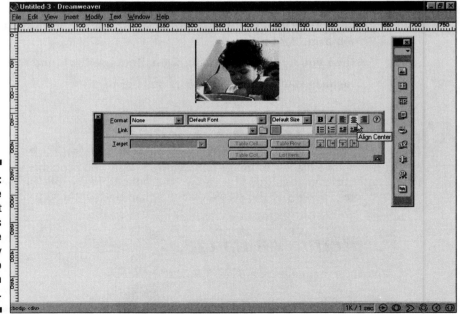

Figure 6-4:
Use the alignment options in the Property inspector to center an image.

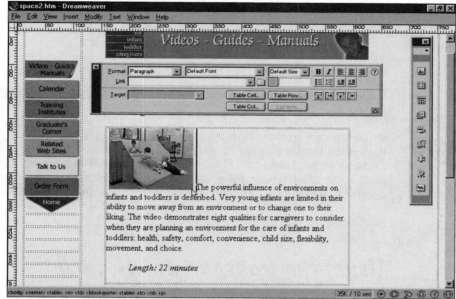

Figure 6-5:
To wrap text around an image, place the image immediately to the left of the text with no spaces between the text and the image.

2. Select the image.

The Property inspector changes to display the image attribute options, as shown in Figure 6-6.

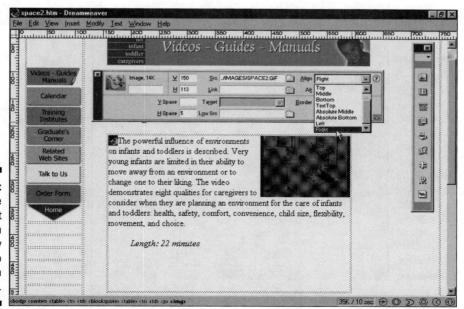

Figure 6-6:
Use the alignment options in the Property inspector to align an image.

3. **In the Property inspector, choose Align⇨Right.**

The image aligns to the right and the text automatically wraps around it (see Figure 6-6).

Creating complex designs with images

The alignment options available in HTML enable you to align your images vertically or horizontally, but you can't do both at once. Positioning images in relation to one another or to text with much precision is also impossible. The way to get around this limitation is to create HTML tables and use the cells in the table to control positioning, as shown in Figure 6-7. This sounds complex at first, but with a little experimentation, you can create almost any page layout. Chapter 7 shows how to use tables to create more complex Web page designs.

Using the transparent GIF trick

You may find it strange that I would suggest you place an invisible image on a Web page, but that's exactly what I show you how to do in this section. A small, transparent GIF is a powerful element in Web page design because you can use it to control the exact position of other elements on a page.

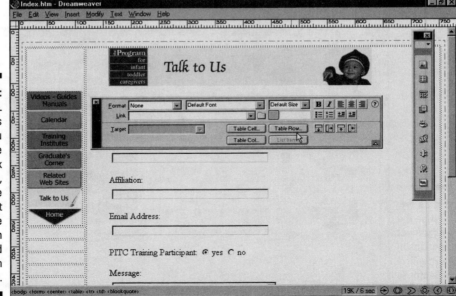

Figure 6-7:
HTML
tables
enable you
to create
complex
designs,
such as the
placement
of the
navigation
bar and
banner on
this page.

If you're not sure how to make a clear GIF, don't worry — I include one on the *Dreamweaver For Dummies* CD-ROM, and you can do whatever you like with it. I always name this image clear.gif and I use one on nearly every Web site I work on.

If you want to make your own, just create a small, solid-color image, save it as a GIF, make that one color transparent, and save the image again. You can make a color transparent in most good graphics programs, including Adobe Photoshop and Microsoft Image Composer. You'll find descriptions of a number of graphics programs that provide this feature earlier in this chapter.

HTML enables you to specify any height and width for an image, regardless of its actual size. Thus, you can use a small transparent GIF with a corresponding small file size (for quick download), and then alter the image attributes for height and width to create exact spaces between other visible elements on your page. Many Web designers recommend that you create a single-pixel graphic for this purpose, but I've found that a 10-x-10 pixel image works best because some older browsers have trouble displaying a GIF that's only one pixel.

Dreamweaver makes it easy to use the transparent GIF trick because it provides easy access to the height and width attributes in the Property inspector. You may also need to specify the alignment of the image to achieve the desired effect.

You can also use a transparent GIF to control spacing around text. This is handy when you want more than just a break between lines of text or other elements, but not as much as you get with the paragraph tag. This is also an ideal way to create larger spaces between elements with down-to-the-pixel design control. The following steps walk you through the process of inserting and sizing a transparent GIF between images, text, or other elements on a page.

1. **Copy the file for the transparent GIF (clear.gif) from the *Dreamweaver For Dummies* CD-ROM to the folder on your hard drive where you're storing your Web site.**

2. **With your page open in Dreamweaver, click to insert your cursor on the page where you want to insert an image or add text.**

   Don't worry if you can't put the cursor *exactly* where you want it; just get as close as you can. You can always reposition it later — that's what the transparent GIF trick is all about.

3. **Choose Insert⇨Image to insert the image.**

   The Insert Image dialog box appears.

4. **In the Insert Image dialog box, click the Browse button.**

   The Select File dialog box appears.

5. **Browse to the file for the image that you want to place on your page, and then double-click it.**

6. **Click OK to close the Insert Image dialog box.**

   The image appears in your workspace.

   In these steps, I insert two image files in addition to the transparent GIF, which I use to control the spacing between them, but you could add text in this step instead of an image and still use the following steps to control the spacing between elements on your page.

7. **Select the Insert Image icon from the Objects palette again.**

   The Insert Image dialog box appears.

8. **Click the Browse button.**

   The Select File dialog box appears.

9. **Browse to the clear.gif file that you copied to your hard drive in Step 1, and then double-click it.**

10. **Click OK.**

    The transparent GIF is inserted on your page.

11. **Select the clear.gif image, and then type 22 in the text box next to the <u>W</u> in the Property inspector to set the width of the image to 22 pixels.**

    I use a value for the width of 22 pixels just for demonstration — you can set the width to any value you want.

    As shown in Figure 6-8, you can see the outline of clear.gif while it's selected. Note that as soon as you deselect the image, it becomes invisible in Dreamweaver. You can always reselect it by clicking in the area until the cursor highlights it.

12. **Now place the third image to the right of the transparent GIF.**

    Just repeat Steps 3 through 5 to insert the image.

    After you insert your third image, you have two images with the space between them held by the transparent GIF, as shown in Figure 6-8.

The clear GIF trick was made popular by Web designer David Siegel. At his site (www.dsiegel.com), you can find more information about how to use this trick to create complex and innovative designs for the Web.

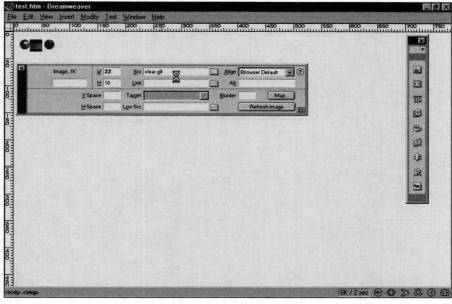

Figure 6-8:
The clear
GIF
highlighted
between
these two
small
globes
controls the
spacing
between
the two
images.

Creating a Background

Background images can bring life to a Web page, adding color and fullness. Used cleverly, a background image can help create the illusion that the entire page is one large image while still downloading quickly and efficiently. The trick is to use a small background image that creates a dramatic effect when it *tiles* (repeats) across and down the page.

When you set an image as the background for your Web page, the browser repeats it across and down the page. This is why background images are often called *tiles,* because they repeat like tiles across a kitchen floor. However, if you use a long narrow image as a background or a large image that's small in file size, you can create many effects beyond a repeating tile.

Kare Anderson's Say It Better Web site (www.sayitbetter.com), shown in Figure 6-9, uses a background image that fills the entire page. The background image creates a stripe of pink down the left-hand side of the page and fills the rest of the page with a peach color. The effect is a rich, colorful page. In this case, the background image wasn't a small image designed to tile horizontally as well as vertically, but a narrow strip that's too wide to repeat horizontally, as shown in Figure 6-10. Many of the clip art collections described earlier in this chapter include background tiles. The numbered steps that follow show you how to use Dreamweaver to place a background image on a Web page.

Figure 6-9: Kare Anderson's Say It Better Web site has a fuller, richer design because a background image fills the entire page.

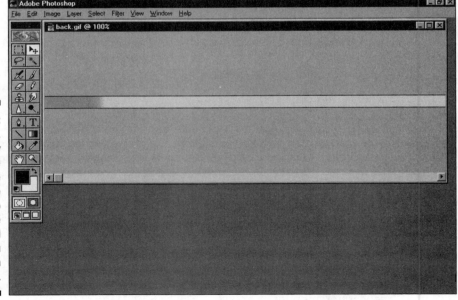

Figure 6-10: The long, narrow image shown here in Adobe Photoshop creates the background image you see in Figure 6-9.

Here's how to set a background on a Web page:

1. Choose <u>M</u>odify⇨<u>P</u>age Properties.

The Page Properties dialog box appears, as shown in Figure 6-11.

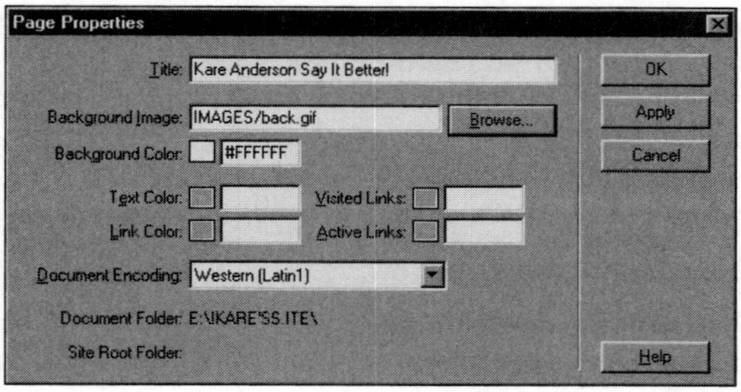

Figure 6-11:
The Page
Properties
dialog box
enables you
to set a
background
image, as
well as a
background
color and
text and link
colors.

Page Properties		×
<u>T</u>itle: Kare Anderson Say It Better!		OK
Background <u>I</u>mage: IMAGES/back.gif	<u>B</u>rowse...	Apply
Background Color: #FFFFFF		Cancel
T<u>e</u>xt Color: Vi<u>s</u>ited Links:		
<u>L</u>ink Color: <u>A</u>ctive Links:		
<u>D</u>ocument Encoding: Western (Latin1)		
Document Folder: E:\IKARE'SS ITE\		
Site Root Folder:		Help

2. Click the <u>B</u>rowse button to the right of the text box next to Back-ground <u>I</u>mage.

The Select Image Source dialog box opens.

3. Browse to find the image you want to use as your background image.

When you insert an image in your Web site, you want to make sure that image is in the same relative location on your hard drive as it will be on your server. If you plan to use your background tile throughout your site, you may want to store it in a common images folder where it will be easy to link to from any page in your site.

4. Double-click the filename of your background image to select it.

The Select Image Source dialog box disappears.

5. Click OK in the Page Properties dialog box to finish.

Note that if you click the Apply button, you see the effect of the back-ground tile being applied to the page without closing the dialog box.

Creating Image Maps

Image maps are popular on the Web because they enable you to create hot spots in an image and link them to different URLs. A common use of an image map is to make a geographic map, such as a map of the United States, link to different locations depending on the section of the map selected. For example, if you have a national bank and want to make it easy for customers to find a local branch or ATM machine, you can create hot spots on an image map of the United States and then link each hot spot to a page listing banks in that geographic location. Dreamweaver makes creating image maps easy by providing a set of tools that enable you to create hot spots and set their corresponding links.

The following steps show you how to create an image map:

1. **Click to insert your cursor in the place on your Web page where you would like to place the image map.**

2. **Choose Insert⇨Image.**

   The Insert Image dialog box appears.

3. **Browse to the image you want.**

4. **Double-click the filename of the image and click OK.**

   The image appears on the page.

5. **Double-click the image to open the Image Property inspector.**

   If you already have the Image Property inspector open, just click the image so that its properties appear in the Image Property inspector.

6. **Select the Map button in the bottom-right of the Image Property inspector, as shown in Figure 6-12.**

   The Image Map Editor dialog box opens.

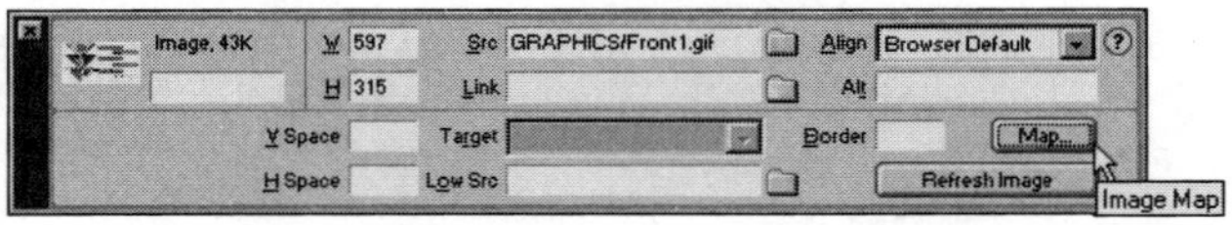

Figure 6-12:
To create an image map, select the Map button from the Image Property inspector.

7. **Choose a shape tool from the top-left of the Image Map Editor dialog box, as shown in Figure 6-13.**

   The shape tools include a rectangle, an ellipse, and an irregular polygon and allow you to specify regions in your image map, called *hot spots,* each with a specific link.

Figure 6-13:
The shape tools in the Image Map Editor make creating hot spots on an image and link them to different URLs easy.

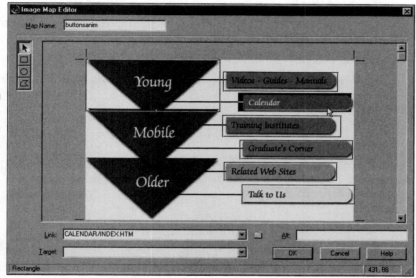

8. **With the shape tool selected, click and drag over an area of the image that you want to make *hot* (link to another page).**

   As you click and drag, you see an outline form around the region that you're making hot. Position the outline so that it covers the area that you want. If you need to reposition the hot area, select the arrow tool from the top-left of the Image Map Editor dialog box, and then move the outline to the location you want. You can also resize it by clicking and dragging any of the corners.

9. **To link a selected hot area, click the Folder icon next to the Link text box (at the bottom of the Image Map Editor dialog box).**

   The Select HTML File dialog box opens.

10. **Browse to find the HTML file that you want to link to the hot spot on your image.**

11. **Double-click the file to which you want to link.**

   The hot spot links to the selected page and the Select HTML File dialog box automatically closes. You can tell that the link has been set because the name of the file and its path appear as text across the hot spot of the image.

12. **To add more hot spots, choose a shape tool and repeat Steps 7 through 11.**

13. **Type a name in the text box next to Map Name at the top of the dialog box.**

   You can call it anything you want.

14. **When you finish creating all the hot spots and associated links for your map, click OK.**

Part III
Advancing Your Site

The 5th Wave   By Rich Tennant

"It says, 'Seth – Please see us about your idea to wrap newsletter text around company logo.' It's signed, 'Webmaster.'"

In this part . . .

*I*f you want to create interesting designs within the confines of HTML, you need to use tables, frames, and style sheets. This part walks you through the maze of nested tables and merged cells, split pages framed with links, and the power and design control that you can achieve only with Cascading Style Sheets.

Chapter 7

Coming to the HTML Table

● ●

In This Chapter

▶ Introducing HTML tables

▶ Going beyond spreadsheets

▶ Creating complex designs

▶ Adding space and creating columns

● ●

*W*hen most people think of tables, they think of spreadsheets and financial data. I've never been a numbers cruncher, but on the Web, tables are for much more than numbers because they help you create complex designs. For example, you can use a table to align elements side-by-side on a page and create columns of text.

If you've ever used a desktop publishing program like QuarkXPress or Adobe PageMaker, you've probably used text and image boxes to lay out pages. Tables work much the same way because you use the table cells (the boxes created by a table) to control the placement of text and images, and you can make the borders of the table invisible, so your viewers don't see the underlying structure of your design when looking at your Web page in a browser. You still won't get the design control you're used to in a desktop publishing program, but you can come much closer *with* tables than without them.

In this chapter, I explore a wide range of uses for HTML tables and show you step-by-step how to create a variety of designs for your Web pages.

Understanding Table Options

You can change HTML table attributes, such as height, width, border size, and spacing, in the Property inspector. Click the border of any table to select it, and the Property inspector displays the table options shown in Figure 7-1. To view all the options, click the expander arrow in the lower-right corner.

Figure 7-1:
Select
a table,
and the
Property
inspector
provides
access to
table
attributes.

- **Rows:** Displays the number of rows in the table. You can alter the size of the table by changing the number. Be careful, though. If you enter a smaller number, Dreamweaver deletes the bottom row — contents and all.

- **Columns:** Displays the number of columns in the table. You can alter the size of the table by changing the number. Be careful, though. If you enter a smaller number, Dreamweaver deletes the column on the right side of the table — contents and all.

- **Width:** Displays the width of the table. You can alter this by changing the number. The width can be specified as a percentage or a value in pixels.

- **Border:** Controls the size of the border around the table. The larger the number, the thicker the border. If you want the border to be invisible, set the border to 0.

- **Align:** Controls the alignment of the table. Options are left, right, and center.

  The best way to center a table is to select the table and choose Text⇨Alignment⇨Center.

- **Cell Space:** Specifies the space between table cells.

- **Cell Pad:** Specifies the space between the contents of a cell and its border.

- **V (Vertical) Space:** Adds space in pixels above and below the table.

- **H (Horizontal) Space:** Adds space in pixels on either side of the table.

- **BG Color:** Controls the background color. Click the color square and select a color from the palette dialog box, or click the color palette icon in the bottom-right of the dialog box to specify any color.

✔ **Border (color):** Controls the border color. Click the color square and select a color from the palette dialog box, or click the color palette icon in the bottom-right of the dialog box to specify any color.

✔ **Light Brdr:** Controls the color of the light area of the three-dimensional border. Click the color square and select a color from the dialog box, or click the color palette icon in the bottom-right of the dialog box to specify any color.

✔ **Dark Brdr:** Controls the color of the shaded area of the three-dimensional border. Click the color square and select a color from the dialog box, or click the color palette icon in the bottom-right of the dialog box to specify any color.

The following icons appear in the bottom left-hand corner of the Property inspector, from left to right:

✔ **Clear Row Heights:** Globally deletes all the height values for the rows in the table.

✔ **Clear Column Widths:** Globally deletes all the width values for the columns in the table.

✔ **Convert Table Widths to Pixels:** Converts the width of the table from a percentage to pixels.

✔ **Convert Table Widths to Percent:** Converts the width of the table pixels to a percentage of the page.

Creating Simple Tables

Back in the days when you had to design Web pages in raw HTML code, even simple tables were difficult to create. The code behind an HTML table is a mess of <TR> and <TD> tags that indicate table rows and table data cells. Finding out how to type in those tags so that they create a series of little boxes on a Web page was never an intuitive process. If you wanted a complex design using tables with uneven numbers of rows or columns, you really faced a challenge.

Thank the cybergods that WYSIWYG editors such as Dreamweaver have made this process so much easier. Even if you enjoy writing HTML code manually, you can appreciate how much simpler Dreamweaver makes it to merge or split cells in a table, to change a background color, or to specify the width of a border. By using the Insert Table icon on the Objects palette, you can quickly create a new table and then use the Property inspector to specify a wide range of table attributes, such as alignment and colors.

Here, I walk you through creating a simple table. For the purposes of these steps, I create a table with two columns and two rows, but you can specify any number of rows and columns that you want.

1. **Click to place your cursor on the page where you'd like to create a table.**

2. **Click the Insert Table icon from the Objects palette.**

   You can also choose Insert⇨Table. The Insert Table dialog box appears, as shown in Figure 7-2.

Figure 7-2:
Use the
Insert Table
dialog box
to create a
table in
your Web
page.

3. **Enter 2 next to Rows, 2 next to Columns, and 100 next to Width, and choose percent in the drop-down list box beside Width; then click OK.**

   This creates the table that's two rows by two columns and spans 100 percent of the screen, as shown in Figure 7-3. Of course, you can enter any values you want for your table.

Aligning columns in a table

When working with lots of numbers, people use tables in word-processing programs and spreadsheets because they can easily align the contents of columns to ensure that numbers line up properly. You don't have as much control in HTML as you have in a program such as Excel, in which you can align numbers to a decimal point. Still, you can align the content of columns left, right, or center.

If you want to convert a table that you've already created in a program such as Word or Excel, you can find some useful utilities described in the sidebar "Converting tables and spreadsheets into HTML," later in this chapter.

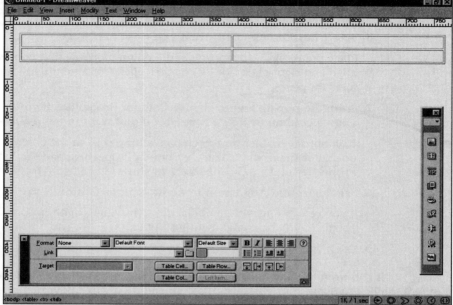

Figure 7-3:
This table
has two
columns,
two rows,
and a width
of 100
percent.

Follow these steps to create a table of financial data with all the data cells aligned to the right to align the numbers. You can also use these steps to align the contents of table cells to the left, center, or top. In these steps, I insert the data into the table after I create it in Dreamweaver. If you've converted a table and just want to align the cells, start with Step 6.

1. **Click to place your cursor where you want to create a table.**

2. **Click the Insert Table icon from the Objects palette.**

   You can also choose Insert⇨Table. The Insert Table dialog box appears (refer to Figure 7-2).

3. **Enter the number of columns and rows you want.**

   For this example, I specified four rows and four columns.

4. **Specify the width in pixels or percent, and click OK.**

   I set my table to 75 percent so that it doesn't fill the entire page. You can set the width to whatever is most appropriate for your design. The table automatically appears on the page.

5. **Click to insert your cursor in a cell and then type to enter the data that you want in each cell.**

   As you can see in Figure 7-4, I entered the heading information across the top row of cells (see "Creating table header cells" later in this chapter). Then I listed several car models and entered the data for each car in the rest of the table.

6. Select the column or row that you want to change.

Place your cursor in any cell in the column or row that you want to align and right-click (for PC) or Ctrl+click (for Macintosh). A pop-up menu appears.

7. From the pop-up menu, choose Column Properties if you want to align a column or Row Properties if you want to align a row.

This option enables you to change all the cells in the column or row at once. For these steps, I chose Column Properties, and the Table Column Properties dialog box appeared, as shown in Figure 7-4.

8. Set Horizontal Alignment to Right, Left, or Center.

If you're working with financial data, the Align Right option often produces the best alignment for numbers.

9. Click OK to finish.

If you want to align one cell in a column or row differently than the others, click to place your cursor in that cell and then move your mouse to click the Alignment icon in the Property inspector to left-, right-, or center-align the cell.

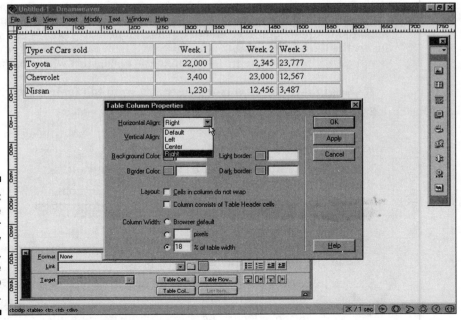

Figure 7-4:
This table is four columns by four rows, with the width set to 75 percent.

Converting tables and spreadsheets into HTML

Manually converting financial data or other spreadsheet information into HTML can be tedious. Fortunately, a few companies have created conversion programs to help automate the process.

If you have tables that you want to convert from Microsoft Excel or Word, Microsoft HTML Assistants can help you. If you use the latest versions of Word or Excel, these assistants are part of the program; if you use an older version of these programs, visit www.microsoft.com to download one of these free add-ons. Microsoft HTML Assistants enable you to save your Word or Excel files as HTML and automatically convert simple formatting, such as bold and italic, as well as complex elements like tables. Then

you can open the file in Dreamweaver to further enhance your design. If you only want part of a file converted, you can copy and paste the elements that you want into your Dreamweaver file.

Another spreadsheet-conversion utility is Two Clicks Instant Tables, an online table-to-HTML converter. Two Clicks is a quick, easy way to convert a little information from a spreadsheet program into HTML (and it's free). To use it, just point your browser to www.twoclicks.com and copy and paste the contents of your spreadsheet into the online form at Two Clicks. The utility automatically generates an HTML table, which you can then copy and paste into your Web page.

Creating table header cells

Often in a table that shows data, such as the one in Figure 7-4, you want header cells that are distinct from the data cells. In HTML, a special tag distinguishes header cells, and Dreamweaver makes it easy to apply this tag. The header cell tag makes its contents bold, and because you can apply the header cell tag to an entire column or row, it's a handy feature.

Follow these steps to create header cells in a table:

1. **Select the column or row that you want to change.**

   Place your cursor in any cell of the column or row that you want to change and right-click (for PC) or Ctrl+click (for Macintosh). The Table Properties dialog box appears.

2. **Change the column or row to header cells.**

   Click to place a check mark in the box next to Row Consists of Table Header Cells in the Table Row Properties dialog box if you want to change a column or row. Figure 7-5 shows how this works.

3. **Click Apply to see the effect, and then click OK to complete the step and close the dialog box.**

Figure 7-5:
The Table
Row
Properties
dialog box
enables you
to format a
row as
header
cells.

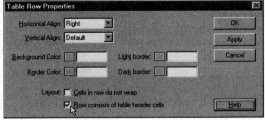

Figure 7-5:
The Table
Row
Properties
dialog box
enables you
to format a
row as
header
cells.

You can further change the formatting of the contents in any table cell the same way you can format any other text or element on a page. Simply select the text and use the formatting options in the Property inspector to make the text larger or smaller, change the font, and more. You have to make these changes one cell at a time. You can keep the Property inspector open at all times or close it by clicking the small box in the top-left corner and open it again by choosing Window⇨Properties.

Using Tables for Spacing and Alignment

As you get more adept at creating Web pages, you may find that HTML tables are a crucial part of creating almost any design that requires more than basic alignment of elements on a page. Using tables, you can get around many of the limitations of basic HTML and accomplish the following design feats:

- ✔ Evenly spaced graphic bullets (little GIFs that can take the place of bullets) next to text
- ✔ Text boxes and fields properly aligned in a form
- ✔ Images placed side-by-side, spaced as far apart as you want them
- ✔ Columns of text that don't span the entire page

In the rest of this chapter, I show you how to use tables to create a variety of page designs including those I just listed.

Anytime you want to use a table to create a great design but don't want the table itself to show, you should turn off the table border. You do that by specifying border=0 in the Table Property inspector. If the inspector isn't already open, choose Window⇨Properties and then click the table to display its properties.

Using tables to evenly space graphic bullets

I quickly get tired of the small, black bullets that HTML code provides. Instead, I prefer to use graphics, colorful circles, and other creative shapes that add life and richness to Web pages. The problem is that controlling the spacing around graphic bullets is hard, and I like to be able to control the spacing of a bulleted list. So, I use tables whenever I create a bulleted list.

Here's how to create a table to align graphic bullets and text in a bulleted list.

1. **Click to place your cursor where you want to start your bulleted list.**

2. **Choose Insert⇨Table.**

   The Insert Table dialog box appears.

3. **Enter 2 next to Columns.**

4. **Next to Rows, enter the number of bulleted items you want to create.**

   I chose to create four rows because I have four items in my bulleted list.

5. **Set the Width to whatever is most appropriate for your design, and then click OK.**

   I set the Width to 75 percent here. A table with four rows and two columns appears.

6. **Click to place your cursor in the top-left cell, and then choose Insert⇨Image.**

7. **Click the Browse button to search your hard drive for the graphic that you want for your bullets.**

   The Select File dialog box appears.

8. **Double-click the name of the image, and then click OK.**

   The image appears on the page.

9. **With the image selected, choose Edit⇨Copy.**

   The image is automatically selected when inserted. If it's not selected, click to select it before continuing.

10. **Click to place your cursor in the next cell, and choose Edit⇨Paste.**

11. **Repeat Step 10 until you've pasted copies of the graphic bullet in all the cells in the left column of your table.**

12. **Click the cell divider in the middle of the table and drag it to the left until the left cell is just a few pixels wider than the graphic bullets.**

    This is easier than it sounds. The result should look about like Figure 7-6.

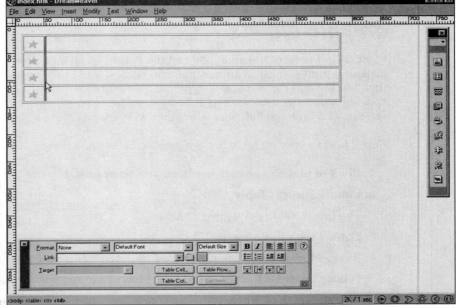

Figure 7-6:
You can just
click and
drag to
resize table
cells and
rows.

13. **Enter your text in the right-hand cell next to each bullet.**

14. **Select the table by clicking anywhere on the border.**

15. **In the Property inspector, set the border to 0 (zero).**

    If the Property inspector is not open, choose Window⇨Properties.

    Setting the table border to 0 makes the table invisible in the browser display. In Figure 7-7, you can see how this bulleted list looks perfectly aligned, thanks to the table, even though you can't see the table borders.

Using tables to design forms

Creating text boxes and pull-down menus for HTML forms is easy in Dreamweaver, but you need to use tables to make them look good. In Chapter 15, you can find lots of information about creating forms, but for now, assume that you've already created a form and that you want to align the text boxes evenly. Here, I use a guest book form — a common, yet simple, form — as an example, but you can use this technique to align other form elements.

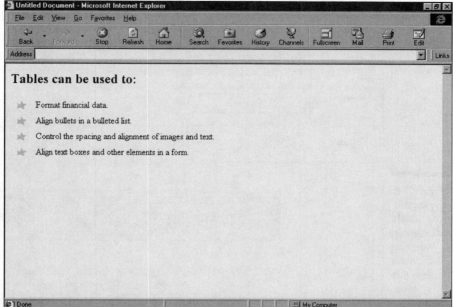

Figure 7-7:
This
bulleted list
uses a table
to align the
bullets; the
table is
invisible
because
the border
was set
to 0.

1. **Open a page that has an HTML form or create an HTML form using the steps in Chapter 15.**

2. **Click to place your cursor where you want to start formatting your form.**

3. **Choose Insert⇨Table.**

   The Insert Table dialog box appears.

4. **Enter the number of columns and rows you need to format your form.**

   I've set the table to two columns and five rows.

5. **Set the Width to whatever is most appropriate for your design, and then click OK.**

   Here, I set the Width to 100 percent. A table with two columns and five rows appears. The table automatically appears on the page when you click OK.

6. **Highlight the text preceding the form's first text field and drag the text into the cell at the top-left of the table.**

   In my example (see Figure 7-8), this means selecting the words **First Name** and dragging them into the first table cell.

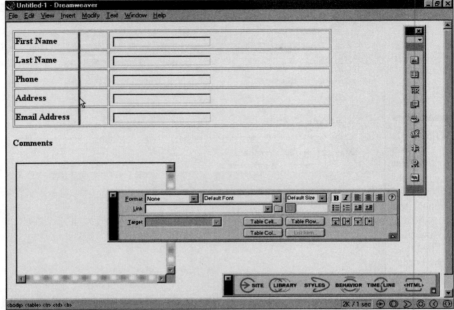

File   Edit   View   Insert   Modify   Text   Window   Help

First Name

Last Name

Phone

Address

Email Address

Comments

Format None   Default Font   Default Size   **B** *I*

Link

Target   Table Cell...   Table Row...

                                            Table Col...   List Item

SITE   LIBRARY   STYLES   BEHAVIOR   TIME LINE   HTML

<body> <table> <tr> <td> <b>   2K / 1 sec

Figure 7-8:
By moving the table's cell divider, you can align the fields in this form.

7. **Select the first text field and drag it to the top-right cell of the table.**

8. **Repeat Steps 6 and 7 for the rest of the form until you've moved all of the form elements into table cells.**

9. **Click the cell divider in the middle of the table and drag it to the left until the left column is just a few pixels wider than the widest line of text.**

10. **Select the table by clicking the border, and set the border to 0 in the Property inspector.**

    When you set the border to 0, the edges of your table change from solid lines to dotted lines so that you can still see where the borders are while you're working in Dreamweaver. When you view the page in a browser, as shown in Figure 7-9, the border of the table is invisible.

You can keep the Property inspector visible at all times, or you can close it by clicking the small box with an X in the top-left corner. To open the Property inspector, choose Window⇨Properties. You can also open it by double-clicking any page element, such as an image or table.

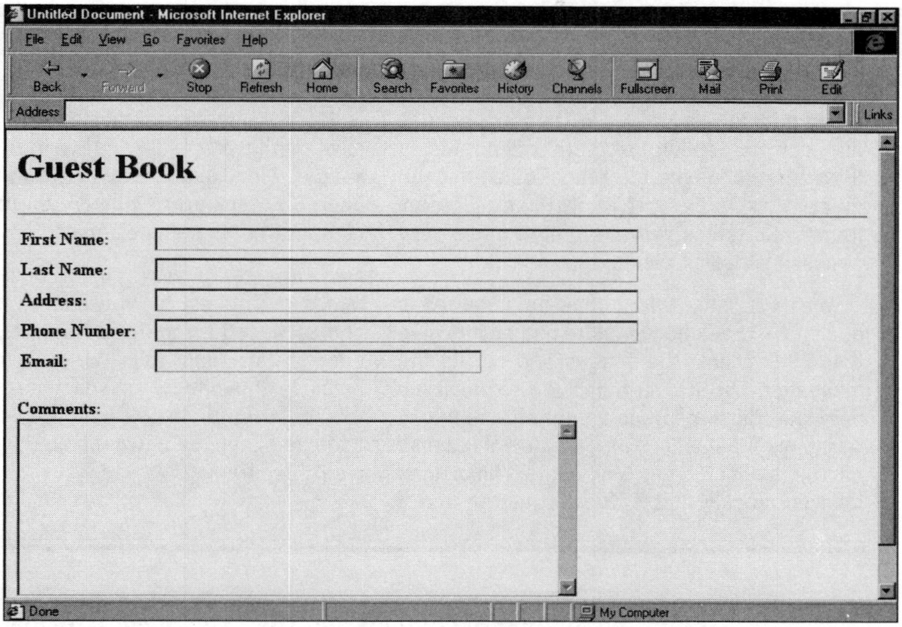

Figure 7-9:
The fields in
the form, as
displayed in
Internet
Explorer,
evenly line
up using a
table with
no visible
border.

Aligning a navigation bar

A common element on Web pages is a navigation bar — a row of images or text with links to the main sections of a Web site. Navigation bars are usually placed at the top, bottom, or side of a page, where users can easily access them, but out of the way of the main part of the page design. Often designers use HTML frames (see Chapter 8) to insert a navigation bar, but you can effectively place a navigation bar on a page by using tables. The sidebar "Why use tables instead of frames?" can help you make the right choice for your Web site.

Here's how to create a table to position a navigation bar on a Web page:

1. **Click to place your cursor in the top-left corner of the page.**

   To provide an example, I place a navigation row in the top-left corner of a page. Even if you want your navigation bar somewhere else, you probably want to create a table that covers most of the page, so the top-left corner is a good place to start.

2. **Choose Insert⇨Table.**

   The Insert Table dialog box appears.

Why use tables instead of frames?

Some people just don't like frames, because they can be difficult to create and confusing for users to navigate. You should also be aware that older browsers can't display frames. So tables provide a more universally accessible design element.

Frames can save a little time because users don't have to reload the entire page every time they click a link; the images and text of the navigation bar stay in their own frame while new material appears in another frame. If you design your page carefully, the download time can be minimal. If you use just text links, they load so quickly that it doesn't matter, and if

you use the same graphics on every page (as most people do in a navigation bar), the linked images reload quickly because they're *cached* (stored in temporary memory on the visitor's computer) the first time a user visits the page.

You can create very similar designs using tables or frames, so you should make your choice based on your goals and your audience. If you want to make sure the largest possible audience can see your page, use tables; if you want to change only part of a page and keep the navigation bar visible at all times, use frames.

3. Enter the number of columns and rows you need to format your page.

I've set the table to two columns and six rows to give myself some room to work on the design of the rest of the page.

4. Set the Width (as a percentage of the total page width) to whatever is most appropriate for your design, and click OK.

Here, I set the Width to 100 percent. A table with two columns and six rows appears.

5. Click to place your cursor in the table cell where you want to insert your navigation bar.

I chose the top-left cell to insert my navigation bar.

6. Choose Insert⇨Image and use the Browse button to locate the image that you want to insert into the table cell.

7. Double-click the filename of the image and click OK.

The image automatically appears in the table cell. Repeat this step to insert multiple images.

Here, I use a series of images that I insert one beneath another, separated by breaks, to create a row of images that runs down the left side of the page, as you see in Figure 7-10. You may also want to merge some of the table cells to better control the placement of other page elements next to the navigation row. The next set of steps shows you how to merge cells.

8. Select the table and set the border to 0 in the Property inspector.

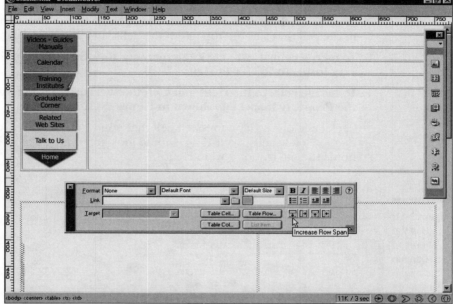

Merging table cells

If you want to create really complex designs, you need to *merge* table cells (meaning that you combine cells in one part of the table). This makes it possible to vary the space in table sections. For example, you may want a long cell space across the top of your table for a banner and then multiple cells underneath it so that you can control the spacing between columns of text or images. The following steps show you how to merge cells in a table:

1. **Click to place your cursor where you want to create the table on your page.**

   If you have already created a table and just want to merge cells, skip to Step 5.

2. **Choose Insert⇨Table.**

   The Insert Table dialog box appears.

3. **Enter the number of columns and rows you need to format your page.**

4. **Set the Width (as a percentage of the total page width) to whatever is most appropriate for your design, and click OK.**

   A table appears on the page.

5. **Click to place your cursor in the table cell that you want to merge.**

   Dreamweaver merges cells down and to the right, so place your cursor in the cell that's at the top-left of the cells that you want to merge.

6. **To merge cells down, click the Increase Row Span icon in the Property inspector (refer to Figure 7-10).**

7. **To merge cells to the right, click on the Increase Column Span icon in the Property inspector, shown in Figure 7-11.**

   Click once on the icon for each cell that you want to merge. After you've merged a few cells, your table should look something like the one that holds the navigation row in Figure 7-12.

Figure 7-11:
Use the
Increase
Column
Span icon
to merge
cells to the
right.

Placing images and text side-by-side

You can apply the steps in the previous section to many designs. After you understand how to merge cells in a table, you can use that ability to create a variety of image and text combinations.

This section takes the navigation row placement a step further by inserting a banner graphic at the top of the page and then inserting text in the body of the page. With designs as specific and complex as these, walking you through every possible combination is impossible. Instead, follow these steps as an example of what's possible. You can use these steps to create exactly this design, or you can change the variables, such as the number of columns and rows or how many cells are merged, to create your own designs.

Follow these steps to insert a banner graphic at the top-right of a page when you have a navigation row on the left and want text in the body of the page. Note that these steps pick up where the steps in the section "Aligning a navigation bar" leave off.

1. **Click to place your cursor in the top-right cell of the table.**

2. **Choose Insert⇨Image and use the Browse button to locate the image that you want to insert into the table cell.**

3. **Double-click the filename of the image and click OK.**

   The image automatically appears in the table cell. Repeat this step to insert multiple images.

4. **Place your cursor in the cell below the cell with the banner and type the text you want displayed.**

   You can also copy and paste text from another source, such as a word-processing program. Using cells next to each other like this enables you to better control the placement of elements. The steps in the next section can help you align cell contents.

Aligning cells

When you insert elements of different sizes in adjacent table cells, the contents often move to the middle of the cell, creating an uneven design. You can counter this by specifying the alignment of the cell. To do so, follow these steps:

1. **Click to place your cursor in the cell that you want to align.**

2. **Click the Table Cell button in the Property inspector.**

   The Table Cell Property inspector appears.

   The Table Cell button is in the bottom part of the Property inspector. If you can't see the bottom part, click the arrow in the bottom-right corner to extend the Property inspector to display all options.

3. **In the Table Cell Properties dialog box, choose the alignment option you want from the Vertical Align pull-down list, as shown in Figure 7-12.**

4. **Click OK.**

   The cell automatically aligns and all of its contents are aligned accordingly.

Creating columns with tables

A page full of text is harder to read on a computer screen than on paper, so breaking up large amounts of text on a Web page is even more important. When text spans the entire width of a computer screen, readers have difficulty keeping their place. One way to make text easier to read is to use tables to put the text into narrow columns.

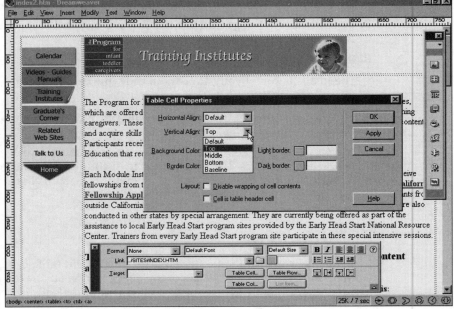

Figure 7-12:
Setting the
Vertical
Alignment
of the left
cell to Top
keeps the
navigation
row at the
top-left of
the page.

If you want your pages to look like a magazine or newspaper, you can create a table with two or three columns of text, but I find that the simplest, and most elegant, solution is often just to create one column and center it on a page.

You can center your column of text to create margins on each side or align the column left or right. Follow these instructions to create a column:

1. **Click to place your cursor where you want to begin the column of text.**

2. **Choose Insert⇨Table.**

   The Insert Table dialog box appears.

3. **Enter the number of columns and rows that you want.**

   I entered 1 for Columns and 1 for Rows to create a single-cell table. You can create as many columns of text as you want.

4. **Set the Width to whatever is most appropriate for your design, and click OK.**

   The table automatically adjusts to the percentage width specified.

   Here, I chose 60 percent; I generally recommend 50 to 75 percent for a column of text.

5. **Place your cursor in the table and type your text, or copy and paste text from another program, such as a word processor.**

6. **Select the table by clicking anywhere on the border.**

7. **In the Property inspector, set the border to 0.**

   If the Property inspector isn't visible, choose Window➪Properties to open it.

8. **With the table still selected, choose Align➪Center from the Property inspector, as shown in Figure 7-13.**

   As you can see in Figure 7-14, the text is centered when displayed in Dreamweaver.

Using nested tables: Tables within tables

Placing tables within tables, called *nested tables,* can help you create the most complex designs. You create nested tables by inserting a table within a cell of another table. In the days when you had to write your own code, this was a daunting task. Today, Dreamweaver makes nesting tables easy, enabling you to create complex designs without ever looking at the HTML code.

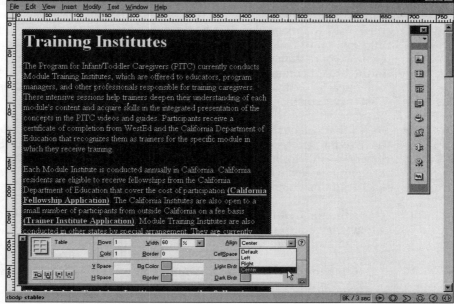

Figure 7-13: You can use the Alignment option in the Property inspector to center a table.

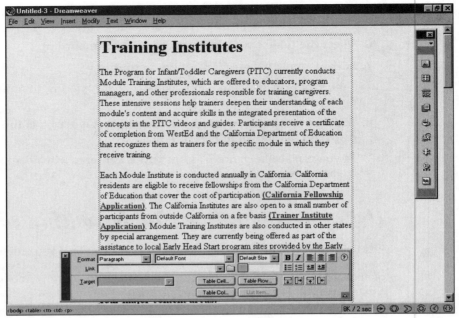

Figure 7-14:
Placing
text in a
table and
centering it
creates a
column
down the
middle of
the page
with
margins on
both sides,
making the
text easier
to read.

Nested tables can get pretty messy. As with all design tricks, don't get carried away and overuse nested tables just because Dreamweaver makes them easy to create. The best Web designs are those that communicate the information to your audience in the most elegant and understandable way. Overuse of certain design elements, including nested tables, can actually get in the way of communicating your message. Make sure that when you use complicated designs, such as nested tables, that your end result is truly the best way to display your information.

Pages that use nested tables take longer to download because browsers have to interpret each table individually. For some designs, the slightly longer download time is worth it, but in most cases, you're better off adding or merging cells in one table, as I explain in the section "Merging cells," earlier in this chapter.

One situation that makes nested tables worth the added download time is when you want to place a table of financial or other data in the midst of a complex page design. Here's how to place a table inside another table.

1. **Click to place your cursor where you want to create the first table.**

2. **Choose Insert⇨Table.**

   The Insert Table dialog box appears.

3. **Enter the number of columns and rows that you need for your design.**

   In this case, I created two columns and three rows.

4. **Set the Width to whatever is appropriate for your design, and click OK.**

   The table is automatically sized to the width you set. I used 80 percent here.

5. **Use this table to create your primary design, and when you're ready to create the nested table, click to place your cursor in the cell where you want to place the second table.**

6. **Repeat Steps 2 through 4, specifying however many columns and rows that you want and the width of the table.**

   The new table appears inside the cell of the first table.

7. **Enter the information that you want in the nested table cells.**

   Figure 7-15 shows an example of a nested table that you can create with these steps.

Figure 7-15:
By placing a table within a table, you can create columnar designs within a table, such as the acting experience on this actor's Web page.

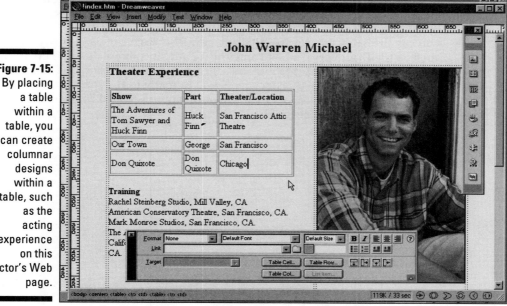

Comparing Tables and Cascading Style Sheets

One of these days, page designs that use tables will be created by using Cascading Style Sheets with X,Y, and Z coordinates for Exact Positioning. These exciting features represent two of the latest additions to HTML supported by Netscape Navigator 4.0 and Microsoft Internet Explorer 4.0.

Dreamweaver really shines when using these new features, which are much more complex than creating HTML tables. So why don't I recommend that you use Exact Positioning and Cascading Style Sheets instead of tables? Because many of your viewers may still use older versions of browsers that don't support these features, and you don't want to leave them out of the loop. Unfortunately, CSS and most of the other DHTML features aren't *backward compatible*. That means that if you use CSS and DHTML to create Web pages, you're limiting yourself to the audience that uses only the latest browsers — and that's still a very small audience.

As more people upgrade to newer browsers, these new features become more viable design options. If you're creating a site that's designed for a sophisticated audience, such as a site with tips for other Web designers, you can probably feel safe using these new features right away. Many sites, such as the Discovery Channel and *The X-Files* sites, have opted to create two sites — one that uses tables and another that uses CSS and DHTML to create powerful, interactive designs. If you're ready to take on this new technology, you can find lots of information about CSS and DHTML in Chapters 9 and 13, respectively.

Chapter 8

Framing Your Pages

● ●

In This Chapter

▶ Introducing HTML frames

▶ Creating frame pages

▶ Knowing when *not* to use frames

▶ Setting targets and links

● ●

*H*TML frames, originally created by Netscape, add a whole range of design possibilities.

Frames add innovative navigation control because they enable you to display multiple HTML pages in one browser window and control the contents of each framed area individually. Designers commonly use frames to create a page with two or more sections and place links in one section that, when selected, display information in another section of the same browser window.

Web pages that use frames, such as the one in Figure 8-1, are split into separate sections — or individual *frames*. All the frames together make up a *frameset*. Behind the scenes, each frame of the frameset is a separate HTML file, which makes a page with frames a little complicated to create — even with Dreamweaver. If you choose to create your frame files in a text editor, you have to juggle multiple pages, working on each frame one at a time, and you can see what you're creating only when you preview your work in a browser. The visual editor in Dreamweaver makes creating frames a lot easier because you can view all of the HTML files that make up the frameset at the same time and can edit them while they display the way they appear in a browser.

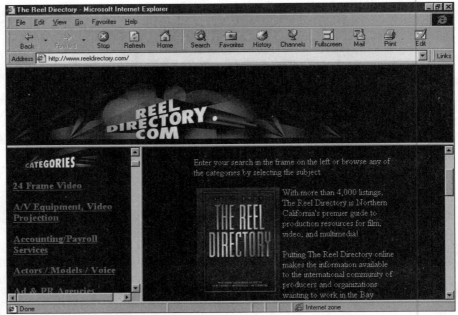

Figure 8-1:
A well-designed, frames-based Web site.

As a navigational feature, frames enable you to keep some information constant, while changing other information on the same page. For example, you can keep a list of links visible in one frame and display the information each link brings up in another frame. As shown in Figure 8-1, ReelDirectory.com, a resource for San Francisco Bay-area filmmakers, uses frames to show viewers a list of categories in the left frame that, when selected, displays listings in the right frame.

Frames look great to many designers, but they're also very controversial. Although frames give you some great navigational features, they also open up a range of design problems and aren't always the best way to organize your site.

For example, you can create as many frames as you want within a browser window. Unfortunately, some people overuse them and create designs that are so complex and broken up that they're neither aesthetically appealing nor easily navigable. Putting too many frames on one page can also make a site hard to read because the individual windows are too small. This has led many viewers to passionately hate frames, and many sites that rushed to implement frames when they were first introduced have either abandoned them or minimized their use.

The most problematic aspect of frames is that they're not backward compatible. That means if a visitor uses an older browser that doesn't support frames, they won't see anything — that's right, they get a blank page — unless you use a special tag called the <NOFRAMES> tag to create an alternative page to supplement your framed page. If you want to ensure that your pages work in older browsers, you can find information about the <NOFRAMES> tag in "Creating Alternative Designs for Older Browsers" at the end of this chapter.

Here's a list of guidelines to follow when using frames:

✔ **Don't use frames just for the sake of using frames.** If you have a compelling reason to use frames, then create an elegant and easy-to-follow frameset, but don't do it just because Dreamweaver makes it easy.

✔ **Limit the use of frames and keep files small.** Remember that each frame you create represents another HTML file. Thus, a frameset with three frames requires a browser to display three Web pages and that can dramatically increase download time.

✔ **Turn off frame borders.** Newer browsers support the ability to turn off the border that divides frames in a frameset. If the section has to be scrollable, the border is visible no matter what, but if you can turn it off, your pages look cleaner. Frame borders are thick and an ugly gray, and they can really break up a nice design. Use them only when you feel it's really necessary. I show you how to turn off frame borders in the section "Changing Frame Properties" toward the end of this chapter.

✔ **Don't use frames when tables are better.** Tables are often easier to create and can provide a more elegant solution to your design needs because they're less intrusive to the design. I include lots of information on creating tables in Chapter 7.

✔ **Don't place frames within frames.** The windows get just too darned small to be useful for much of anything, and the screen looks horribly complicated. You can also run into problems when your framed site links to another site that's displayed in your frameset. The sidebar "Resist using frames when you link to other people's Web sites" provides many more reasons to limit using frames inside of frames.

Understanding How Frames Work

When you create a Web page with frames in Dreamweaver, you need to remember that each frame area is a separate file, and you need to save each frame area as a separate page. You also want to keep track of which file is displayed in which section of the frame so that you can set links.

Resist using frames when you link to other people's Web sites

I understand that most people don't want to lose viewers to another site when they set a link, but that's the nature of the Web. If your site is designed well, you shouldn't have to worry about losing people. Instead, you should guide them around your informative site and then politely help them to other resources that they may find of interest — and let them go. Frames keep users captive and often leave them so annoyed with you for taking up part of their browser area with your site that you do yourself more harm than good in trying to keep them.

If you insist on using frames when you link to another site, do so discretely by placing a small, narrow frame across the bottom of the screen or the left side, not a wide band across the top and certainly not more than one frame that still contains information from your site. Not only is this rude and ugly, but it's gotten a few Web sites sued because the people they linked to felt that the designers were making it look like their content belonged to the site using the frames.

Another reason not to use frames when you link to another site is that many other sites use frames, too, and you can quickly create a mass of frames within frames that makes it difficult for users to find their way through information. Not everyone realizes that you can get out of frames — if you haven't figured it out yet as a user, you can always right-click in your browser in Windows or click and hold in your browser on a Mac, and then in the pop-up menu that appears, choose the option to open the frame in a separate window. Now that you know this trick, you can get out of a framed situation, but don't count on your users knowing how to do this if they get annoyed.

Figure 8-2 shows a simple frameset example with three frames, each with a different HTML page and the text Page 1, Page 2, and Page 3, so that I can clearly refer to them in the numbered steps that follow.

In addition to the files that display in each frame, another HTML file makes up a frameset. This page isn't visible in the browser, but it describes the frames and instructs the browser how and where to display them. This gets a little complicated, but don't worry. Dreamweaver creates these pages for you. I just want to give you a general understanding of all the files you're creating so that the steps that follow make more sense.

To help you understand how this works, use the frameset in Figure 8-2 as an example. In this frameset, you see three frames with three different HTML pages displayed in those frames. The fourth HTML file that makes up the frameset is behind the scenes, describing how the frames should be displayed, whether they should be on the left side of the page or the right, and how large they should be. That fourth file contains other information as well, such as the name assigned to each frame section. The name of each

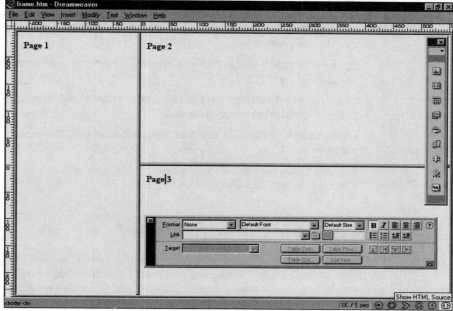

Figure 8-2:
This is an
example
of simple
frameset.

frame is used to set links so that you can specify which frame a new HTML file should *target,* or open into. I cover more about linking frames in "Setting Targets and Links in Frames" later in this chapter.

Creating a frame in Dreamweaver

You create a frame in Dreamweaver by splitting a single HTML file. When you do that, Dreamweaver automatically generates an untitled page with the <FRAMESET> tag and then additional untitled pages that display in each frame that you create. This is important to understand because you have to save and name each of these pages as a separate file, even though Dreamweaver makes it look like you're working on one page that's broken into sections.

To create a simple frameset in Dreamweaver, such as the one shown in Figure 8-2, follow these steps:

1. **Choose File⇨New to start a new page.**

2. **Choose Modify⇨Frameset⇨Split Frame Left.**

   You can also choose Split Frame Right, Up, or Down. Split Frame Left or Right divides the page vertically. Split Frame Up or Down divides the page horizontally.

   In this example, the page splits into two sections.

3. **Click inside the right frame area to make it active.**

4. **Choose** <u>M</u>odify⇨<u>F</u>rameset⇨Split Frame <u>U</u>p, <u>D</u>own, <u>L</u>eft, or <u>R</u>ight **to divide the page again.**

   In this example, I chose Split Frame Up. The right frame divides into two sections.

5. **Click to select the bar that divides the frames and drag it until the page is divided the way you want.**

6. **To edit each section of the frameset, click inside the frame that you want to work on.**

   You can type, insert images, create tables, and add any other features just as you would to any other page.

Saving files in a frameset

Dreamweaver gives you multiple save options with framesets. You can save an individual HTML file displayed in a frame by choosing File⇨Save just as you would save any other individual page, and Dreamweaver automatically generates a different number for each file that makes up a frameset — such as UntitledFrame-1.htm, UntitledFrame-2.htm, and so on. You can change the filenames to anything you want.

If you want to save all the files that you've created in your frameset at the same time, choose File⇨Save All. Dreamweaver prompts you to save each page.

To save only the page that defines the frameset, choose File⇨Save Frameset. Remember that this page doesn't display in any of the frames; it simply defines the entire display area, specifying which of the other pages displays in each frame, as well as the position and size of the frames. Make sure that you choose a name for this page that's distinct from the names of the frame section pages.

Carefully name the files that make up your frameset in a way that helps you keep them in order. When you get into setting links in the next section, you may find that the filenames you choose for your frameset are crucial for the process of organizing links among framed documents, and even more complex than with regular HTML files.

Setting Targets and Links in Frames

One of the best features of frames is the ability to manipulate the contents of each frame separately. This feature opens a wide range of design possibilities that can improve navigation for your site. One very common way to use a frameset is to create a frame that displays a list of links to various pages of your site, and then open those links into another frame on the same page. Doing so makes it possible to keep a list of links constantly visible, and can make navigation a lot simpler and more intuitive.

Setting links from a file in one frame so that the pages they link to open in another frame is like linking from one page to another, and that's essentially what you're doing. What makes linking a frameset distinctive is that, in addition to indicating which page you want to open with the link, you have to specify which frame section it should *target* (open into).

But before you can set those links, you need to do a few things: First, you need to create some other pages that you can link to. That part's easy. You can do that by clicking in any frame and choosing File⇨New, or you can choose File⇨New Window and create additional pages outside the frameset. It really doesn't matter. Either way, you create a new, distinct HTML file. I prefer to create them within the frameset so that I can see how they look next to the pages that I link them to. But if you create the new files as completely separate pages, you can still link them into any frame area in your frameset.

The other thing you have to do before you can set links is to name each frame so that you can specify where the linked file should load. This makes more sense after you see how it works, as I show in the next section.

Naming frames

For the following steps, use the simple frameset you created in the section "Creating a frame in Dreamweaver."

1. **Choose Window⇨Frames to open the Frames dialog box.**

2. **If the Property inspector isn't already open, choose Window⇨ Properties.**

3. **Click to place your cursor in the area of the Frames dialog box that corresponds to the frame you want to name.**

   Figure 8-3 shows the Frames dialog box with each frame named. The Frames dialog box, which appears on the left of the figure, is basically a small copy of the main page. Use this dialog box to indicate which frame you're working on in the Property inspector, the dialog box shown at the bottom of the figure, which is where you make any changes to the frame's properties.

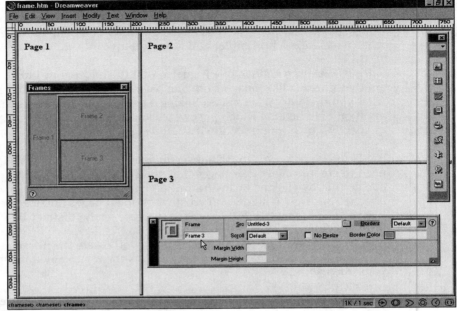

Figure 8-3:
The Frames
dialog box
enables you
to name the
frames in
your
frameset.

4. In the top-left of the Property inspector, type the name you want for the frame in the text box that appears just under the word Frame.

In the example in Figure 8-3, I use the names Frame 1, Frame 2, and Frame 3 to correspond to the pages and their page names. You can call your frames anything you want. I often name frames with descriptive words like Top, Left, Center, or Bottom.

5. Save each file.

Refer to the section "Saving files in a frameset," earlier in this chapter, for more info. This is a good time to make sure that each HTML file displayed in a frame is saved. The best way to do this (and keep track of your files) is to put your cursor in each frame separately, and choose File⇨Save and then name the HTML page. I've chosen to name these pages page1.htm, page2.htm, and page3.htm so that I can easily keep track.

I like to save my work on a regular basis so that I never lose more than a few minutes of work if my system crashes or the power goes out. Beware, however, that when you work with frames, you need to save each page separately. To do so, click to place your cursor in the frame you want to save and choose File⇨Save.

Creating new pages in a frame

Before you can set links, you have to create new pages. Follow these steps to create a new page within a frame in your frameset:

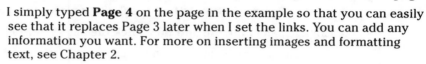

1. **Click to place your cursor inside the frame in which you want to create a new file.**

   Using the example shown earlier in Figure 8-3, I put my cursor in Frame 3 because Frame 3 is where I want to add pages that I'll link to from Frame 1.

2. **Choose File⇨New.**

   A new, blank page appears in the frame area.

3. **Add the text, images, or other information that you want on the page.**

   I simply typed **Page 4** on the page in the example so that you can easily see that it replaces Page 3 later when I set the links. You can add any information you want. For more on inserting images and formatting text, see Chapter 2.

   You can add any elements to a page in a frame that you would add to any other HTML page.

4. **Choose File⇨Save.**

   I called my file page4.htm in keeping with the naming convention I started earlier.

5. **Repeat these steps to create as many pages as you want.**

   I went on to create Page 5 and Page 6 so I have a few pages to set links to when I go through the steps in the next section.

When you want to open a page in a frame, click to place your cursor inside the frame and choose File⇨Open in Frame. If you simply choose File⇨Open, you open the page by itself in a new Dreamweaver window.

Setting links to a target frame

Setting links in a frameset requires some preliminary work. If you jumped to this section without creating a frameset, as described in the section, "Creating new pages in a frame," or without having named your frames, as described in "Naming frames" (both earlier in this chapter), you need to go back and start with those steps.

If you already have a frameset and just want to get better at setting links, this section is where you want to be. Setting links in a frameset is like setting any other links between pages, except that you need to specify the target frame. (That's why you need to take the time to name each frame — now you can use those names as targets.)

In the following steps, I continue to use the sample frameset shown earlier in Figures 8-2 and 8-3. I set three links in Page 1 that will open Pages 3 through 6 in the Frame 3 area of the frameset. If this seems confusing, don't fret. It's easier to understand after you try the following steps:

1. **Click to place the cursor inside the frame in which you want to create your links.**

   As you can see in the example shown in Figure 8-4, I've added text for links to Pages 4, 5, and 6.

2. **Highlight the text or image you want to link.**

3. **In the Property inspector, click the folder icon.**

   The Select HTML file dialog box appears.

4. **Use the Browse button to find the file to which you want to link.**

5. **Click to select the file and then click the Select button.**

   The name of the file appears in the Link text box in the Property inspector.

6. **From the pull-down menu next to Target in the Property inspector, choose the name of the frame you want the link to open into.**

   In keeping with my example, I chose Frame 3, as you can see in Figure 8-4.

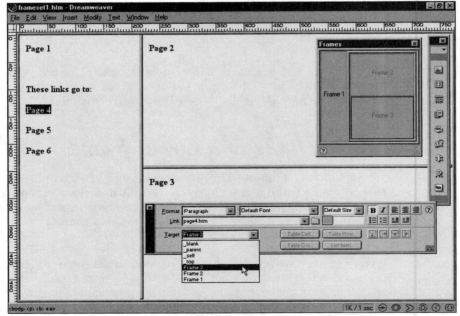

Figure 8-4: Use the Target pull-down menu to specify the frame that you want your linked page to open into.

The result, as shown in Figure 8-5, is that when you select the linked text called "Page 4" that appears in Page 1, page4.htm displays in Frame 3. Don't get overwhelmed by the complexity of all these numbers. Study Figures 8-2 through 8-5 and follow the steps outlined in this and the previous sections and you should be able to create your first frameset. After you go through these steps, this all makes more sense. You can then adapt these steps to any type of frameset that you may want to create.

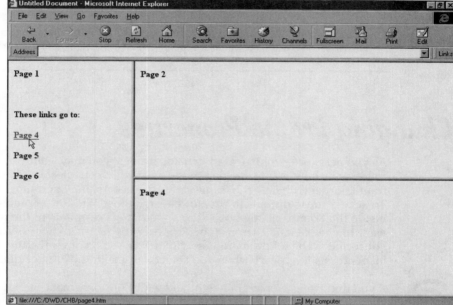

Figure 8-5:
The links in this simple frameset example cause Page 4 to open in Frame 3 when the linked text "Page 4" is selected in Frame 1.

Comparing target options

You have many options when you target links in a frameset. As I show in the section "Setting links to a target frame" (earlier in this chapter) you can specify that a linked page should open in another frame within your frameset. In addition, you can set linked pages to open in the same frame as the page with the link, to open a completely new page, and even to open a second browser window. Table 8-1 provides a list of target options and what they mean. You can find all of these options in the Target pull-down menu of the Property inspector.

The Target pull-down menu in the Property inspector is only active when you select a linked image or section of text.

Table 8-1	Understanding Frame Target Options
Target Name	*Action*
_blank	Opens the linked file into a new browser window.
_parent	Opens the linked file into the frameset parent of the page that has the link. If no parent file exists, the link opens in the same frame as the original page. (The *parent* is the window that contains the frameset.)
_self	Opens the linked file in the same frame as the original page.
_top	Opens the linked page into the full Web browser window, replacing the entire framed document with the linked file.

Changing Frame Properties

As you get more sophisticated in using frames, you may want to further refine your frames by changing properties, which enables you to turn off frame borders, change the frame or border colors, limit scrolling, and so on. To access these options in Dreamweaver, choose Window⇨Frames, click inside the Frames dialog box in the area that corresponds to the frame you want to change, and then use the Property inspector to access the options I describe in the following four sections. Figure 8-6 shows the Property inspector as it appears when you select a frame in the Frames dialog box.

If you don't see the margin height and width options, make sure that you click the small arrow in the bottom-right corner of the Property inspector.

Changing frame borders

The best thing I think you can do with a border is to turn it off. You can do so by choosing No from the Borders pull-down menu in the Property inspector. Your other options include Yes, which forces the borders to be visible, and Default, which usually means that they display but follow the default setting of the browser used by your viewer.

You can make global border settings using the Property inspector shown in Figure 8-6, or you can change these settings for a particular border in your frameset by selecting that frame border, which displays the Property inspector shown in Figure 8-7.

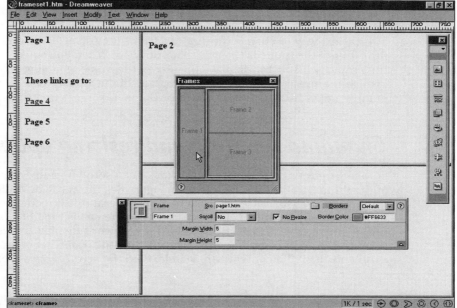

Figure 8-6:
The
Property
inspector
provides
access to
frame
properties
only when a
frame is
selected in
the Frames
dialog box.

Figure 8-7:
Change the
settings for
borders on
a frame-by-
frame basis.

If you choose to keep your borders visible, you may want to change the color by selecting the Border Color square and then choosing a color from the Dreamweaver palette.

If you select a specific border, the Property inspector also enables you to specify the border width, as shown in Figure 8-7. Simply enter a value in pixels in the Border Width text box to change the width of the selected border.

Changing frame sizes

The easiest way to change the size of a frame is to select the border and drag it until the frame is the size that you want. When you select the border, the Property inspector displays the size of the frame, enabling you to change the size in pixels or as a percentage of the display area by entering a number in the text area next to Row or Column.

Changing scrolling and resizing options

Scrolling options control whether a viewer can scroll up and down or left and right in a frame area. As shown in Figure 8-8, the scrolling options for frames are Yes, No, Auto, and Default. As a general rule, I recommend leaving the scroll option set to Auto because then a visitor's browser can turn scrolling on if necessary. That is, if the viewer's display area is too small to see all the contents of the frame, then the frame becomes scrollable. If all the contents are visible, then the scroll arrows aren't visible.

Figure 8-8:
This pull-down menu lets you control frame-scrolling options.

If you set this option to Yes, the scroll arrows are visible whether they're needed or not. If you set it to No, they won't be visible, even if that means your viewer can't see all of the contents of the frame. Default leaves it up to the browser. In most browsers, the Default option results in the same display as the Auto option, but Default can result in the scroll bar always being visible or never being visible.

Notice also in Figure 8-8 the No Resize option. If you place a check mark in this box, then a visitor to your site can't change the size of the frames. If you leave this box unchecked, then your user can select the border and drag it to make the frame area small or larger, just as you can when you develop your frames in Dreamweaver. Generally, I like to give viewers control, but I often check the No Resize option because I want to ensure that my viewers don't alter my design, especially because some viewers may do so accidentally.

Setting margin height and width

The Margin Height and Margin Width features enable you to specify the amount of margin space within a frame. I generally recommend that you set this to at least 2 pixels and make it larger if you want to create more space around your content. Adding margin space is especially important if you turn the borders off because margins separate the content in your frames when displayed in a browser. If the frames are turned off, adding margin space can replace the separation that would have been created by the frame.

Creating Alternative Designs for Older Browsers

Frames provide some great navigational options, but they can also provide the worst possible navigation nightmare. That's because they're not *backward compatible*. For example, if you create a frameset on your site and a visitor tries to access your page with an old browser — such as an early version of the AOL browser or Netscape 1.1, both of which are still used on the Web today — they won't see the contents of any of your frames. In fact, if you don't provide an alternative, they won't see anything at all.

So what's the alternative? It's called the <NOFRAMES> tag, and Dreamweaver makes it easy to create this option for low-end users. The <NOFRAMES> tag enables you to create an alternative page that displays in browsers that don't support frames. The contents of the <NOFRAMES> tag are stored in the frameset file. A browser that supports frames ignores the content of the alternative page because it knows not to display anything that appears in the <NOFRAMES> tag. A browser that doesn't support frames ignores the contents of the Frameset and displays all of the content contained within the <NOFRAMES> tag.

Fortunately for you, you don't have to know much about how this all works; you just need to know that you should use the <NOFRAMES> tag in Dreamweaver if you want to ensure that your pages look okay to people with older browsers.

To create an alternative page for older browsers using the <NOFRAMES> tag, open any document that uses frames and follow these steps:

1. **Choose Modify⇨Frameset⇨Edit NoFrames Content.**

   A new Document window opens with "NoFrames Content" at the top.

2. **Edit this page as you would any other page by inserting images, typing text, creating tables, and adding any other features you want (except frames, of course).**

   Your goal is to create an alternative page that can be viewed by people using older browsers. The alternative page can be as simple as instructions for how viewers can get a newer copy of Internet Explorer or Netscape Navigator, or as complex as a copy of the page you created in frames, re-created as well as you can without frames.

   You can find information about adding images and formatting text in Chapter 2.

3. **To return to your frameset, choose Modify➪Frameset➪Edit NoFrames Content.**

   The check box next to the Edit NoFrames Content option disappears and the frames page again appears.

If you create an alternative page, don't forget to update it when you make changes to your frameset.

Chapter 9

Cascading Style Sheets

● ●

In This Chapter

▶ Introducing Dynamic HTML

▶ Comparing Web browsers

▶ Creating styles

▶ Applying styles

● ●

*C*ascading Style Sheets (CSS) — just the name should send chills down the spine of anyone with a graphic design background. If you're not familiar with the concept of style sheets, you're sure to appreciate the benefits — styles sheets can save lots of time and make creating a consistent look and feel throughout a Web site much easier.

Like many such timesavers, however, style sheets are much more complex to create than basic HTML formatting. Fortunately, Dreamweaver takes care of creating the code for CSS, providing an intuitive interface that enables you to choose fonts, colors, styles, and other formatting, without worrying about the programming code that makes it all work.

Style sheets are just a part of Dynamic HTML, which uses scripting languages in the Document Object Model to create dynamic effects and global styles. If this still seems a little confusing, don't worry. It'll make more sense as you find out what you can do with these powerful new HTML features. For more on the Document Object Model, see the sidebar "What is the Document Object Model?"

In this chapter, I introduce you to CSS and to CSS-P (the addition that enables precise positioning of elements on a Web page). I also walk you step-by-step through creating and applying styles sheets in Dreamweaver. In Chapter 13, you can find lots more information about using Dreamweaver to create other Dynamic HTML features, such as applying behaviors to create rollover effects and changing elements over time to create animations.

What is the Document Object Model?

The Document Object Model, part of the World Wide Web Consortium's proposed HTML 4.0 specification, makes every element on a page an identifiable object. The properties of that object are then readable and writeable, meaning that you can use a scripting language, such as JavaScript, to change, hide, or move the elements' attributes. This ability is what makes possible most of the DHTML effects, such as dynamically changing text and images.

Appreciating Style Sheets

Style sheets are powerful tools because they enable you to define a set of formatting attributes and then apply them to as many elements on a page or throughout a Web site as you want. For example, you can define a Headline style as bold, blue, and centered, and then you can easily apply that style to every headline in your Web page. This saves you time because instead of formatting every headline with three steps — to make it bold, centered, and blue — you can apply the Headline style and all three changes occur at once.

You can save even more time if you decide to change one of the style attributes. If, one fine day, you decide that all your headlines should be purple rather than blue, you can change the style definition for Headline and all the text on your site that you formatted with the Headline style changes from blue to purple. One simple change to the style can save you hours, even days, if you ever find yourself in a redesign (and believe me, every good site goes through several redesigns).

Understanding style sheet differences in Web browsers

The differences in the way Netscape Navigator 4.0 and Internet Explorer 4.0 support Cascading Style Sheets can be extremely frustrating. The good news is that style sheets are great for design consistency and making fast changes throughout a page and even an entire site. The bad news is that style sheets are one of the newest additions to HTML and not all browsers support them. The worse news is that style sheets aren't backward compatible, meaning that if you use this cool new design feature and someone visits your site using an older browser, such as Netscape Navigator 3.0, they won't be able to see any of the formatting that you created with a style sheet.

Now for the even worse news. Even if your viewers use a newer browser, they won't necessarily see the same formatting. That's because Netscape and Microsoft haven't agreed on how they should implement and support style sheets.

For example, in Internet Explorer 4.0, you use JavaScript to change attributes, such as font color and size, after a page has loaded. This can add powerful effects to your site, such as changing the color of a link when a user moves the cursor over it. But this feature doesn't work the same way in Navigator because Navigator 4.0 doesn't support changes to attributes. On the other hand, both 4.0 browsers enable you to swap images, so you could create a similar effect by using two images of different colors. Fortunately, you don't have to know what browser supports what features. Dreamweaver takes care of that for you by enabling you to target browsers and limit design options to features supported by target browsers.

Dreamweaver works hard to try to solve these problems with browser differences. When you work with Dynamic HTML, Dreamweaver creates complex code in the background designed to take the best advantage of the features supported by each browser. If you look at the code, it may look a bit more complex than necessary sometimes, but that's because Dreamweaver creates these tags in ways that both browsers can interpret them. And this is true not only for DHTML. As you can see in Chapter 14, the best way to insert many multimedia files, such as Shockwave and Flash, is to use a combination of code that's designed to compensate for the differences between browsers.

Using font tags without style sheets

Before you jump into what you can do with style sheets, you should have a basic understanding of how you can apply some of these formatting features without style sheets. Unless you're designing your site for an audience that you know uses the latest browser, you're still better off directly applying formatting features — such as font face, color, and size — than using style sheets.

In Chapter 2, I give you instructions on directly applying the most basic formatting options, such as bold and italic. In this section, I show you how to use Dreamweaver to specify fonts without using style sheets. In the next section, I get into specifying fonts as part of a style sheet definition.

Understanding the <FONT> tag

You can use the <FONT> tag to specify size, font face, and color. All of these options are attributes of the <FONT> tag, so you specify them in the Property inspector in Dreamweaver. But before you start applying these options, you should understand a little about how they work.

HTML specifies font sizes relative to a given browser's default font size. The actual size of the default font varies from browser to browser and from platform to platform. For example, Netscape Navigator defaults to Times Roman 12-point type, but users can change the default to any font and size in the browser's preferences. In most browsers, the standard default size is HTML Font Size 3. If you're used to regular font sizes, 3 sounds like it's a really small font size, but it's about the same as Times 12 point on the Mac and Times 14 point on the PC. That's why the default size option in the Property inspector in Dreamweaver is the equivalent of font size 3.

You can change that default to any font size between 1 and 6, with 6 being the largest. You also have the option in HTML of setting the font size using +1 through +6 or –1 through –6. Using these options enables you to specify a font size relative to the default of the browser, even if it's something other than font size 3. For example, if you set the font size to +2, it displays at +2 larger than whatever the default font size is, even if the viewer has chosen to make that default size the equivalent of Times 24 point.

When you specify a font face in Dreamweaver, you override the default font of the browser. But for the font to display, it must be available on the viewer's computer. If you specify that you want to use Helvetica, but your viewer doesn't have Helvetica, then the browser reverts to the default. To help get around this problem, HTML enables you to specify multiple font faces and then prioritize their use. For example, if you specify Helvetica, you may also specify a similar font, such as Arial, as your second choice. Then, if Helvetica isn't available, the browser looks for Arial. If Arial is on the viewer's hard drive, the browser uses it to display the text. You can even take this a step further and choose a family of fonts, such as serif or sans serif, as one of your options. Then the browser at least tries to use a font in the same family if none of the fonts you've chosen is available.

Dreamweaver provides a list of common fonts and families under the font option in the Property inspector. You can also edit this list to add fonts and combinations of fonts. Figure 9-1 shows the Font List dialog box where you can change and edit the list of available fonts.

Figure 9-1:
The Font
List dialog
box makes
it easy to
edit the
fonts you
can apply
with
Dreamweaver.

Applying the <FONT> tag in Dreamweaver

Dreamweaver makes applying any font, or combination of fonts, and setting font sizes and colors easy. Follow these steps to apply all these attributes to text:

1. **Highlight the text that you want to change.**

2. **In the Property inspector, choose a set of fonts from the pull-down font list.**

   The font is automatically applied to the text. Remember that if you don't find the font or fonts that you want, you can edit this list (see "Understanding the <FONT> tag" earlier in this chapter).

3. **With the text still highlighted, choose the size you want from the Font Size pull-down menu in the Property inspector.**

   You can choose a size from 1 to 6 or specify sizes relative to the default font size by choosing + or –1 through 6.

4. **With the text still highlighted, choose the Text Color area in the middle of the Property inspector.**

   The Text Color area is right below the Font Size box.

5. **Choose any color from the color palette, as you see in Figure 9-2.**

   This color palette is limited to Web-safe colors (those that best display on both the Macintosh and Windows operating systems). If you want to create a custom color, choose the icon that looks like a painter's palette in the bottom-right of the color swatch palette.

Creating Style Sheets in Dreamweaver

When you get into creating and using style sheets, you use some of the most complex and advanced features of Dreamweaver. Thus, creating styles takes a little more time to grasp than applying basic HTML tags, even tags as complex as tables and frames. Still Dreamweaver makes it much easier to define style sheets than to write them by hand, a task much more like programming than creating other HTML tags.

To help you get the hang of using Dreamweaver to create style sheets, I first walk you through the screens that define styles and give you an overview of your options as you create styles. After the following sections on each aspect of style sheet creation, you find specific numbered steps that walk you through the entire process.

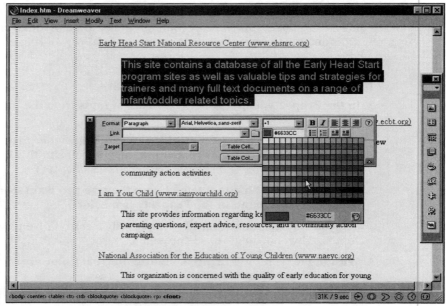

Figure 9-2:
Use the
Property
inspector to
set font
size, face,
and color.

Understanding style types

You can define two different kinds of styles: HTML tag styles and custom styles. The difference is that a custom style is a completely new set of formatting attributes that you can apply to any text block identified with a Class attribute. Don't worry about this too much because I get into it more later in the chapter. For now, you should know that when you define a custom style, you give it a Class name and then you use that name to apply the style to any text block on the page. This means that you can call a custom style anything you want and create new ones anytime that won't necessarily affect anything else on the page.

In contrast, you create HTML tag styles by redefining existing HTML tags. That means that you change how common HTML tags format text throughout your page and even your Web site, if you want to define it that way. The result is that if you redefine a tag, such as the <H1> tag, all the text already formatted with the <H1> tag automatically changes to reflect your new styles definition.

Using the Edit Style Sheet dialog box

To create either HTML tag styles or custom styles, choose Window➪Styles to open the Styles palette, and then click on the Style Sheet button at the bottom of the dialog box to open the Edit Style Sheet dialog box that you see in Figure 9-3.

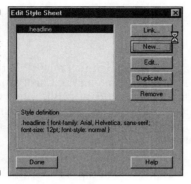

Figure 9-3:
The Edit Style Sheet dialog box provides options for creating, editing, and removing styles.

The Edit Style Sheet dialog box includes several options:

- ✔ **Link** enables you to link to or import an external style sheet (a separate text file that defines a style) so that you can apply it to the page or even the entire site that you're working on. You can find more information on external styles in "Creating and Linking to External Style Sheets" at the end of this chapter.

- ✔ **New** enables you to define one of three types of style sheets. You can find these explained in detail in "Defining styles" later in the chapter.

- ✔ **Edit** enables you to change an existing style. For more information, see "Editing an Existing Style" later in the chapter.

- ✔ **Duplicate** creates a copy of a selected style that you can then redefine as any one of the three style options.

- ✔ **Remove** enables you to delete a defined style.

The Undo feature doesn't work with the Remove option in the Edit Style Sheet dialog box. Before you select the Remove button, make sure that you really want to get rid of the style.

Understanding New Style options

If you choose the New button in the Edit Style Sheet dialog box, the New Style dialog box, shown in Figure 9-4, opens, giving you these options:

Figure 9-4:
The New
Style dialog
box.

✔ **Make Custom Style (class)** enables you to define a new style that you can apply to any section of text on a page, using the Class attribute. All custom style names must begin with a period, which Dreamweaver automatically inserts as you name the style. If you choose this option, another dialog box appears, which I explain in "Creating a custom style: Step-by-step" later in this chapter.

✔ **Redefine HTML Tag** enables you to create a style that changes the formatting associated with an existing HTML tag. This option also opens yet another dialog box where you can choose an existing tag to redefine. For more information on this option, see "Redefining HTML tags" later in this chapter.

✔ **Use CSS Selector** enables you to create sub-styles associated with other attributes for any section of the document identified by a valid CSS selector. Options include a.active, a.hover, a.link, and a.visited.

Defining styles

When you choose to make a custom style or to redefine an existing HTML tag, the Style Definition dialog box opens. This is where you decide how you want your style to look by selecting the attribute options. This dialog box includes eight panels, each with multiple options that you can use to define different style elements.

You don't have to make selections for all the options in each panel. Any options that you leave blank remain in the browser's default. For example, if you don't specify a text color, the text displays as black.

Don't be frustrated by options in these panels that Dreamweaver doesn't yet support. If they don't display in Dreamweaver, they almost certainly won't work in any of the current browsers. The good news is that Macromedia is looking ahead, building these options into Dreamweaver so that they'll be ready when these features are supported. Keep an eye on Macromedia's Web site at www.macromedia.com for changes and updates to Dreamweaver, as well as for news about changing standards and support for these CSS features.

The Type panel

The Type panel (see Figure 9-5) enables you to specify the following formatting options:

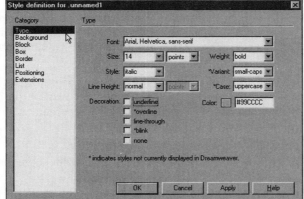

Figure 9-5:
The Type panel in the Style Definition dialog box.

✔ **Font** specifies a font, font family, or series of families. You can choose to define a new font option and then specify that option for your new style.

✔ **Size** defines the size of the text. You can choose a specific point size or use a relative size, expressed as small, extra small, and so on.

✔ **Style** enables you to choose whether the text appears as Normal, Italic, or Oblique.

✔ **Line Height** enables you to specify the height of a line that the text is placed on (you graphic designers usually call this *leading*). The 4.0 browsers don't support this feature, and it can cause problems in older browsers. So, for now, you should probably avoid this.

✔ **Decoration** enables you to specify whether text is underlined, overlined, or displayed with a strikethrough. You can also choose to make the text blink, which makes it flash on and off.

Use the Decoration options sparingly, if at all. Links are automatically underlined, so if you underline text that isn't a link, you risk confusing viewers. Overlined and strikethrough text can be harder to read, so use these options only if that is your intention. And, by all means, resist the blink option; it's distracting and can make the entire screen harder to read.

✔ **Weight** enables you to control how bold the text displays by using a specific or relative boldness option.

✔ **Variant** enables you to select a variation of the font, such as small caps. Unfortunately, Dreamweaver doesn't display this attribute in the Document window.

✔ **Case** enables you to globally change the case of selected words, making them all uppercase or lowercase or with initial caps. Unfortunately, Dreamweaver doesn't display this attribute in the Document window either.

✔ **Color** defines the color of the text. You can use the color square icon to open a Web-safe color palette in which you can select predefined colors or create custom colors.

The Background panel

The Background panel (see Figure 9-6) enables you to specify a background color or image for a style.

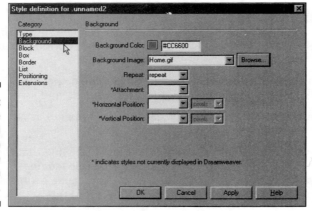

Figure 9-6: The Background panel in the Style Definition dialog box.

✔ **Background Color** specifies the background color of an element, such as a table.

✔ **Background Image** enables you to select a background image as part of the style definition.

✔ **Repeat** determines how and if the background image tiles across and down the page. In all cases, the image is cropped if it doesn't fit behind the element.

Repeat options are as follows:

- *No repeat:* The background displays once at the beginning of the element.

- *Repeat:* The background tiles vertically and horizontally behind the element.

- *Repeat-x:* The background repeats horizontally, but not vertically, behind the element.

- *Repeat-y:* The background repeats vertically, but not horizontally, behind the element.

✔ **Attachment, Horizontal Position,** and **Vertical Position** are not yet supported by Dreamweaver.

Some of the CSS features that are available in these panels don't yet display in Dreamweaver because they're not supported by browsers, even though they're part of the proposed standard. Although you can apply these features, you're best to avoid them because they won't work when your pages display in a browser.

The Block panel

The Block panel (see Figure 9-7) defines spacing and alignment settings for tags and attributes.

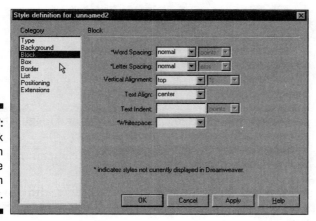

Figure 9-7:
The Block
panel in
the Style
Definition
dialog box.

✔ **Word Spacing** is not yet supported by Dreamweaver.

✔ **Letter Spacing** is not yet supported by Dreamweaver.

✔ **Vertical Alignment** works only with the <IMAGE> tag in Dreamweaver. It specifies the vertical alignment of an image, usually in relation to its parent.

✔ **Text Align** specifies how text aligns within an element.

✔ **Text Indent** specifies how far the first line of text indents.

✔ **Whitespace** is not yet supported by Dreamweaver.

The Box panel

The Box panel (see Figure 9-8) defines settings for tags and attributes that control the placement of elements on the page.

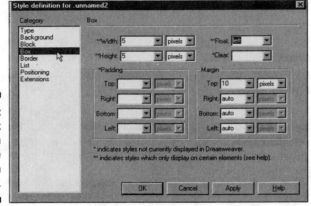

Figure 9-8:
The Box panel in the Style Definition dialog box.

✔ **Width** and **Height** enable you to specify a width and height that you can use in styles that you apply to images or layers.

✔ **Float** enables you to align an image to the left or right so that other elements, such as text, wrap around it.

✔ **Clear** enables you to control how an image interacts with a layer. If a layer appears on the clear side, the element with the clear setting moves below it.

✔ **Padding** is not yet supported by Dreamweaver.

✔ **Margin** enables you to define the amount of space between the borders or edges of elements.

The Border and List panels

The Border panel defines settings, such as width, color, and style, for the borders of elements on a page. The List panel defines settings, such as bullet size and type, for list tags. Dreamweaver doesn't currently support any of these features.

The Positioning panel

The Positioning panel (see Figure 9-9) enables you to change a tag or block of text into a new layer and specify its attributes. When applied, this style uses the tag specified for defining layers in the Layer preferences. The default in Dreamweaver for layers is the <DIV> tag. You can change this by editing the Layer preferences, but the <DIV> tag is the most universally supported, so you're best to stick with it.

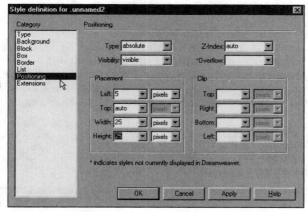

Figure 9-9:
The Positioning panel in the Style Definition dialog box.

✔ **Type** enables you to specify the position of a layer as absolute, relative, or static.

• *Absolute* positioning uses the top and left coordinates entered in the Placement text boxes on this screen to control the position of the layer relative to the top-left corner of the Web page.

• *Relative* positioning isn't supported by Dreamweaver.

• *Static* positioning keeps the layer in the place where you insert it on the page.

✔ **Visibility** enables you to control if the browser displays the layer. Combined with a scripting language, such as JavaScript, you can use this feature to dynamically change the display of layers. The default on most browsers is to inherit the original layer's visibility value.

- *Inherit:* The layer has the visibility of its parent.
- *Visible:* The layer displays.
- *Hidden:* The layer doesn't display.

✓ **Z-Index** controls the position of the layer on the z coordinate, meaning how it stacks in relation to other elements on the page. Higher numbered layers appear above lower numbered layers.

✓ **Overflow** tells the browser how to display the contents of a layer if it exceeds its size.

- *Visible* forces the layer to increase in size to display all of its contents. The layer expands down and right.
- *Hidden* cuts off the contents of the layer that don't fit and doesn't provide any scroll bars.
- *Scroll* is not yet supported by Dreamweaver.
- *Auto* is not yet supported by Dreamweaver.

✓ **Placement** defines the size and location of a layer, in keeping with the setting for Type. The default values are measured in pixels, but you can also use pc (picas), pt (points), in (inches), mm (millimeters), cm (centimeters), or % (percentage of the parent's value). Don't use a space between the number and abbreviation — for example, use 7pc.

✓ **Clip** enables you to specify which part of the layer is visible by controlling what part of the layer is cropped if it doesn't fit in the display area.

The Extensions panel

Extensions include filters and cursor options, but Dreamweaver doesn't yet support them.

Creating a custom style: Step-by-step

Here's how to use Dreamweaver to define a style for headlines. If you want to create different styles for other elements, follow these same steps but change the specific attributes.

You can leave any attributes unspecified if you don't want to use them. If you don't specify them, the browser uses its own default. For example, I don't recommend using any of the Decoration options because they can distract and confuse viewers.

1. **Choose Window⇨Styles.**

2. **Select the Edit Style Sheets button in the Styles palette.**

3. **In the Edit Style Sheet dialog box, choose New.**

4. **Select the Make Custom Style (class) radio button.**

5. **Enter a name for the style.**

   Dreamweaver gives you a default name that begins with a period. Don't delete it by mistake. You can name the style anything you want.

6. **Click OK.**

   The Style Definition dialog window automatically opens.

7. **Choose the Type panel option on the left side of the dialog box.**

8. **Choose a font set from the Font pull-down list.**

   If you want to use fonts that aren't on the list, choose the Edit Font List option of the pull-down list to create new font options. (For more about how to create font sets, see "Understanding the <FONT> tag" earlier in this chapter).

9. **Choose the size that you want for your headline.**

   Large headlines are generally 24 or 36 point. You may prefer to choose a relative size, such as large or larger.

10. **Choose a Style from the pull-down menu.**

    Italic and Oblique are both good for making text stand out on a page.

11. **Choose Bold from the Weight pull-down menu to make your headline thicker and darker.**

12. **Ignore Variant and Case because Dreamweaver doesn't support them.**

13. **Select a color by clicking the Color square and choosing a color from the color swatches.**

    Sticking to the color swatches is best because it ensures that you use a Web-safe color. You can also create a custom color by clicking the icon that looks like a painter's palette in the bottom-right corner of the swatch area.

14. **Click OK when you're finished.**

    Your style is automatically added to the Styles list.

You can apply styles in the Styles list to any Web page or selected text block. For more on how to use styles, read "Applying Styles" later in this chapter.

Redefining HTML tags

The Redefining HTML Tags option opens the Style Definition dialog box that I describe earlier in this section. All the style options have the same effect. The difference is that when you create a custom style, you start a completely new style with its own unique name. When you redefine an HTML tag, you change the attributes associated with an existing HTML tag, such as <B> (bold), <HR> (horizontal rule), or <TABLE> (table).

To redefine a tag, choose the tag that you want to change from the pull-down list in the New Style dialog box (see Figure 9-10), and then define how you want to change it by using the Style Definition dialog box. Be aware that when you redefine an existing HTML tag, any text that you've already formatted with that tag changes to reflect the new definition.

Conflicting styles

Be careful when you apply more than one style to the same text (something that is easier to do than you may realize). The problem is that styles often conflict and, because browsers aren't all consistent in the way they display styles, the results can be inconsistent and unexpected.

For the most part, Netscape Navigator 4.0 and Internet Explorer 4.0 display all the attributes applied to an element, even if they're from different styles, as long as the styles don't conflict. If they do conflict, browsers prioritize styles depending on how they're defined.

Here's an example to help you get the idea. You define a custom style called .headline as red and centered and apply it to a selection of text. Then you decide you want that text to be bold, so you apply the bold tag independently by selecting it from the Property inspector. You have now used two different types of styles, but because they don't conflict, all of them take effect and your text becomes bold, centered, and red. If, however, you decide that you want this text aligned left, instead of centered, and apply left alignment directly from the Property inspector, then you have a conflict.

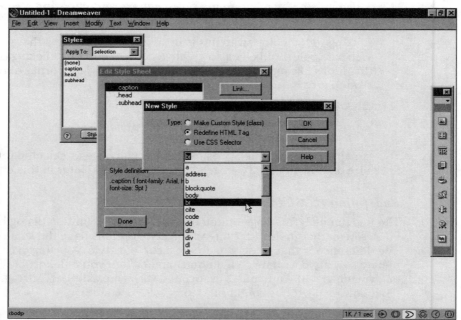

Figure 9-10: The Redefine HTML Tag option includes a list of the HTML tags included in Dreamweaver.

If a direct conflict exists, custom styles overrule regular HTML tag styles. The browser also gives priority to the attribute of the style that's inserted closest to the text. This can get really hard to juggle if you're applying defined styles, trying to keep track of standard HTML tags, and then trying to sort out how the browser prioritizes them. It gets worse with time, too, because these styles and priorities are sure to change and evolve. Your best bet is not to apply conflicting styles. Either go back and redefine an existing style, apply regular HTML tags individually, or create a new style. Remember that you can use the Duplicate option to make minor alterations easily.

Editing an Existing Style

You can change the attributes of any style by editing that style. This is a major advantage of style sheets because you can make global changes to a page or even an entire Web site by changing a style that you applied to multiple elements. Be aware, however, that everything you defined with that style will change.

Remember that you can also create new styles by duplicating an existing style and then altering it. Then you can apply that new style without changing elements that are already formatted on your pages.

Follow these steps to edit an existing style:

1. **Choose Text⇨Custom Styles⇨Edit Style Sheet.**

   You can also access this by clicking on the Edit Style Sheet button in the Styles palette.

2. **Select the style that you want to change in the Edit Style Sheet dialog box and click Edit.**

   The Style Definition dialog box for that style appears.

3. **Make a selection on the left side of the dialog box to open a particular panel, such as Type or Border, and then specify the style changes you want to make.**

   You can find descriptions of all the style options in "Defining styles" earlier in this chapter.

4. **When you've made all the changes you want, click OK and the style automatically redefines to reflect your changes.**

   At the same time, all elements that you defined with that style automatically change.

Applying Styles

Defining styles is the complicated part. Applying them after you've defined them is easy. You simply select the elements that you want to affect and then choose the predefined style you want to apply.

Follow these steps to apply a style:

1. **Highlight the text to which you want to apply a style.**

   If you want to apply a style to the body of a page, skip to Step 2.

2. **Choose Window⇔Styles.**

   The Styles palette opens, as shown in Figure 9-11.

3. **From the Apply To pull-down menu, choose Selection.**

   If you want to apply a style to the entire page, choose Body from the Apply To pull-down menu.

4. **Select the style that you want to apply from the list in the Styles palette.**

   The style is automatically applied to the selection.

You can also apply a custom style by selecting the text you want to change, choosing Text⇔Custom Style, and choosing a custom style from the submenu.

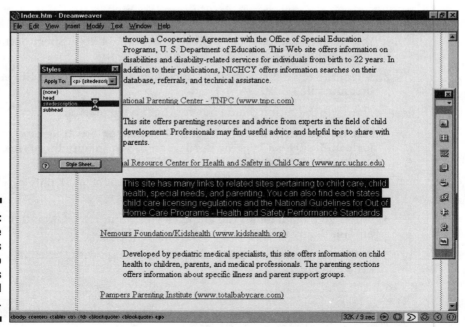

Figure 9-11:
Use the Styles palette to apply styles to selected text blocks.

Creating and Editing External Style Sheets

External style sheets enable you to create styles that you can apply to pages throughout a Web site. This is when style sheets really save time because you can define styles for common formatting options, such as headlines, captions, and even images, and make applying multiple formatting options to elements faster and easier. This also makes global changes easy because when you can change the external style sheet, you globally change every element to which you applied the style throughout the site.

You create external style sheets almost exactly the same way you create other style sheets, except external style sheets are saved in separate text files instead of being imbedded in an HTML document. When you use Dreamweaver to create an external style sheet, Dreamweaver automatically links the style sheet to the page that you're working on. You can then link it to any other Web page in which you want to apply the style definitions.

Follow these steps to create or link to an external style sheet:

1. **Select Window⇨Styles.**

   You can also click the Styles button on the Launcher.

2. **Choose the Style Sheet button in the Styles palette.**

   The Edit Style Sheet dialog box appears.

3. **Click the Link button.**

   The Add Remote Style Sheet dialog box appears.

4. **Use the Browse button to locate the external file that you want to link to the page.**

   You can also manually type in a path to any file.

5. **To create a new external style sheet, choose the Browse button. But instead of locating a file to link to, type a new name in the text box next to File Name.**

   You can use the Browse option to select the folder that you want the new file to reside in. Note that all external style sheets must end with the extension .css.

6. **Choose Link or Import and then click OK.**

   Import and Link serve similar functions, but Link is the better choice because it works in more browsers and provides more features.

When you create a new style sheet, you need to edit the file to define styles. The name of the external style sheet appears with the word *link* in the list of styles in the Edit Style Sheet dialog box. To edit that file and define styles, follow these steps:

1. **Select Window⇨Styles.**

   You can also click the Styles button on the Launcher.

2. **Click the Style Sheet button in the Styles palette.**

   The Edit Style Sheet dialog box appears.

3. **Select the name of the external style sheet you want to change and click the Edit button.**

   You can also double-click the style sheet name to select it and open the Style Definition dialog box.

4. **Click the New button to define a new style in the external style sheet.**

   You can now define styles for the external style sheet as you would for custom styles. I explain the style options in "Creating Style Sheets in Dreamweaver" earlier in this chapter. You can define as many styles as you want.

5. **Click Save when you finish defining styles.**

   Click Done to close the Edit Style Sheet dialog box.

Changing Style Sheet Preferences

Dreamweaver is so good at taking care of things for you that you should leave style sheet preferences alone, unless you really know what you're doing. The only change you can make in style sheet preferences controls whether or not Dreamweaver writes styles using *shorthand* (a more concise way to write the code that creates a style). If you're experienced at writing the HTML code for style sheets and prefer using shorthand, you may want to make this change because it makes editing styles manually easier. I don't recommend it, however, because some older browsers don't correctly interpret the shorthand and Dreamweaver does such a good job of creating styles for you that you shouldn't need to edit them yourself.

Part IV
Writing It Out: Dreamweaver Text Editors

The 5th Wave — By Rich Tennant

"Hold your horses. It takes time to build a home page for someone your size."

In this part . . .

1 **I**f you prefer working in the raw HTML code, this part is for you. Jump right in to the HTML text editor of your choice with introductions to BBEdit for the Macintosh crowd and HomeSite for you Windows users.

Chapter 10

Getting into HTML

● ●

In This Chapter

▶ Viewing source code

▶ Naming files

▶ Understanding HTML tags

● ●

Dreamweaver is so evolved as a Web design program that, for the most part, you really don't need to know HTML (Hypertext Markup Language). However, in some cases, you may bump up against some of the limitations of Dreamweaver and may need to tweak the HTML for one of your pages. Dreamweaver provides a number of options for doing this: It has a built-in HTML editor and also has the tried-and-true HTML editors HomeSite (for Windows) and BBEdit (for Macintosh) bundled with it.

When you first look at the code behind a Web page, you may be overwhelmed by what you see and decide that learning all these "hieroglyphics" isn't worth it. But having a basic understanding of HTML — what it looks like, where it comes from, and why it works the way it does — is helpful no matter what you do on the Web. Even if you don't want to edit HTML code, understanding a little about how HTML works can help you appreciate what Dreamweaver has to offer and help you understand its limitations. And, of course, if you want to tweak your HTML, you need to understand what all those hieroglyphics do.

If you've never worked in HTML before, this chapter gives you the basics to help make sense of HTML. If you're an old pro at HTML, you may find this chapter to be a welcome refresher course. And if you really want to get into HTML, check out *HTML 4 For Dummies* by Ed Tittel and Stephen N. James (published by IDG Books Worldwide, Inc.).

Appreciating Roundtrip HTML

If you like to write your own code, but still want the advantage of a WYSIWYG editor once in a while, you'll appreciate what Macromedia calls Roundtrip HTML — if you open a file in Dreamweaver that you created in another program, Dreamweaver never automatically changes your code just because it doesn't recognize the code you've written. This is crucial to sophisticated developers because sometimes they create a special tag or combination of tags and don't want another program to alter their work. Unlike many other HTML editors on the market, Dreamweaver respects HTML code no matter what. (It will, however, let you know when you enter code that it considers invalid.)

When Dreamweaver comes across HTML code that it doesn't understand, it assumes that you've made a mistake. When that happens, Dreamweaver alerts you to the possible mistake by highlighting those tags in yellow in the WYSIWYG editor window as well as in the HTML Source window. Dreamweaver displays any content between the yellow highlighted tags as regular text, complete with HTML brackets, because it can't understand what you intended. If you find that you've made a mistake in your code and correct it, Dreamweaver integrates the correction and displays your format-ted content properly. If you want to keep the code the way you've written it, just ignore the yellow highlighting — Dreamweaver won't change it.

Accessing HTML code

You have two ways to access HTML code in Dreamweaver. The most inte-grated way is by using the built-in HTML Source editor — to get to it, choose Window➪HTML. The HTML window is a basic text editor that's fully inte-grated into Dreamweaver — if you type in new text or apply any formatting in the WYSIWYG editor, you immediately see your changes reflected in the HTML Source window. If you add tags or text in the text editor, the WYSIWYG editor displays the results after you save the file. You can easily move back and forth between the two editing environments, and you can learn HTML code this way, too. Try applying bold or centering some text in the WYSIWYG editor, and then notice that the <B>...</B> and <CENTER>... </CENTER> tags appear in the text editor. This impressive feature provides an interactive way to learn HTML and is a great way to keep track of what Dreamweaver is doing when you apply formatting in the WYSIWYG editing environment.

The other way to work in HTML with Dreamweaver is to use the HTML text editor that's bundled with Dreamweaver. This program — either HomeSite (for Windows) or BBEdit (for Macintosh) — is a sophisticated text editor designed for writing HTML code.

Both programs provide a list of tags that you can easily insert into your HTML file, as well as wizards and other features for creating more complex code, such as tables and frames. Keep in mind that any changes you make to your Web page in these programs don't immediately show up in the Dreamweaver window. You must first save your work, leave the text editor, and then return to Dreamweaver. When you toggle back to the WYSIWYG editor in Dreamweaver, you're prompted with a dialog box stating "This file was edited outside of Dreamweaver. Do you want to reload it?" Click Yes to see your changes reflected in Dreamweaver. (You can keep both Dreamweaver and the text editor open at the same time and move back and forth between them.) You can find lots more information about working with BBEdit in Chapter 11 and with HomeSite in Chapter 12.

Understanding basic HTML

HTML uses *tags* (set off in brackets like these <>) to format words and images on a page. You insert HTML tags around words and image descriptions to specify how these elements should display in a browser. For example, if you want something to appear as bold type, simply put the tags <B> and </B> on either side of the words that you want to appear bold.

Most tags have an *open tag* — or *start tag* — followed by a similar *close tag* — or *end tag*. The close tag is distinguished by the forward slash (/) to indicate that the formatting should stop. Together, these tags tell the browser where your formatting should begin and end.

Viewing HTML document source code

Many people suggest that you can learn HTML by looking at the source code of Web pages. Most browsers give you the option to display the HTML code behind any Web page that you're viewing. In Netscape Navigator, choose View⇨Document Source; in Internet Explorer, choose View⇨Source. Although looking at Web pages can be a great way to learn new tricks, be aware that it's also a way to pick up bad habits.

You'd be surprised at how many people make mistakes in their HTML code or use redundant HTML tags. Fortunately — or unfortunately, as the case may be — many browsers forgive this and do a decent job of displaying the page, even if its creator forgot a closing tag here or left out a set of quotation marks there. The problem is that other browsers, and even other versions of the same browser, may have trouble displaying pages with these same errors, distorting the intended view or even crashing when the browser gets confused by bad syntax. So be forewarned — just because a page looks okay in Netscape Navigator or Internet Explorer doesn't mean the code behind the page is without errors.

Some HTML tags may seem strange to you at first, especially if you're used to formatting text for print. That stems in large part from the fact that HTML was designed to be so universally functional that nearly every computer on the planet could display pages created for the Web. But not every computer has the same size monitor or the same fonts. So you're generally limited to *relative* descriptions in HTML. For example, instead of making an absolute description for a font, such as "headline 24-point, bold," you use a heading tag. The heading tags all show emphasis for the text that you enclose in them relative to one another. Heading 1, written <H1>, is the largest heading size; then come <H2>, <H3>, and so on, down to <H6>, which, somewhat counter-intuitively, is the smallest heading size. The actual size of the headings varies for different types of computers and Web browsers, but relative to each other, heading 1 clearly shows more emphasis than heading 2, and so on, down to heading 6.

The advantage of relative tags is that they enable the browser and the user to decide how a Web page should display, taking best advantage of the system, while still providing general guidelines about the importance of elements on a page. In Netscape Navigator, for example, the default font is Times, but users have the option to use any font that they prefer. So, for one viewer, <H1> may be 24-point Times and bold, but for another, it may be 30-point Helvetica. But no matter which font your viewers select, <H1> is always going to be bigger than <H2>, and so on down the line. Your job as Web designer is to organize the page so that the information and layout make sense at any setting, and then try to get over your frustration at not having more control!

Having introduced HTML this way, I have to warn you that things are changing quickly. As graphic designers demand greater control, HTML is evolving. Today, some HTML tags enable you to set the exact font face, color, and size. That's a welcome and exciting part of the evolution of the language, but it's also a reason to exercise caution. Keep in mind that not everyone on the Web has the latest browser or a fast computer and modem, and for users who do, they may not have the same fonts as you do on their computers. So your design may not appear on their computers exactly the way you intend.

Fortunately, the creators of Dreamweaver considered this problem. You can choose the level of HTML that you want to use and test your pages in Dreamweaver to identify tags and features that may not be supported in different browsers. You can use this feature by choosing File➪Check Target Browsers and then selecting the browser level that you want to verify. The current options in Dreamweaver are Netscape Navigator 2.0, 3.0, and 4.0, as well as Internet Explorer 2.0, 3.0, and 4.0.

Writing HTML for different browsers

The saving grace of browser differences is that when a browser doesn't understand an HTML tag, the browser ignores it. So, if you're considering using a feature that adds to your design, such as font face or background colors in a table, you shouldn't hesitate just because not all browsers can view it. Your only real loss in most cases is that outdated browsers won't display it. Often this simply means that your users with the newest browsers enjoy the benefit of the feature and users with older browsers don't even know what they're missing.

However, you need to watch out for inconsistent support and the problems that using the latest tags can cause. For example, if you use a black background and white text in a table, you may find that some browsers can't display the black background within a table, but still display the white text, making it unreadable against the light gray or white background that the browsers do display.

When you get into the more sophisticated features supported by Dreamweaver, such as DHTML and Cascading Style Sheets, browser differences can be even more serious. A powerful animation effect and sophisticated interactivity that displays well in the latest browsers may not display at all in older browsers, such as Netscape Navigator 3.0 and Internet Explorer 3.0, both of which are still common on the Web. Dreamweaver tries to help you avoid this problem by providing its File⇨Check Target Browsers feature, but you still have to change or remove these features yourself if you want your pages to work well in older browsers. Many designers today are creating two versions of pages — one that works in older browsers and another with the latest features for newer browsers. Dreamweaver 1.2 includes conversion features to help automate the process of creating a second version of your Web pages that work in older browsers. You can find more information about those features, as well as the Check Target Browsers feature, in Chapter 13.

Your best bet is to test your pages by previewing them in a variety of browsers. Dreamweaver gives you a list of the features that won't work, but until you see your designs in an older browser, you can't appreciate what they look like or what is left of your designs when the more advanced tags are ignored. Often, by experimenting with combinations of tags and using tags that maintain some of your design when other tags don't work, you can salvage you work and create pages that look great in the newest browsers and are still presentable in older browsers. Use the Check Target Browsers feature as a guide, but use the actual browsers to view your pages to make sure that they look okay to you.

Two Web sites are a big help for solving this issue of how your pages look in various browsers:

- ✔ BrowserWatch (www.browserwatch.com) can help you find out about the variety and limitations of the browsers that your viewers may use.

- ✔ Shareware.com (www.shareware.com) provides access to older versions of browsers. If you no longer have a copy of Navigator 2.0, for example, you should be able to find it at this Web site.

Creating a Simple HTML Page

HTML code is just text in a document — the same way anything else you type is text in a document. This means that you can use any word-processing program to create an HTML document — SimpleText, NotePad, Microsoft Word, Corel WordPerfect, or any one of the other 250 or so word-processing programs out there. Simply type in the tags that you see in the following section, and you can create a Web page. For this chapter's examples, I recommend using the HTML Source editor built into Dreamweaver, because you can easily see what you create in the WYSIWYG editor of Dreamweaver.

You should also get in the habit of previewing your work in a browser. Dreamweaver does an excellent job of displaying HTML code accurately in its WYSIWYG editor, but if you view your pages in different browsers, you can begin to appreciate the differences in the way tags display. Because you can try something in HTML and then look at it right away in a browser to see the effect, figuring out HTML is relatively easy.

Word processing programs, such as Microsoft Word, save files in a special file format that browsers can't read. If you use a word-processing program to create an HTML file, make sure that you save the file as Text Only. If you work on a Windows 3.x machine, change the .txt file extension to .htm (in Windows 95, 98, and NT, it's now okay to use .html). On a Macintosh or UNIX system, use .html.

The simplest HTML document

All HTML documents start and end with the same basic code. At the top of the page, you should put the open <HTML> tag to indicate to a browser that this is an HTML document. Similarly, at the very end of the page, use the close HTML tag </HTML>. Follow the open <HTML> tag with the header information — the <HEAD> tag. Put the <TITLE> inside the <HEAD> tag. The

<TITLE> tag often confuses people because the text within it doesn't display in the Web page itself. Instead, the contents of the <TITLE> tag appear in the browser's title bar. After closing the title and the header, open the body text of the document with — surprise! — the <BODY> tag. All the words, images, and other HTML code that make up the document go between the <BODY> and </BODY> tags.

A very simple HTML document looks like this:

```
<HTML>
<HEAD><TITLE>A Simple HTML Page</TITLE></HEAD>
<BODY>
This is a simple HTML document.
</BODY></HTML>
```

To distinguish the tags from the text, I've written all the tags in this chapter in uppercase. I recommend you stick to that model to make your code easier to read, but you can write HTML in either uppercase or lowercase or even mix cases without incident. Dreamweaver enables you to choose which you prefer in preferences and then leaves the case the way you type it if you add tags manually.

The <P> and <BR> tags

I included the line breaks in the simple HTML example for clarity. You can put all the line breaks that you want in HTML code without affecting how the document appears in a browser. To create line breaks that do appear in a browser, use the paragraph (<P>) or break (<BR>) tags. The break tag inserts a line break. The paragraph tag adds even more space by breaking the line and adding another blank line below it. In Figure 10-1, you see how the <P> and <BR> tags in the following code example display differently.

```
<HTML>
<HEAD><TITLE>Paragraph and break tags</TITLE></HEAD>
<BODY>
Remember that the spaces and returns in HTML code don't
          affect the display. You have to use break and
          paragraph tags if you want the returns to show
          up in the browser. Even though I didn't put any
          returns around this break tag <BR> or this <P>
          paragraph tag in the code, the lines break when
          displayed in the browser.
Similarly, the return in this code before the beginning of
          this sentence doesn't appear in the display in
          the browser.
</BODY></HTML>
```

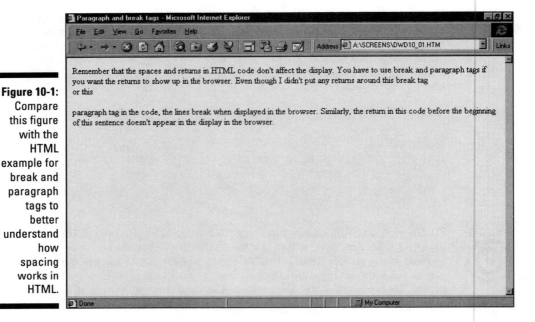

Figure 10-1:
Compare
this figure
with the
HTML
example for
break and
paragraph
tags to
better
understand
how
spacing
works in
HTML.

Because you can use two different kinds of line breaks, Dreamweaver offers two ways of using the Enter key (the Return key on a Macintosh) to insert them in your pages when you are working in the WYSIWYG environment. Simply pressing the Enter key inserts a <P> tag, but if you want a <BR> tag, you have to hold down the Shift key while pressing the Enter key (on the Mac, hold the Option key while pressing the Return key). This makes choosing between the two tags as you work in Dreamweaver easy. It also means that you don't need to memorize these tags or try to remember which tag is which because Dreamweaver takes care of that for you. If you're working in the HTML Source window or in BBEdit or Homesite, the Enter key inserts space in the text file but doesn't insert a <P> or <BR> tag.

The <HR> tag

Another tag that you can use to create space on a Web page is the <HR> or *horizontal rule tag*. The <HR> tag creates a gray, sometimes three-dimensional-looking line that can act as a divider on your Web page. The <HR> tag creates a thin line that goes all the way across the page. To insert one using the WYSIWYG editor, choose Insert⇔Horizontal Rule. In a text editor, simply type **<HR>** (there is no close tag). The <HR> tag attributes (available from the Property inspector) enable you to control the height, width, and alignment of the line. Using these options enables you to make the line thicker and specify how far it stretches across the page. When you fill in each of those boxes, the editor automatically generates code that looks something like this:

```
<HR WIDTH="50%" SIZE="4" ALIGN="CENTER">
```

The <BODY> tag

The <BODY> tag, which designates the main area of the page, includes attributes to specify background color, text color, and other features that can make a dramatic difference in how your page looks. You can write the <BODY> tag simply as <BODY> with no attributes, in which case the browser displays its default colors. Dreamweaver automatically generates this simple <BODY> tag when you create a new page. In most browsers, the default is a gray or white background, black text, and blue links that turn red after they're selected. Using attributes, you can change these colors. The following code would create a page with a white background, green text, and black links:

```
<BODY BGCOLOR="#FFFFFF" TEXT="#0E7769" LINK="#000000">
```

Just so you know, BGCOLOR stands for background color; the "#FFFFFF" is a *hexadecimal* (a computer number system) color code that specifies that the background should be white.

Fortunately, you don't have to worry about hexidecimal color codes because Dreamweaver calculates them for you when you choose a color from a color palette or color wheel in the WYSIWYG editor. You can set text and link colors the same way.

In the following example, all the tags introduced in this chapter so far are used on one page. Notice the colors in the <BODY> tag, the use of the horizontal rule, and the spacing created by the <P> tags. Figure 10-2 shows this code displayed in Internet Explorer.

```
<HTML>
<HEAD><TITLE>Attributes</TITLE></HEAD>
<BODY BGCOLOR="#FFFFFF" TEXT="#0E7769" LINK="#000000">
<P ALIGN=CENTER>This text should be centered because I use
            the center attribute in the paragraph tag.
            Because of the attributes used in the body tag,
            the background of this page is white and the
            text is green. (You can't tell that from the
            black and white image in Figure 10-2, but if you
            type this code into Dreamweaver and display it
            in a browser, it will be green.)
<P>This text should not be centered and should be separated
            by a return and space. Below, you can find the
            horizontal rule tag with its attributes.
<P>
<HR WIDTH="50%" SIZE="4" ALIGN="CENTER">
<BR>
```

(continued)

(continued)

```
The horizontal rule inserts a gray line. I've set this line
        to be thicker (size "4") and narrower than the
        default. It's also a little hard to see against
        the white background.
</BODY>
</HTML>
```

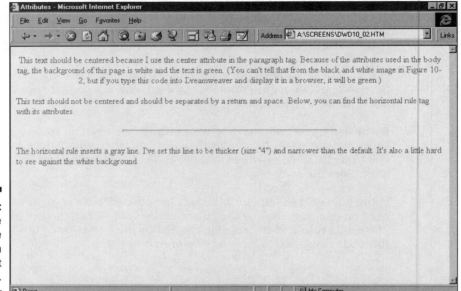

Figure 10-2:
How the
example
appears in
Internet
Explorer.

Setting hyperlinks

Perhaps the most magical feature made possible by HTML is the ability to
link to another page with hyperlinks. Many people who are new to HTML
think it must be really complicated to set hyperlinks to other pages in a Web
site and even harder to set links to another site on the Web. Fortunately, it's
not that complicated, but it is a little more involved than just putting bold
tags around text.

The comment tag

A special tag that you should know about is the comment tag (`<!--comment-->`), which enables you to include information in your HTML document that you don't want displayed to your viewers. You can use comment tags anywhere in the document; you generally use them if you want to make notes to yourself or to someone else who may work on the file. The browser ignores all text between the `<!--` and `-->`, so you have to make sure that all your comments appear between them. The comment tag doesn't use a closing tag because all its contents appear between the brackets.

In the Dreamweaver WYSIWYG editor window, comment tags appear in a small yellow box with an exclamation point. To add a comment tag in the WYSIWYG editor, choose Insert⇨Comment. You can also type your comments manually in the HTML Source window, HomeSite, or BBEdit.

Dreamweaver automates the process of setting links to make it easier. However, understanding the basics of how links work behind the scenes helps you appreciate how links get broken and how to fix them. I start with the easy part, even though you may think it's hard at first.

You set links by using the `<A HREF>` tag, which I call the *link tag*. The link tag does have a close tag, but it's just `</A>`. The attribute for the link tag is the URL of the location where the link goes. If you want a link from the word *Macromedia* on your Web page to the Macromedia Web site, the code looks like this:

```
<A HREF="http://www.macromedia.com">Macromedia</A>
```

Creating links from one page in your Web site to another gets a little more complicated. The tag is the same, but instead of specifying the full URL of a Web site, you indicate the name of the page that you're linking to. For example, if you want to link from your home page to a page called help.html, the tag looks like this:

```
<A HREF="help.html">This text links to the help page</A>
```

Setting links to pages in your own Web site may seem pretty straightforward, but it gets more complicated. The link tag in the previous example looks simple because the files are in the same folder. But you may not want to keep all the files in your Web site in one place. Instead, I recommend you organize them in separate folders for the same reason that you probably don't like all your papers in one file folder in your file cabinet or all your files in one folder on your hard drive. However, when an HTML file isn't in the same folder as the file you want to link it to, you have to write a slightly more complicated link tag that specifies the path to the page. Check out Chapter 4 for more on organizing your Web site's files and directories.

To set a link to a file within another folder, you need to include in the path the folder name as well as the filename. Thus, to go from an index.html file in the Web site to tools.html in the books folder, the link looks like this:

```
<A HREF="books/tools.html">
```

This path tells your browser that the tools.html file is in the books folder on your hard drive or server. Fortunately, Dreamweaver automatically sets link paths like this one when you use the browse feature to set links in the WYSIWYG editor. (The browse feature is accessible by clicking on the folder icon in the Property inspector. Then you simply locate the file you want and select it, and Dreamweaver figures out the path for you.) You can find the steps you need to create all kinds of links with Dreamweaver in Chapter 2. BBEdit and HomeSite also provide assistance with link setting. You can find information about their features in Chapters 11 and 12 respectively.

Naming the Main Page

You should name the home page in your Web site index.html, because most servers are set up to serve the index file when somebody types just your domain name (for example, if you just type www.macromedia.com). If you don't have an index file, the browser displays a list of all the files and folders in your site instead.

Relative versus absolute links

You should set local links, those that go to HTML documents or other files within your own Web site, as *relative*, rather than *absolute*. An absolute link looks something like this: `<A HREF="http://www.your_name. com/file_name.html">`. The same hyperlink set as a relative link looks like this: `<A HREF="file_name.html">`.

Reserve absolute links — full URLs including the `http://` — for links to other Web sites.

I can give you two good reasons for using relative links within your Web site: First, you want to be able to test your links on your local hard drive. If you use absolute links, the files have to reside on the server in order for the links to work, because otherwise, your browser will try to go to the Web address to find what it wants. Second, absolute links make the browser work harder and often take longer to load because the browser has to request the domain name each time, instead of just going directly to a nearby file.

Most servers use index.html as the main page, but some use index.htm or default.html (especially those running Microsoft software). If you're unsure, ask your system administrator or Internet service provider.

The main file in your site isn't the only place that you should name a file index.html. This technique also works for the main HTML page in other folders, especially if you want to provide a direct address to that section of the site. For example, if you want to create a special section for a product and your sales force wants to go directly to that page, you can create a folder using the product name. Then, using index.html as the main file, all a visitor needs in order to access the page is the folder name added to the URL.

Here's what it could look like: Say your domain name is www.close.com, and you want "friends" to be an easily accessible section. If you create a folder called friends and make best.html the main page, the URL would have to be www.close.com/friends/best.html. If you rename best.html to index.html, then a visitor to the site could enter www.close.com/friends as the URL, and the browser automatically loads the page.

Cross-platform issues and testing

Before you send your Web site to your Web server, testing your links on your local hard drive is a good idea. If you've set relative links, you can test your links by simply opening any linked HTML file on your computer with any browser and selecting the hyperlinks to move through the site.

Testing is almost as big a part of Web design as creating the HTML in the first place. You should always thoroughly test your work before you put it online. But be aware that just because your graphics and links work on your hard drive, they may not work on the server. Cross-platform differences become especially important in testing.

UNIX, Macintosh, and Windows computers have distinct naming require-ments that can cause problems when you move a site from one computer to another. This surprises many new developers because HTML files are ASCII text and can be opened by any text editor on any computer system. The links, however, aren't so universal.

For example, you can call files "just about anything you want.html" on a Mac server; however, on a UNIX server, you can't have spaces or special charac-ters in filenames, and you must make sure that the case is the same in the hyperlink as in the filename. You can also use long filenames on Windows 95, 98, and NT, but if you work in DOS or Windows 3.*x*, you should limit yourself to the *8.3 rule* (say "eight-dot-three"), which requires that none of your filenames have more than eight characters and none of the extensions more than three.

The most common problems occur when you create a Web site on a Macintosh or Windows computer and then send it to a UNIX server. Because most of the servers on the Internet are UNIX machines, you need to be aware of one of the biggest differences right away: UNIX systems are case-sensitive, and Windows and Macintosh aren't. That means that you can create a file called index.html and refer to it in your HTML links as `INDEX.HTML` and it works on a Macintosh or Windows system but not on a UNIX server. Many HTML authors have tested and retested their work locally only to see all their links fall apart when they put the site online. If you use Dreamweaver's link features, it makes sure that the case is the same in the code and the filename, but if you change the case in a filename or manually enter the name in the wrong case, you can cause broken links on a UNIX server.

Getting help with HTML Rename!

HTML Rename! is a software program designed to help you deal with filename problems. If you've already built a site and haven't been careful about the filenames, or if you're moving a site from one system to another and need to change the filenames, HTML Rename! can save you hours of time and trouble. This is also a great tool if you have developers working on different platforms — for example, if all your designers use Macs and all your programmers use Windows and UNIX.

HTML Rename! automatically converts any filenames so that they conform to a specific file-naming convention. For example, if you built a site on a Macintosh or Windows machine without realizing that you couldn't use special characters or spaces when you published your site to a server, this program can go through and strip out all the special characters for you.

HTML Rename! can process an entire Web site at once, even if you have hundreds or thousands of pages, and it not only changes the filenames, it also changes their references in the HTML code so that all your links still work. The ability to automatically find all link references is a crucial and invaluable aid because pages in a Web site can be linked from multiple locations.

HTML Rename! works with a wizard that walks you through the process, first selecting the folder with the Web site that you want to change and then choosing the filename convention you want (such as Windows 3.*x* or UNIX). You have the option of letting HTML Rename! automatically change all the filenames for you, or you can set it to alert you to filenames that are problematic and then rename them yourself. Either way, you get a chance to review all the name changes at the end of the process, so you can ensure that you like them. As a bonus, the report it generates also lists any broken links or files that are not referenced anywhere in your site.

Chapter 11

Introducing BBEdit

● ●

● ●

*M*acintosh users who want to write their own HTML code will be delighted to find that Dreamweaver includes BBEdit, the most popular HTML text editor on the market. Macromedia was clever when it integrated the power of its WYSIWYG-editing environment with the well-known HTML text editor. BBEdit and Dreamweaver work together so that any changes you make in one program show up in the other. That means you can easily move back and forth between the two programs, using the text editor when you want to see your code and the graphical Dreamweaver environment when you want to design without worrying about the HTML.

In this chapter, I introduce you to BBEdit and include step-by-step instructions for creating many HTML features.

BBEdit Basics

The HTML Tools palette in BBEdit provides access to a wide range of shortcuts for common HTML tags and attributes. In this section, I walk you through some of the common things that you'll want to do with BBEdit. Of course, if you prefer, you can always type in all the HTML markup by hand instead of using shortcuts. But who wants to do that when BBEdit makes inserting markup tags so easy? Using BBEdit to insert your tags ensures that you never make any typos or miss any part of the necessary code.

Creating a new Web page

The following steps show you how to create a new page in BBEdit:

1. **Select the New Document button on the HTML Tools palette (see Figure 11-1).**

   A dialog box opens in which you can set attributes for the HTML header, including the page title and metatags (see Figure 11-2).

2. **Click Create.**

   BBEdit creates a new page with the appropriate HTML document tags, like the page in Figure 11-3.

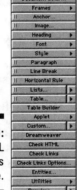

Figure 11-1:
The HTML
Tools
palette.

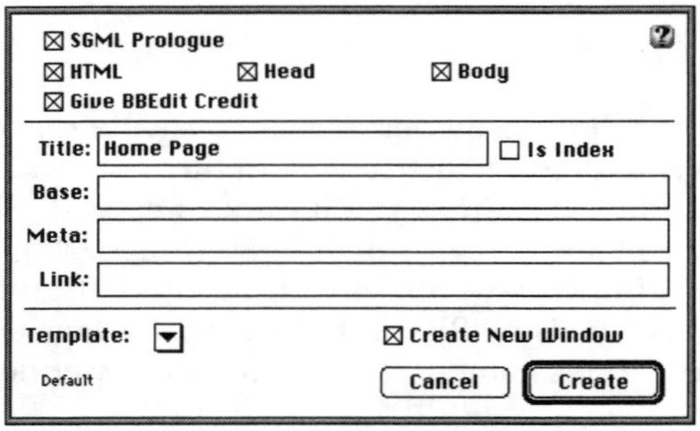

Figure 11-2:
The HTML
header
dialog box.

Figure 11-3:
A new page
created in
BBEdit.

3. **Choose File⇨Save and give the document a name that ends in .htm or .html.**

   You can actually give the file any name you want, but adding the .html extension tells BBEdit to color-code your HTML tags.

4. **In the Save dialog box, click the Options button and choose the Line Breaks option appropriate for your system.**

   For example, if you plan to upload your file to a UNIX server, you should save it with UNIX line breaks.

5. **Click OK to close the Options dialog box. Click Save to finish saving your file.**

Setting background and text colors

Here's how to use BBEdit to change the background and text colors of a Web page:

1. **Select the Document Color button on the HTML Tools palette.**

   A color picker appears for choosing background, text, and tag colors.

2. **Choose colors for the document background (BGCOLOR), the default text color (TEXT), links (LINK), visited links (VLINK), and active links (ALINK). Click Insert when you're done.**

   You may choose from the small number of default colors, or double-click a color swatch to change it.

   You can also choose a background image.

3. **Click OK.**

Creating frames

If you want to use HTML frames in your Web pages, first create the frameset and frame pages and then edit each one individually, as you would any other page, by following the steps throughout the rest of this chapter.

Here's how to create a frameset page:

1. **Click and hold down the Frames button on the HTML Tools palette, and select Frameset.**

   A dialog box appears.

2. **Choose Rows or Columns to define how you want the page divided.**

3. **Type in the number of frames and click OK.**

Next, create the frame sections of your page. Follow these steps to specify the name and placement of each frame in the frameset:

1. **Choose Frames⇨Frame from the Tools palette.**

   In the dialog box, use the File button to specify the HTML page that you want displayed in that frame. Browse until you find the file that you want and double-click it. BBEdit enters the name and folder path of the file you selected in the Frame box.

2. **Type the name of the frame in the Name text box and click OK.**

   This is important because the name is used to target the frame area when you set links.

3. **Repeat Steps 1 and 2 for each frame in the frameset.**

Adding and formatting text

Adding text to your Web page with BBEdit is easy. Just click to insert your cursor on the page wherever you want the text to appear, and start typing. Then, to add HTML formatting, highlight the target text and select one of the following buttons on the HTML Tools palette:

- **Heading:** Use this button to assign heading levels 1 through 6.

- **Font:** Use this button to change the color or size of text.

- **Style:** Use this button to assign styles, such as Bold, Strong, and Center.

You can also use the Tools palette to insert HTML tags, such as paragraph marks, line breaks, and horizontal rules, as well as more complex HTML structures, such as tables and lists. You can find out more about these features later in the chapter.

If you're new to HTML, make sure that you check out *HTML 4 For Dummies* by Ed Tittel and Stephen N. James (published by IDG Books Worldwide, Inc.).

Creating hyperlinks

Hyperlinks make the Web go 'round. BBEdit makes it easy to create links by providing a browse feature that you can use to automatically enter the path and filename that you want in the link tag. Follow these steps to use the link features in BBEdit:

1. **Select the text or image that you want to link.**
2. **Click Anchor on the HTML Tools palette.**

   The Anchor dialog box appears.

3. **Click the File button and locate the file that you want to link to.**
4. **Double-click the filename.**

   BBEdit enters the file information into the HREF box (the link tag box). You can also manually type text for the link in the HREF box.

To add an internal reference anchor, type a name for the anchor in the Name box. This enables you to refer to a particular place within the HTML document. To reference an internal anchor, type # followed by the anchor name in the HREF box. For more on internal anchors, check out Chapter 2.

The target box is included for setting links when you're working with HTML frames. To open a link in a specified frame window, type the appropriate window reference (name) in the Target box. To find out more about frames and how Dreamweaver makes it easy to create frames in its WYSIWYG editor, see Chapter 9.

5. **Specify the appropriate prefix based on the type of hyperlink in the Scheme pop-up menu.**

   Choose mailto: for an e-mail link, and http:// for a hyperlink to another Web site. BBEdit places the selected prefix at the beginning of the HREF text. You just need to type in the rest of the URL or e-mail address.

BBEdit automatically converts any Internet address into a properly formatted hyperlink. Just select the address and click the Anchor button on the HTML Tools palette.

Inserting graphics

Graphics add color and style to your Web pages. Inserting them with BBEdit involves a very similar process to setting links. Follow these steps to insert images on your pages:

1. **Click to insert your cursor on the page where you want to insert the image.**

2. **Select the Image button on the HTML Tools palette.**

   The Image dialog window opens displaying the contents of your hard drive.

3. **Use the File button to locate the graphic that you want to link to.**

4. **Select the graphic file that you want to insert and click Open.**

   BBEdit enters the file and path information into the Image text field in the Image dialog box.

   BBEdit automatically determines the size of your image file and inserts the height and width in the Size area in the Image dialog. If you want to change the specified size, enter a new height and width in pixels.

5. **Assign any other relevant attributes, such as alternative text or border.**

   If you want to change an image tag that you've already placed in your document, select the entire image tag (including the ⟨ and ⟩), and then click the Image button on the HTML Tools palette to edit the settings.

6. **Click the Insert button to finish.**

HTML tools tricks

You can drag any button on the HTML Tools palette that has a grip-strip (two vertical bars on the left of the button) onto the open BBEdit window for automatic placement. This enables you to quickly insert a tag, such as a paragraph or break tag, onto a page.

Did you accidentally make the HTML Tools palette disappear? In the Tools menu, scroll down to HTML Tools⇨HTML Tools Palette. And voilà! It's back.

If the HTML Tools palette takes up too much screen real estate, use the small pop-up menu at the top-left of the palette to make the buttons thinner. The same pop-up menu enables you to customize which tools show on the palette.

Making a table

In addition to the table-building features in Dreamweaver, BBEdit offers two completely different ways to build a table. The first is the Table tool in the HTML Tools palette, which works similarly to the other HTML tools by assisting you as you work in the HTML code. The second method for building tables in BBEdit is the recently added Table Builder feature, a standalone WYSIWYG program that, like Dreamweaver, works with BBEdit.

In the following section, I show you how to create a table with the Table tool. However, because Dreamweaver provides a much better environment for building tables, I don't cover the standalone WYSIWYG program in BBEdit. You can find out more about the table feature of Dreamweaver in Chapter 7.

Creating a table with the Table tool

The Table tool makes creating HTML tables easy. Follow these steps to add a table to your Web page:

1. **Click to insert your cursor on the page where you want to add a table.**

2. **Click the Table button in the HTML Tools palette.**

   A dialog box appears with options for the entire table.

3. **Select Generate Table Shell to create a complete table structure.**

   BBEdit generates the HTML code for a table, including row and cell tags, with room for you to insert the appropriate content into each cell.

4. **Enter the number of rows and columns that you want to start with, and assign other table attributes as desired. Click Insert when you're done.**

   BBEdit generates a complete table structure.

5. **In the HTML table tag structure, type the contents of the table (or add images, styles, anchors, and so on).**

6. **To insert additional rows, cells, headers, or captions into an existing table, place the cursor at the insertion point and click the pop-up menu button just to the right of the Table button.**

   Making a selection from the pop-up list instantly adds the appropriate tags to the document.

7. **Enter the appropriate attributes and click OK.**

   BBEdit inserts the necessary tags.

Converting tab- or comma-delimited text into a table

Most spreadsheet programs enable you to convert data into tab- or comma-delimited format — that is, text sections separated by tabs instead of the borders of a table. Many databases also let you export data as tab- or comma-delimited. BBEdit automatically converts tab- or comma-delimited data into an HTML table, making it possible to automate the otherwise tedious task of converting columns of numbers of information from a database into an HTML table.

1. **Use Copy and Paste to insert tab-delimited text onto your Web page and then select the text.**

   Each row should be on a separate line, and a tab should separate the text from each individual table cell.

2. **Click and hold down the small arrow to the right of the Table button on the Tools palette.**

3. **From the pop-up menu that appears, select Convert.**

   The Conversion dialog box appears.

4. **Specify whether the original text was tab- or comma-delimited, and whether the top row or left-most column should be formatted as a header.**

5. **Click Convert to finish.**

   BBEdit inserts the appropriate tags to convert the text into an HTML table.

Previewing a page in a Web browser

Since BBEdit isn't a WYSIWYG editor, previewing your file in a Web browser, such as Netscape Navigator or Internet Explorer, is important to make sure that it displays as you intend. Fortunately, the Preview tool provides a handy way to check your work for you.

1. **Before previewing, save the file to disk.**

   BBEdit enables you to preview only the most recently saved version of the file. If you've made changes since you last saved, these changes won't show up in the browser preview.

2. **Click the Preview button in the HTML Tools palette.**

   BBEdit launches your default browser and loads the file into the browser window.

On the Mac, the default browser setting is typically saved by a program named Internet Config (if using Mac OS 8, especially). If you don't have Internet Config installed, Mac OS sets the default to the program that best matches the file type (usually the most recently installed browser). For more on the ins and outs of Mac OS 8, check out *Mac OS 8 For Dummies* by Bob LeVitus (published by IDG Books Worldwide, Inc.).

3. **To preview the file in a different browser, click the arrow to the right of the Preview button and select a browser from the pop-up list.**

   You can modify this list by using the Web Browsers section in Edit⇨ Preferences.

Beyond the Basics

BBEdit offers a number of powerful features to make HTML editing easier, including advanced search-and-replace capabilities, special characters, and more. In this section, I show you how to use these features.

Search and replace

The Find function in BBEdit is extremely robust. In addition to the standard find and replace options found in most word processors, the program offers fast and flexible search and replace across large collections of files, even multiple folders. That makes BBEdit an ideal tool for making global changes to a Web site. For more technically savvy users, the advanced searching options (called *grep* — a UNIX-speak acronym for Global Regular Expression Print) provide the ability to search for complex patterns in text, rather than specific text strings. You can find more on grep searches in "Making sense of grep searches" later in this chapter.

Using basic search-and-replace features

The basic Find command in BBEdit works much like the find functions in other word processors. Follow these steps to use basic search-and-replace features:

1. **Choose Search⇨Find.**

   The Find dialog box appears.

2. **Enter the text you want to locate in the Search For: text box and the text you want to replace it with in the Replace With: text box.**

3. **Choose any relevant options, such as Selection Only (to search only highlighted text) or Start at Top (to search the entire file regardless of where the cursor is).**

4. Click the Find or Replace button.

If you click Find, BBEdit locates the first occurrence of the text string in the open document and highlights it. If you click Replace, BBEdit replaces the first occurrence with the replacement text that you entered. If you want to continue, choose Search⇨Find Again. Click the Replace All button if you want to replace all the matching text on the page.

Searching across many files

One of the most powerful features in BBEdit is the ability to search and replace text across multiple documents with one command. You can search through a particular folder, through multiple folders and subfolders, or search all the windows that you have open in BBEdit.

1. Choose Search⇨Find.

The Find dialog box appears.

2. Enter the appropriate text in the Search For: and Replace With: boxes.

3. Click the check box next to Multi-File Search.

If you don't see the bottom part of the window, as shown in Figure 11-4, click the arrow just to the left of Multi-File Search.

The What: pop-up menu enables you to search either a specific folder on your hard drive or just the files currently open in BBEdit.

4. To search an entire folder, choose Other from the pop-up menu next to Folder:.

An Open File dialog box appears.

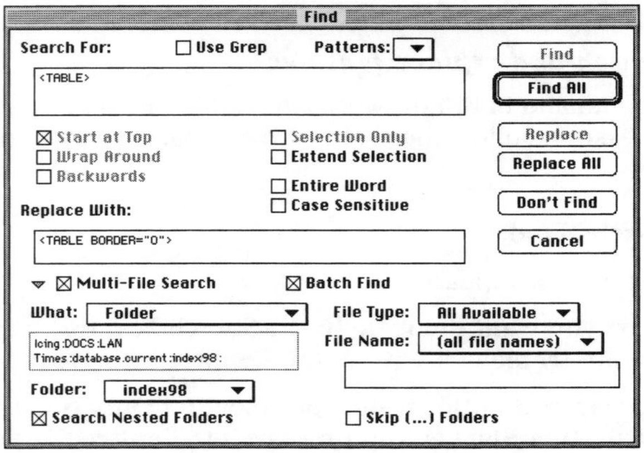

Figure 11-4:
The multiple file search-and-replace options.

5. **Locate the folder you want to search through and double-click it.**

   BBEdit searches through every file in the specified folder.

6. **To search subfolders within the main folder, click the check box next to Search Nested Folders.**

7. **Use the File Type: and Filename: options to further narrow down the file types that you want to search.**

   For example, you may choose to search only files that end with the extension .html.

8. **When you've made your selections, click the appropriate button in the top-right corner of the dialog box to continue with the operation.**

   Find gives you the first occurrence of your search string, while Find All displays all the occurrences at once. Replace finds the first occurrence of the search string and replaces it, while Replace All finds and replaces all occurrences across the set of files that you specified. For more details on these options, see "Using Batch Find" next.

Using Batch Find

When doing multifile search and replace, leaving the Batch Find option on is generally easiest. Without Batch Find, BBEdit opens each file one at a time and waits for you to continue the operation. With Batch Find selected, BBEdit automatically performs the search and replace on the complete set of files without your having to do anything else.

If you do a Find without a Replace, BBEdit collects all the lines in all the files in which it finds the desired text and displays a list in the Search Results browser window (see Figure 11-5). For more information on navigating the Search Results window, see the sidebar "BBEdit browser windows."

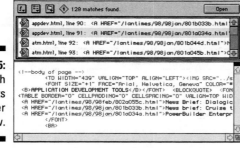

Figure 11-5:
The search
results
browser
window.

BBEdit browser windows

BBEdit often uses a special double-paned window called a browser — not to be confused with a Web browser like Netscape Navigator. You see a BBEdit browser window when you do a multifile batch find, check your HTML syntax, or open the BBEdit glossary. The top pane of a browser contains a list of items that you can click for navigation; the bottom pane displays the content of the item you select in the top pane. Double-clicking items in the top panel opens the file to which the item refers.

You should test your search before do the entire batch find. The multifile search capabilities in BBEdit are a powerful tool, but you can wreak havoc on your files by executing an incorrect search routine. You should test your search a few times before applying it across a large document or many documents.

To do so, enter the search-and-replace terms, and click the Find button. BBEdit highlights the found text. Next, choose Search⇨Replace to execute a single replace. Check to make sure that you get the desired result. To be on the safe side, try it a few more times. When you're satisfied that you're on the right track, either choose Search⇨Replace All to execute your search on a single document, or choose Search⇨Find to execute a multifile search and replace.

Searching for special characters

For more complex searches, you may want to search for special characters and replace them with HTML tags. For example, you could search for all the returns in a file and replace them with paragraph tags. Table 11-1 provides a list of special characters that you can search for and the search string you need to use.

Table 11-1	Special Search Characters
Meaning	*Special Character*
Carriage return	\r
Line feed	\n
Tab	\T
Page break	\f

Storing patterns

If you have a commonly used search-and-replace pattern, you can store it permanently and then reuse it when needed. After entering the appropriate search-and-replace strings in the Find dialog box, click the Pattern: pop-up menu at the top of the dialog box and choose Add This Pattern to store the pattern. To reuse the pattern, just select it from the Pattern: pop-up menu. To modify a pattern you've already saved, choose Add This Pattern and type in the same name as you used before. This replaces the old pattern with the new one.

Making sense of grep searches

The term *grep* comes from the wild and wonderful world of UNIX, where almost everything is subject to the programmer's control. BBEdit has taken the powerful grep pattern-matching language from UNIX and made it available to humble Mac users through the Use Grep option in the Find dialog box. Grep syntax isn't for the faint of heart, but if you can handle some terse syntax, it's a powerful tool.

When may you find grep more useful than the simple search-and-replace options you find in most text editors? Say that you want to find every occurrence of a heading level 1, 2, or 3, and automatically create an anchor based on the heading text — no matter what the text. A grep search is the right tool for the job. Explaining the complexity of grep syntax would take an entire book in itself, and it's beyond the scope of this book. But you can get a handle on using grep searches in BBEdit from the BBEdit Help Guide or the BBEdit manual.

File management

In addition to the Macintosh File menu standards, BBEdit provides some extra helpers for file management. These features include the following:

- ✔ **An FTP client:** Using the Open from FTP Server and Save to FTP Server items in the File menu, you can directly access and change files on a remote server.

  The FTP function in BBEdit is slow because it makes a new connection every time it accesses the server; you may find it faster to use a dedicated FTP client, such as Fetch or Anarchie, to transfer files. You should also be aware that if you save a file to an FTP server, the file isn't automatically saved to your local drive.

- ✔ **Automatic file backup:** If you choose File➪Backup Options and File➪Make Backup Now, BBEdit creates incremental backups of your file that are date- and version-stamped. This feature enables you to backtrack to previous versions of a file.

Status bar

The status bar at the top of each document window contains a number of useful options and pieces of information about your document. Table 11-2 explains each option. In addition to these buttons, the status bar lists some important information about the document itself: the date and time last saved, and the directory path of the file on the hard drive or remote server.

Table 11-2	Status Bar Functions
Button	*Function*
◆	The black diamond indicates that the file has changes that haven't yet been saved to disk.
✎	You click the pencil to make the file read-only.
▦	The Window Options pop-up menu (which mirrors options in Edit➪Window Options) enables you to soft-wrap text to prevent lines from going off the right side of the window, display line numbers, show invisible characters such as tabs and returns, and auto-indent to automatically indent new lines to the same level as the previous line.
▣	The File pop-up menu provides a quick way to set the type of line breaks (Macintosh, UNIX, or DOS) for the file. Choose the option appropriate to the type of server that you plan to send your Web pages to.
▤	Clicking the document button switches to the Finder and opens the folder containing the active BBEdit file.
▮	The key button hides or shows the status bar.

Setting BBEdit preferences

The Preferences menu contains a wide (and, unfortunately, rather poorly organized) set of options to control default settings for the program. To access the different sections of the preferences, choose Edit➪Preferences and then select an item in the scrolling list on the left. Some of the more useful settings for Web coding include the following:

✔ **Editor:** Editor (see Figure 11-6) enables you to set default Window Options preferences, such as Soft Wrap and Auto Indent. It also turns Syntax Coloring on, so that HTML tags appear color-coded.

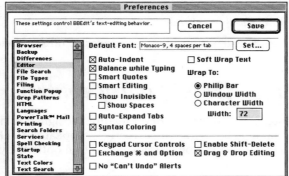

Figure 11-6:
The Editor
panel of the
BBEdit
Preferences
dialog box.

✔ **Filing:** Filing enables you to set a default line break type (Mac, UNIX, or PC) for BBEdit documents.

✔ **Grep Patterns:** Over time, you may accumulate quite a collection of stored search-and-replace patterns. This panel enables you to delete obsolete patterns or modify existing ones.

✔ **HTML Preferences:** HTML Preferences enables you to specify whether tags are set in uppercase or lowercase. It also enables you to specify a default remote server and local root directory for your Web documents.

✔ **Text Colors:** Text Colors specifies how different types of HTML tags display in BBEdit. You can choose different colors for General tags, Anchors, and Images.

✔ **Web Browsers:** Web Browsers creates a list of available Web browsers that you may want to use to preview your pages.

Understanding text cleanup functions

The Text menu provides several useful tools for cleaning up text and controlling how it appears. This menu includes the following:

✔ **Change Case:** This handy menu item converts text to uppercase or lowercase, and capitalizes words, sentences, or lines.

✔ **Insert Line Breaks:** If the Soft Wrap option is turned on, this command inserts a hard line break at the end of each line on the screen. This may be useful for some types of file transfers, particularly when pasting text into e-mail messages.

✔ **Remove Line Breaks:** This removes all line breaks from the file.

✔ **Hard Wrap:** This is similar to Insert Line Breaks but enables you to specify how long the lines should be.

✔ **Entab or Detab:** These options convert spaces to tabs and vice versa.

Appreciating HTML quality control

Several HTML debugging options — BBEdit features designed to help you "fix" HTML code that may be written incorrectly — appear in the HTML Tools palette. You can find additional HTML correction options by choosing Tools⇨HTML Debugging.

To have BBEdit check your HTML syntax, choose Check HTML from the Tools palette. If BBEdit finds more than one error, it opens a new browser window called HTML Syntax Errors and shows a sequential list of the errors. Don't be alarmed if the number of errors seems huge; often fixing the first one or two makes the rest disappear. Try rechecking the HTML after you correct the first couple of errors.

You can also have BBEdit check the links to files on your hard drive; just click the Check Links button on the Tools palette. If you've specified a root folder on your hard drive, as I explain in "Setting BBEdit preferences" (earlier in this chapter), you can have BBEdit check all the HTML files in the root directory by selecting Tools⇨HTML Debugging⇨Check Site Links.

Finding more cool HTML tools

The HTML Tools section includes many other features, including the following:

✔ **Text Translation:** Choosing Tools⇨HTML Utilities⇨Translate converts special characters, such as curly (or smart) quotes, to their ASCII equivalent; adds HTML paragraph tags between paragraphs; strips out control characters and gremlins (those mystery characters that show up occasionally); and converts special characters to HTML entities.

✔ **Entities:** Want to insert the HTML code for an ampersand (&) or any other special character? Click the Entities button on the HTML Tools palette and select the special character of your choice.

✔ **Web Color Palette:** Choosing Tools⇨HTML Utilities⇨Web Color Palette opens a window with color swatches for the browser-safe color palette. Click or drag a swatch to insert the appropriate HTML code for that color.

The Windows List

The Windows List, as shown in Figure 11-7, available from the Windows menu, helps to keep you organized when you have multiple BBEdit windows open at once. All the open files appear in the window. A black diamond next to the filename indicates that the file has been modified since you last saved it. To bring a file to the foreground, double-click its name. You can select multiple files by holding down the Shift key and selecting each one. Then use the buttons across the top of the Windows List to save, close, or print all the selected files at once.

Figure 11-7:
The
Windows
List.

Adding custom HTML to the Tools palette

Want to add tags that aren't available in the BBEdit HTML Tools, without typing them manually each time? The Custom Markup tool enables you to do just that. The interface is rather complex, but here's a simple way to add your own tags to the Tools menu.

As an example, BBEdit doesn't offer a tool for applying specific fonts or font sets to text. To add this feature to the Tools menu, follow these steps:

1. **Choose Tools⇨HTML Custom Markup⇨Custom Markup.**

   The Custom Markup dialog box appears.

2. **Select Undefined and click the Edit button.**

   The Define Custom Markup dialog box, as shown in Figure 11-8, appears.

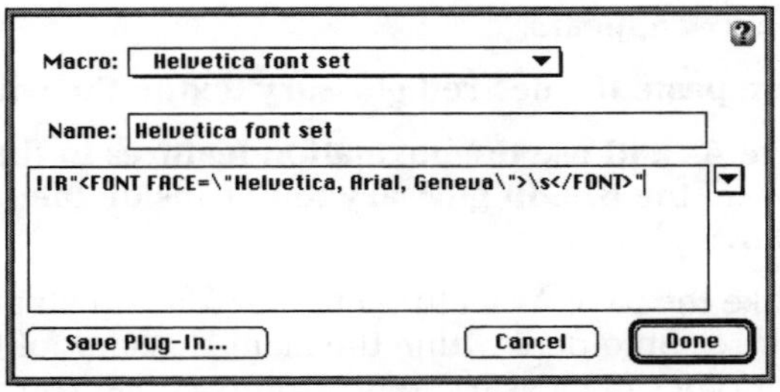

Figure 11-8:
Use this
dialog box
to define
your own
personal
style!

Macro: [Helvetica font set ▼]

Name: [Helvetica font set]

[!IR"<FONT FACE=\"Helvetica, Arial, Geneva\">\s</FONT>" ▼]

[Save Plug-In...]   [Cancel]   [Done]

3. **Type** Helvetica font set **in the Name: field.**

4. **In the markup field, type the appropriate code for the custom tag (refer to Figure 11-8).**

   Your custom tag should start with ! IR, which tells BBEdit to replace the selected text.

   You need to enclose the rest of the tag in double quotes.

5. **To add the new tag to the Tools menu, click the Save Plug-In button.**

   Give the tag an obvious name, such as Helvetica Set. You should save the file within the Plug-ins folder in the BBEdit application folder. You may want to create a new folder in Plug-ins called Fonts and save several different font tags in it. This shows up as a nicely organized hierarchical menu in the Tools menu (you have to quit and restart BBEdit for the new plug-in to show up).

   You can also simply save the tag as Custom Markup and access it through the Custom Markup menu.

6. **To apply your new tag, highlight the target text, and then either select the custom tag from the Tools menu or choose Tools⇨ Custom Markup⇨Custom Markup.**

Using the glossary

Another timesaver is the glossary, which is similar in function to the Library in Dreamweaver. Glossary entries can be simple bits of text or very complex combinations of paragraphs, tags, and code. You can store these in the glossary, the same way that you save things in the Library in Dreamweaver, to provide easy access to them when you want to add them to other pages in your site.

Creating a glossary entry

Follow these steps to create a new glossary item and save it so that it's easy to use when you work with any file in BBEdit:

1. **Choose File⇨New⇨Text Document.**

   A new BBEdit window appears.

2. **Enter or copy and paste the desired glossary text in the window.**

3. **Choose File⇨Save As and use the navigation features in the Save As dialog box to locate the BBEdit glossary folder inside the BBEdit application folder.**

   This works just like the Save As feature in other Macintosh programs. You can even create subfolders within the main glossary folder to organize different types of glossary items (for example, you may create different glossaries for different projects).

4. Give the file a descriptive name and save it.

You don't need to include a special file extension.

Assigning hotkeys to glossary entries

The BBEdit Glossary is designed to save time. Take this a step further by assigning hotkeys to create keyboard shortcuts that make inserting the contents of glossary entries quick and easy. Follow these steps to create hotkeys:

1. From the Windows menu, choose Glossary.

A BBEdit browser window, like the one shown in Figure 11-9, appears.

Figure 11-9:
A BBEdit
Glossary
browser
window.

2. In the top pane of the glossary window, double-click the appropriate folder to find the entry you want.

Use the Folder: pop-up menu to navigate back up the folder hierarchy.

3. Select the glossary entry and click the Set Key button.

4. Input the keystroke that you want to assign to the entry.

The shortcut is automatically set. The next time you type that keystroke or key combination, the glossary entry contents appears on your page.

Inserting a glossary entry into a BBEdit file

You can insert glossary entries on any page you're working on by following these steps:

1. Click to insert your cursor where you want to insert the contents of the glossary entry.

2. Choose Windows⇨Glossary to open the glossary.

You can keep the glossary window open while you work in BBEdit to make accessing glossary entries easier.

3. **Click to highlight a glossary entry from the glossary window and then click the Insert button.**

   Or you can simply press a hotkey combination if you assigned one. The text appears in your document.

Creating custom HTML tags with the glossary

In addition to simply inserting text into your files, the BBEdit Glossary enables you to create custom HTML tags or sets of tags. Using the glossary in this manner is very similar to using the Custom Markup tool (see "Adding custom HTML to the Tools palette" earlier in this chapter). Each method has its advantages: The glossary provides a simpler syntax, while the Custom Markup tool enables you to conveniently organize your tags in the Tools menu. To create a new tag with the glossary, follow these steps:

1. **Create a new glossary file, as described earlier in "Creating a glossary entry."**

2. **Type the special keyword #select# between the tags to represent the selected text.**

   For example, to create the same font tag described in "Adding custom HTML to the Tools palette," your glossary file would contain `<font face=helvetica>#select#</font>`. (Refer to Figure 11-8.)

3. **Follow the rest of the steps earlier in this chapter for saving glossary entries and assigning keywords.**

   To apply a custom HTML glossary entry, select the text or image that you want to apply the tag to and then type the hotkey, or select the entry from the glossary window to apply the tag.

Saving Time with BBEdit Tips

The following BBEdit tips can save you much time and tedium:

✔ Use command keys for frequently accessed HTML Tools: ⌘+Ctrl+A for Anchors, ⌘+Ctrl+I for Images, and ⌘+Ctrl+P for browser preview.

✔ Use the multifile search-and-replace feature to change text across a large number of files. For industrial-strength search and replace, get familiar with the grep-based search language.

✔ Take advantage of the built-in HTML syntax checker.

✔ Set the preferences so that HTML syntax is color-coded, which makes it much easier to read.

✔ Use the glossary or Custom Markup to add HTML tags, such as font sets, that BBEdit doesn't provide.

✔ Remove soft wrapping to get an overview of document and table structure.

✔ Use Auto Indent to keep your code neat and readable, especially for tables.

✔ Use the Windows List to manage multiple open windows.

✔ Use the Windows Option pop-up menu in the status bar to make sure that your documents are saved with the appropriate line breaks.

✔ Take advantage of the nearly limitless Undo's and Redo's — they work even after you save a file.

Chapter 12

Introducing HomeSite

*W*hen all you PC users need to work with HTML code, you'll be glad to find that a powerful HTML editor, HomeSite, comes with Dreamweaver for Windows.

An *HTML editor* is a tool that enables you to work directly in the HTML code of a Web page. It's not a WYSIWYG editor, meaning that when you work in HomeSite, you can't see how your page really looks until you view it in a browser. In this chapter, I focus on using HomeSite independently of Dreamweaver so that you can work in HTML code directly.

Why would you want to look at the HTML code when you have a great WYSIWYG editor in Dreamweaver? The answer is that some people just prefer doing some or all of their page design work in HTML code. They feel that they have more control, and they like to see what's happening behind the scenes. But even if you don't *always* want to work in HTML code, you may find that, at times, using a text editor can give you an advantage. For example, you may want to add a special combination of tags that Dreamweaver doesn't support, or you may want to use a new tag that's not yet included in Dreamweaver.

Appreciating an HTML Text Editor

You can find many kinds of text editors, from simple text editors, such as Notepad (the little text editor that comes with Windows 95 and 98) to sophisticated word processors such as Microsoft Word and Corel WordPerfect. A good HTML editor, such as HomeSite, is different from a plain-text editor because it offers many tools designed to help you build a Web page in HMTL.

You don't have to be a super-techie to appreciate the advantages of an HTML text editor. HomeSite helps you create HTML code exactly the way you want it. Unlike WYSIWYG editors, a text editor doesn't impose a certain structure or layout of code, and it enables you to have ultimate control over how you want your page to look. A good text editor offers features that provide useful, but not imposing, tools for creating HTML code. For example, HomeSite gives you a list of HTML tags that you can insert around text, a table wizard, and even a frames wizard. HomeSite color-codes HTML tags, making it easier to distinguish them from the rest of the code. It also provides powerful search-and-replace capabilities, as well as the ability to customize the tools for your own personal preferences.

You can always create your pages in HomeSite and then work on them in the WYSIWYG editor in Dreamweaver later. Dreamweaver is integrated with HomeSite so that you can move back and forth between these two editors. Changes made in one automatically appear in the other as long as you save the file that you're working on.

Finding the Toolbars and Menus

Before you start coding, you should acquaint yourself with the HomeSite menus and toolbars. This section explains each menu and toolbar so that you can understand the different tools and features of HomeSite.

Menus

At the top of the screen, the menu bar provides easy access to all the features you find in the toolbars, as well as a few others that are only available from the menu.

The File menu

Under the File menu, you find most of the familiar Windows file options, such as New, Open, Close, Save, and Save As. In addition, you find such useful options as:

- ✔ **Open from the Web:** Enables you to open files from a remote Web server.

- ✔ **Insert:** Enables you to insert an entire file into your HTML page.

- ✔ **Reopen:** Enables you to open documents that you've opened before.

- ✔ **Save as UNIX:** Enables you to save your file in the UNIX format. The UNIX format is different from the PC format, so this feature is valuable if your Web server is a UNIX-based server.

Many Internet service providers (ISPs) have UNIX servers, so being able to save your files in UNIX format eliminates the possibility that your ISP's Web server won't be able to read your files. UNIX files are different from Windows files in that they don't have a carriage return at the end of each line. It may sound minimal, but such differences have caused a myriad of problems on some Web servers.

The Edit menu

The Edit menu contains the famous Undo and Redo options, as well as the Cut, Copy, Paste, and Select All options, which function in HomeSite the same way they do in any Windows program. Specific to HomeSite are the Indent and Unindent options, which enable you to indent (or unindent) your HTML code so that it's easier to read. This is a common practice for people who work with HTML code — it can make reading the code much easier. The indent and unindent features only affect the layout of the HTML code and not the way the text displays in a Web browser.

You also find the Convert Tag Case option under the Edit menu. This option converts your tags to uppercase or lowercase, depending on which you prefer. I usually code with all-uppercase tags because it's easier to distinguish them that way.

Another HTML-specific feature is Strip All Tags. This option removes the HTML tags from your document, leaving the plain text. This is useful if you want to reuse text for other purposes.

Finally, you can Go to Line from the Edit menu. That means that you can jump to a specific line in the file (HomeSite numbers each line of text).

The Search menu

You can find some goodies in the Search menu. Besides the regular Find and Replace options, you also have an Extended Find and Replace option. This option enables you to search an entire Web site for a word or string of words and tags to replace.

The Replace Extended Characters option enables you to replace a special character, such as a trademark symbol, with its appropriate HTML equivalent. The Replace Double Spacing with Single Spacing option does exactly what you would think it would do.

The Tools menu

The Tools menu contains many of the greatest features of HomeSite, including a spell checker that functions the way the spell checker of Microsoft Word functions, except that it ignores text contained within HTML brackets if you tell it to.

The Tools menu also provides access to three Quick tools — these tools generate HTML text quickly and enable you to automate some common tasks. The three Quick tools are Quick Anchor, Quick Image, and Quick Font. Each feature uses a dialog box to gather information about the element (anchor, image, or font). You type the information, and the code is automatically generated for you. Figure 12-1 shows the Image dialog box.

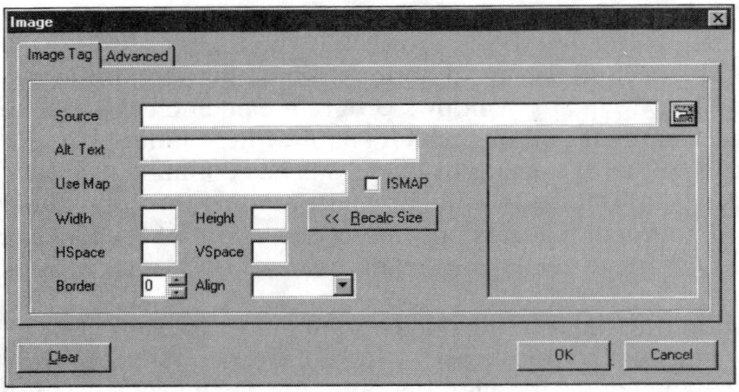

Figure 12-1:
The Image
dialog box
appears
when you
choose
Quick
Image.

The last four tools in the Tools menu have more to do with site management than HTML coding:

- ✔ **Document Weight:** This tool tells you how large your file is and how long it takes to download over a variety of modems.

- ✔ **Verify Links:** This tool checks to make sure that your links are valid.

- ✔ **Import HomeSite 2.5 Custom Tags:** This tool enables you to import tags that you created in earlier versions of HomeSite.

- ✔ **Validate HTML:** This tool enables you to validate your HTML code to make sure that it's correct. I cover more about this tool in "Advanced Features to Explore" later in this chapter.

The Tags menu

The Tags menu contains some of the more widely used tags in HTML. You can also find the same tags on the Tag toolbar, which I discuss in "Toolbars" later in the chapter.

The only tag that you may not recognize is the ASP (Active Server Pages) tag, which is used when you're retrieving information from a database. The ASP tag is beyond the scope of this book, but if you're interested in reading about Active Server Pages, check out *Active Server Pages For Dummies* by Bill Hatfield (published by IDG Books Worldwide, Inc.). And for more information on HTML in general, check out *HTML 4 For Dummies* by Ed Tittel and Stephen N. James (published by IDG Books Worldwide, Inc.).

The View menu

The View menu is where you choose how you want your workspace — the area where you create and edit your pages — to look. Like many other programs that use toolbars and palettes, you have the option to view whichever toolbars you like simply by clicking the option. If you find that these toolbars take up more of your screen than you want, you can turn them off and choose to make them visible only when you need them. The View menu also includes an option that enables you to view your document in a browser.

The Options menu

The Options menu enables you to set your preferred settings for using HomeSite. You can specify your toolbar layout, whether you want your code to automatically wrap (if you're coding in JavaScript, you don't want this option), and much more. If you go to the Settings option, you can choose what kinds of options you want in your Tag toolbar, such as the color of the coded text. This enables you to apply a different color for each tag and specify your preferred font for coding and other display options for the HTML code.

The Help menu

The Help menu contains several options for help, including an HTML reference, Cascading Style Sheet reference, HTML 4.0 specification, Allaire technical support information, and a section on customizing the HomeSite environment.

Of all the Help options, the HTML reference is probably the most valuable. This option has a very complete explanation of HTML, including a listing of every tag supported by both Microsoft Internet Explorer and Netscape Navigator.

Toolbars

Toolbars provide easy point-and-click access to popular features. In this section, I introduce you to the toolbars in HomeSite. As you go through this section, run your cursor over each toolbar so that you can see the various button options for each toolbar.

The Main toolbar

The Main toolbar, as shown in Figure 12-2, has a sampling of the major functional features of HomeSite, such as New File, Save File, Cut, Copy, Paste, Find, Replace, Help, and more. These options can also be found under several menu options.

Figure 12-2:
The Main
toolbar.

The Tag toolbar

The Tag toolbar, as shown in Figure 12-3, has buttons for most of the HTML tags you need. You can find most, but not all, of these tags in the Tag menu.

Figure 12-3:
The Tag
toolbar.

The Editor toolbar

The Editor toolbar (see Figure 12-4) has buttons that enable you to customize how your HTML is formatted as you type it. Options on this toolbar include the following:

Figure 12-4:
The Editor
toolbar.

✓ **Toggle Browser:** This option switches between the HomeSite browser and editor.

✓ **Toggle Word Wrap:** This option switches between text wrapping and not wrapping within the HomeSite window.

✓ **Show Line Number:** This option inserts line numbers on each line of HTML.

✓ **Tag Completion:** This option automatically adds a close-tag to an HTML tag. For example, if you begin to type the font close-tag `<FONT>`, HomeSite automatically inserts a font-close tag `</FONT>`. You can continue to type the text between the tags. HomeSite doesn't alter the position of your cursor when it automatically completes the tag, so the experience isn't as awkward as it sounds. Try it for yourself — you're bound to get addicted to it (it's less typing for you).

✓ **Tag Insight:** This button is a very useful tool. When selected, it provides a pull-down menu that displays all possible attributes for a tag. To access the pull-down menu, just click the tag and then hit the Spacebar. A pop-up window appears in the HomeSite main window (see Figure 12-5).

✓ **Tag Tips:** This option displays basic syntax information for a tag when you place the cursor in the start tag.

✓ **Block Indent/Unindent:** This option indents your code, making it easier to read. When you select the unindent option, the indented text becomes left justified.

✓ **Full Screen:** This option displays the main window of HomeSite as the full screen, without the toolbars or left pane.

✓ **Palette:** This option displays several palettes of colors to choose from when specifying background or font colors. These palettes are considered *safe* palettes, meaning that you can display them across all computer platforms, on all browsers (Internet Explorer and Navigator).

✓ **Macromedia Dreamweaver:** This option toggles you to Dreamweaver. If the Macromedia Dreamweaver button isn't visible in HomeSite, make sure that you check the Enable Dreamweaver Integration check box by choosing Options➪Settings➪Dreamweaver.

Figure 12-5:
The Tag
Insight
button
allows you
to access
all possible
attributes
for a
selected
HTML tag.

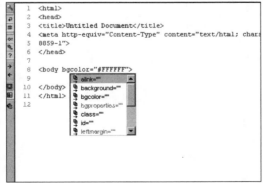

Working with HomeSite

The HomeSite workspace consists of the menus and toolbars described earlier in this chapter and two display windows: the directory window and the main window. When you open HomeSite, you open the entire workspace. See Figure 12-6 to see the workspace with most of the toolbars displayed.

The directory window

The directory window is the left-most window that you see when you open HomeSite. The directory window gives you quick access to all your HTML documents and Web graphics. If you want to open and edit a document, all you need to do is double-click it in the directory window, and it opens in the main window. You can also drag and drop files into the main window (such as image files, sound files, and animations).

Right-clicking a document displays the pop-up document properties menu. This menu enables you to copy or rename an HTML document. It also enables you to display a document's properties, including a list of all external links. In addition, if you right-click an image or multimedia file and then choose Edit in the pop-up menu, that file opens in its associated application.

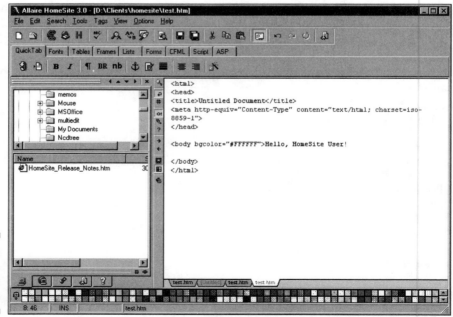

Figure 12-6:
The
HomeSite
workspace.

You can display five different views in the directory window. You switch between these views by clicking one of these five buttons directly underneath the directory window:

✔ **Local:** This is a view of your file system on your hard drive, where you keep local copies of your HTML files.

✔ **Remote:** This option shows files that reside on a remote Web server.

✔ **Projects:** This option lists all HTML files that you group together as projects. For example, if you're working on a Web site for a shoe store named Shoe Biz, you would create a project called Shoe Biz, and this project would contain all your HTML files.

✔ **Tag Snippets:** If you find yourself reusing the same blocks of code, such as a font size, color, and face, you can save that code as a tag snippet. When you do this, you have easy access to this code simply by switching to the tag snippet view of the directory window.

✔ **Help:** This option displays the Help options.

The main window

The main window is the right-most window that you see when you open HomeSite. The main window is where you create your HTML pages. You can switch from Edit mode, which is the mode that you use when creating your pages, to Browse mode, which you use when you want to see how your page looks in a browser, by selecting the Toggle Browser button on the Editor toolbar.

Pages and projects

With HomeSite, you can organize your HTML pages into projects, which are directories with pages specific to that project. Projects are useful if you're creating several different Web sites at once, enabling you to view each site as its own project, which you can then manage and publish. To create a new project, follow these steps:

1. **Switch to the Projects view in the document window, and then right-click and select Create Project from the File menu.**

   The Project Wizard appears. This wizard is very simple, and it guides you through creating a new project or importing one that was created in HomeSite or Dreamweaver.

2. **Name your project.**

   When you do this, a new project is added to the project tree, like the one in Figure 12-7. You can change a project's name at any time by right-clicking it and selecting Rename Project.

Figure 12-7:
The project
view of the
directory
window.

You can add files to the projects that reside on your hard drive by following these steps:

1. **Select the project by clicking it.**

   A Root Folder associated with the selected project appears in the directory window.

2. **Right-click the Root Folder to display a pop-up properties menu and choose Add documents to folder.**

   The Open HTML File dialog box appears.

3. **Select a document to add to the project, or hold down the Shift key to add multiple documents; then click Open to add the file.**

   If you wish to add the document in the editor to the project, choose Add Current Document to Project from the pop-up properties dialog box.

4. **Open a document in a project simply by double-clicking it, or select Open All Files in Project from the project's pop-up properties menu to open every document a project contains.**

Creating a New Page

You have two options when you create a new page. You can use the standard Default template, or you can use the Blank document to get a completely blank document. The difference is that the New template has the minimum set of HTML tags that you need to create a new document. These are the <HTML>, <HEAD>, <TITLE>, and <BODY> tags, as well as a Document Type tag that your Web server uses to establish what version of HTML you use.

HomeSite uses the latest standard, HTML 3.2. I recommend that you use the New template, unless you're working an unusual format or creating something other than an HTML page.

To create a new page using the New template, select the New Page icon at the top-left corner of the Main toolbar. A new HTML page appears in the main window. You can see what the New template looks like in Figure 12-8.

Figure 12-8:
The New
template.

If you want to choose the Blank template, follow these steps:

1. **Choose File⇨New.**

   The New Document dialog box appears.

2. **Choose the Blank document template.**

   A completely blank page appears in the main window.

Using the Quick features

The Quick features enable you to add chunks of code to your document by filling out a dialog box screen instead of typing all the code yourself. This option comes in handy when you're adding links, images, and fonts, because these tags have many attributes, which can be tedious to type.

Adding images

Figure 12-9 shows the Quick Image tool dialog box, which provides an input field for important attribute information, such as size, alternative text, and targets. To use the Quick Image tool, follow these steps:

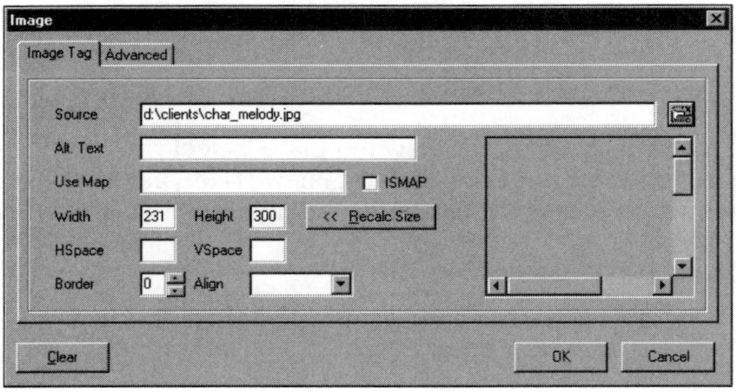

Figure 12-9:
The Image
dialog box.

1. **Choose Tools⇨Quick Image.**

   You see the Image dialog box.

2. **Browse to an image by clicking the folder icon.**

   HomeSite fills in the height and width information.

3. **Fill in the alternative text field and any other fields you like.**

   Use alternative text to provide a text description of the image in case the image can't display in a user's browser.

Creating links

Use the Quick Anchor tool to make an image a hyperlink. Here's how:

1. **Highlight the code for the image that you want to make a hyperlink.**

   The image code may look something like this:

   ```
   <IMG SRC="/Clients/char_melody.jpg" WIDTH=231
          HEIGHT=300 HSPACE=0 VSPACE=0 BORDER=0
          ALT="Picture of Melody">
   ```

2. **Choose Tools⇨Quick Anchor.**

   The Anchor dialog box appears (see Figure 12-10).

3. **Fill in the appropriate information in the dialog box and click OK.**

   The full anchor tags appear around the image code like this:

   ```
   <A HREF="/Sega/Characters/Melody.html"><IMG SRC="
          Clients/char_melody.jpg" WIDTH=231 HEIGHT=300
          HSPACE=0 VSPACE=0 BORDER=0 ALT="Picture of
          Melody"></A>
   ```

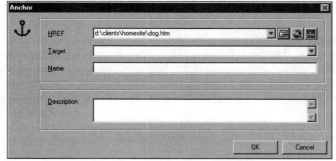

Figure 12-10:
The Anchor
dialog box.

Specifying fonts

To specify attributes for the font that you want to use for text, use the Quick Font tool.

1. Choose Tools⇨Quick Font.

The Tag Editor - FONT dialog box appears (see Figure 12-11).

Figure 12-11:
The Tag
Editor -FONT
dialog box.

2. Select a size, a color, and a typeface from the pull-down menus.

3. Click Apply.

The dialog box disappears, and the code for the font attributes that you just specified appears in the main window. Everything should work fine except that you need to add some text to see what the font looks like.

4. Enter some text in between the <FONT> **and** </FONT> **tags.**

If you have some text already input and want to format it using the Quick Font tool, highlight the text and follow Steps 1 through 3.

Browsing your work

One of the most useful features in HomeSite is the ability to view (or browse) your HTML documents as they appear to your Web site visitors. The default internal browser in HomeSite doesn't support more recent HTML features (such as frames and style sheets), but you can use Microsoft Internet Explorer as your default browser instead to overcome the HomeSite browser's limitations.

To use Internet Explorer as your default browser, follow these steps:

1. **Choose Options⇨Settings.**

   The Settings dialog box appears.

2. **Click the Internal Browser tab.**

   The setting for the internal browser appears.

3. **Place a check mark in the box next to Use Microsoft Internet Explorer as HomeSite's Internal Browser.**

   This changes the default browser to Internet Explorer.

4. **Click OK.**

To preview your page using the default browser, simply click the Toggle Browser button on the Editor toolbar.

But what if you want to use Netscape Navigator instead? In addition to the internal browser, you can also maintain a list of external browsers. To set up Netscape Navigator or another browser as an external browser, choose Options⇨External Browsers. You can add as many external browsers as you like by choosing Add and then browsing to the program by clicking the folder icon.

Use the Browse button on the Main toolbar to display the HTML file that you're working on in the external browser. If you've specified more than one external browser, a menu appears so that you can choose which browser to use. If you specified only one browser, clicking this button opens the browser directly without prompting you to make a choice.

Creating tables

Creating tables with HomeSite is fun. You can use either the Tag toolbar to select the number of columns and rows you want, or the Quick Table button feature (the last button on the table portion of the toolbar). The Quick Table functions the way the Table tool in Microsoft Word does — you click and hold the cursor, and then select how many rows or columns you want. Using the Table Wizard, you can specify how many rows and columns you want in a dialog box, as shown in Figure 12-12. To get to the Table Wizard, click the Tables tab of the Tag toolbar (it's the first button on the toolbar).

A word of caution: Make sure that you know exactly how you want your table to look. As soon as the Table Wizard creates the table code, the only way to edit it is through tinkering with the HTML code — you can't go back and change the Table Wizard settings. If you find that you made a mistake with your table, the easiest thing to do is delete the table and start the Table Wizard again from scratch.

For more on creating tables in Dreamweaver, see Chapter 7.

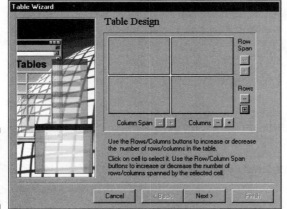

Figure 12-12:
The Table
Wizard
dialog box.

Creating frames

HomeSite has a Frame Wizard that takes you through the steps to creating those tricky framesets. The Frame Wizard walks you through several screens in which you choose a layout for your frameset, as well as the HTML pages that you want to appear in each frame. When you're finished, the wizard creates the HTML code for the frameset page.

As with the Table Wizard, as soon as you create the frameset code in HomeSite, you can't edit it using the Frame Wizard. You need to edit the HTML code directly in the main window, or you can start over from scratch by deleting the HTML code for the frames and starting the Frame Wizard again.

To use the Frame Wizard, follow these steps:

1. **Click the Frames tab of the Tag toolbar.**

   The Tag toolbar displays the different Frames buttons.

2. **Click the Frame Wizard button (it's first button on the toolbar).**

   The Frame Wizard dialog box appears (see Figure 12-13).

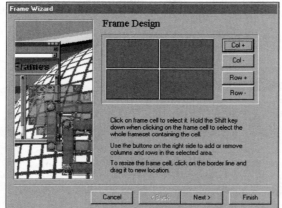

Figure 12-13:
The Frame
Wizard
dialog box.

3. **Choose a layout for your frameset.**

4. **Add or decrease columns or rows by holding the Shift key down when selecting frames.**

5. **Choose Next when you're satisfied with your layout.**

   The Frame Attributes dialog box appears. Notice that the boxes for the frame attributes are grayed out; you have to select a frame to be able to fill in attributes.

6. **Click a frame to activate it.**

   When you do this, the text boxes for the attributes of this frame go from gray to white, which means that you can now enter the attributes.

7. **Choose a file to load inside the frame by clicking the folder icon and browsing to a file. When you find one, click Open.**

   The file is now linked to the frame. Now you're back in the Frame Attributes dialog box.

8. **Enter a value (in pixels) for the margin width and height of each frame.**

9. **Choose whether you want the frame to be scrollable by choosing yes, no, or auto from the pull-down menu.**

10. **Repeat Steps 6 through 9 for each frame you have.**

11. **Click Finish to see the code of your frameset.**

For more on using frames in Dreamweaver, check out Chapter 8.

Advanced Features to Explore

Now that you're a HomeSite expert (well, almost), I urge you to experiment with at least two of HomeSite's advanced features: creating custom toolbars and validating your HTML code.

Creating custom toolbars

Custom toolbars are shortcuts to blocks of code, and they're a great place to keep special tags or combinations of tags that you frequently reuse. Imagine that on several Web pages, you use the same table structure. You can create a toolbar button that automatically inserts the entire table — in just a single click! All you need to do then is fill in the contents of the table cells.

You can also create custom toolbars for scripts that you reuse over and over again, as well as for certain text blocks.

Validating your code

When you validate your code, you make sure that it fits within the rules of the latest HTML specification. Then, no matter what browser reads your file, the file displays exactly how you intend.

An *HTML specification* represents the rules of HTML as agreed upon by the World Wide Web Consortium. The W3C is a group of industry leaders who work together to develop HTML specifications that everyone (users, software vendors, and hardware vendors) can use without fear that "their" HTML code won't work with someone else's software, browser, or computer.

With HomeSite, you can validate your HTML. To do this, click the Validate HTML button (the big red H) on the Main toolbar. When you do this, the validator lists possible invalid HTML code in a frame that appears at the bottom of the workspace. Figure 12-14 shows the results of running the validator.

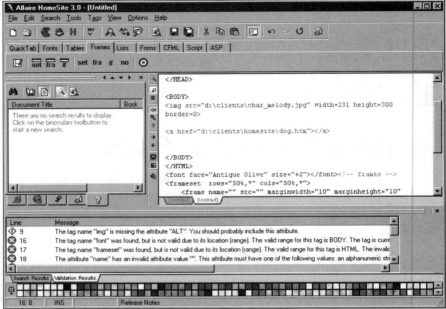

Figure 12-14:
Here's
what the
validator
spits out
when you
check your
HTML code.

To go to a specific line where a problem exists, just double-click it in the list. Because the word-wrap setting may cause the line numbers not to match those of the validator output, HomeSite automatically turns off the word-wrap setting.

Ten Great HomeSite Features and Tips

More and more people are using HomeSite, both with Dreamweaver and as a standalone editor. I asked my favorite HTML guru, Greg Meyers, to give me his top-ten favorite features and tips for using HomeSite.

✔ **Internal browser:** Being able to click the Browse tab and look at your changes without having to save them is a great feature. It saves time and takes less of a toll on your computer system because you only need to have one program open to both edit and view your page.

✔ **Document weight:** This feature helps you keep your file sizes small. By choosing the document weight option, you can see how big your file is, not only the HTML text, but also the images and applets embedded into the page. You can also see how long the page takes to download over 14.4 or 28.8 modems.

✔ **Custom toolbar:** This toolbar helps if you often use the same set of tags or commands.

✔ **Tag toolbar:** After you get familiar with the Tag toolbar, you'll be amazed at how often you use it. Simply pressing a button when you want a certain tag is a great convenience.

✔ **Color-coding of HTML tags:** Sometimes HTML code looks like a big blur of text. To be able to use color so that you can tell the difference between an anchor tag, its text, and its attributes is a big help.

✔ **Color bar:** The color bar is a big timesaver in figuring out hexadecimal values from RGB values.

✔ **Extended search and replace:** This feature makes sitewide changes a snap.

✔ **Keyboard shortcuts:** A full keyboard shortcut section exists in the Help menu for people who prefer using the keyboard to using the mouse.

✔ **Project feature:** This feature makes working on several Web sites easy because you can organize them all in the directory window.

✔ **Listmaker:** Ever wonder how to make nested lists? Try the listmaker — it really works!

Part V
Making It Cool

The 5th Wave   By Rich Tennant

"No, Thomas Jefferson never did 'the Grind,' however, this does show how animation can be used to illustrate American history on the Web."

In this part . . .

Bring your Web pages to life with the interactive features made possible by Dynamic HTML. Add animations, sound, and video by linking a wide range of multimedia files to your Web pages. And finally, use HTML forms to create search engines, online shopping systems, and so much more.

Chapter 13

Adding Interactivity with Dynamic HTML

• •

In This Chapter

▶ Looking into the future

▶ Using a timeline

▶ Applying behaviors

▶ Adding ActiveX controls

• •

Dynamic HTML (DHTML) has received so much hype and attention that you'd think you could do anything with it, including your laundry. Well, DHTML isn't quite powerful enough to take over your domestic duties, but it does add a range of functionality to a Web page that has been impossible with any other technology. Oh sure, you can create interactive animations with other technologies, such as Java or Shockwave for Director, but DHTML animations work much faster. And, yes, designers have used JavaScript to add dynamic effects to Web pages for a while, but now you can actually affect the attributes of tags, meaning that you create many more kinds of effects and make them happen more quickly.

All in all, DHTML deserves most of the hype because it takes Web page design to another level of interactivity and multimedia without compromising download times. Like any new Web technology, however, DHTML has a few problems. The biggest one is browser compatibility. At the end of this chapter, I tell you how Dreamweaver makes designing pages that work in different browsers easier, even if you use the latest features. The rest of this chapter shows you how to use layers, behaviors, and timelines to create complex DHTML features, such as animations.

Understanding DHTML

DHTML is exciting because it adds so many possibilities to Web design, from global style formatting with Cascading Style Sheets (covered in detail in Chapter 9), to fast-loading animations, and other interactive features made possible with the addition of layers and timelines.

DHTML brings dramatic improvements to Web design by providing more precise design control. Using DHTML, you can position elements (text, images, and others) exactly where you want them on a page by specifying their distance from the top and left side of a page. Dreamweaver refers to these as Top and Bottom, but in HTML, they're officially called X,Y coordinates. A third positioning option, the Z coordinate, adds the ability to stack elements on top of one another.

DHTML also enables you to use a scripting language, such as JavaScript or VBScript, to control any element or attribute of an element. That means you can dynamically change the size or color of text, the alignment of an image, or any other attribute of an HTML tag. When I say you can change those dynamically, I mean you can make those changes happen automatically, after a page loads, or you can assign the action to be triggered by an event, such as the click of a mouse. What is unique in DHTML is that the entire page doesn't have to reload for these changes to take effect, they happen right on the same page — that's what makes them dynamic.

Designers have been using JavaScript to create some of these effects for a while. For example, you've probably seen sites where images change when you move a cursor over them. DHTML takes tricks, like that "roll over" effect, a step further by adding many more events and actions. DHTML is, however, much more complicated to write than regular old HTML 3.2. Even HTML frames, which are complex by many Web design standards, look relatively simple when compared to JavaScript and the kind of code you have to write to create DHTML. This is where Dreamweaver really shines — Macromedia has successfully created a WYSIWYG design environment that you can use to create these complex DHTML features without ever having to look at the code (unless you want to, of course).

Three powerful features in Dreamweaver make creating DHTML features possible — layers, behaviors, and the timeline. All these features are covered in this chapter and you'll find step-by-step instructions for using all of them. But before you get into each section, it's helpful to understand what each of them has to do and how they can all work together to create the most advanced features.

Think of a layer as the container (like a ship that contains passengers, except layers are usually transparent to the viewer). Then break down behaviors as events and actions. For example, hitting an iceberg could be an event the same way clicking on a graphic is an event. The ship sinking could then be considered an action, the same way a graphic moving across a page is an action. Finally, think of a timeline like the schedule on the ship. The ship leaves port at a certain time and passes the islands at another time, all on schedule. The timeline in Dreamweaver enables you to control the actions and events over time, like you're creating a schedule of events for your page. At the Fabric8 Web site, shown in Figure 13-1, Web designer Olivia Ongpin uses DHTML layers and actions to move the mannequin around the front page and display a bubble with text when the user moves a cursor over links. Check out her latest designs at www.fabric8.com.

Figure 13-1:
Web designer Olivia Ongpin uses the DHTML features in Dreamweaver to create layers and attach behaviors that bring her Fabric8 Web site to life.

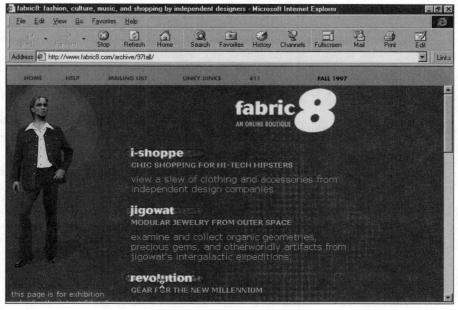

Working with Layers

Think of a *layer* as a transparent box or a container you can use to hold images, text, and other elements. This box is handy because you can manipulate all its contents together, move them on top of another layer, or make them visible or invisible as a collection. If you're familiar with Adobe Photoshop, you should have a general concept of how layers work. DHTML layers are very similar; you can move them around to position elements exactly where you want them, use them to overlap elements on a page, or turn them on and off to control visibility. If you're new to layers, you may want to use the following numbered steps to experiment a little with creating layers, adding images and other elements, and moving them around.

By using the positioning controls, you can place layers in exact locations on a page for precise design control. You can treat each layer as if it's a separate page that can be manipulated independently and can contain anything from text to images to plug-ins to tables and even other layers.

Creating layers

Follow these steps to create a layer:

1. **Choose Insert➪Layer.**

   A box, representing the layer, appears on the page.

2. **Move the cursor into the Document window and drag any of the corners of the box to resize the layer.**

Adding elements, and moving and resizing layers

To add images or text to a layer, follow these steps:

1. **Click to insert your cursor inside the layer.**

2. **Choose Insert➪Image.**

   The Insert Image dialog box appears.

3. **Click the Browse button, locate the image file that you want to insert, click to highlight the filename, click the Select button, and then click OK.**

   The image appears inside the layer.

4. Click to insert your cursor anywhere in the layer area and enter some text.

As you can see in Figure 13-2, I entered the word *Questions* next to a button image with a question mark on it. You can type in any text you want and place it anywhere in the layer.

5. Highlight the text and format it by using the text formatting options in the Property inspector.

You can choose any formatting option available for any other text. In this case, I chose Heading 1 from the pull-down list, as you can see in Figure 13-2.

6. Select the image and use the Property inspector to make any desired formatting changes to it.

In this example in Figure 13-2, I chose Align⇨Top from the Align option in the Property inspector to achieve the positioning shown.

7. Click the box that appears at the top-left of the layer area to select the layer.

You know that you've achieved this because the "handles" (the little black squares that appear at the corners and in the middle of each side) appear.

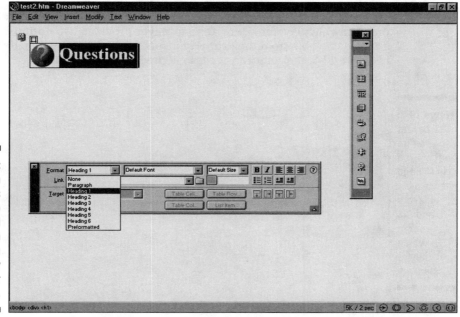

Figure 13-2:
You can add images and text to layers and format them as you would any similar element.

8. **Click any handle and drag to resize the layer.**

As a general rule, you should always size layers so that their contents just fit within its boundaries because positioning it on the page becomes easier.

9. **To move a layer, click the box that appears at the top-left of the layer and use it to drag the layer to any place on the page.**

Because layers use exact positioning, you can move them to any precise location on a page, and they display in that exact location in browsers, such as Navigator 4.0 and Internet Explorer 4.0, that support DHTML.

In addition to using the click-and-drag method to move a layer, you can change a layer's position by entering a number in the position boxes, marked with L (for left) and T (for top) in the Property inspector.

Stacking layers and changing visibility

A powerful feature of layers is the ability to stack them on top of each other and make them visible or invisible. When I get into the section on adding behaviors later in this chapter, I show you how to use these features in combination with behaviors to create animations and other effects. Here, I help you get the hang of moving layers and changing layer visibility.

To stack layers, simply drag one layer on top of another. To control the order in which layers appear, Dreamweaver provides two options: the Z index available from the Property inspector, and the Layers palette, shown in Figure 13-3, that you can access via the Windows menu.

Figure 13-3:
The Layers palette enables you to change the visibility of layers and the order in which they're stacked.

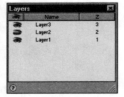

Follow these steps to stack layers and change their order and visibility:

1. **Select the layer by clicking anywhere within the border of the layer.**

2. **Click the small box in the top-left corner of the layer and drag the layer to reposition it.**

   You can use drag-and-drop to move the layer anywhere on the page, including on top of another layer. When the layer is where you want it, release the mouse button.

3. **Choose Window⇨Layers to open the Layer palette.**

   If you're familiar with layers in Adobe Photoshop, you may find some similarities here, such as the eye to show a layer is visible and the ability to drag layers around to reposition them.

4. **Reposition the layers by selecting the name of a layer in the Layer inspector and dragging it up or down.**

   Layers are automatically named layer1, layer2, and so on, as they're created. You can rename a layer by double-clicking the name to select it, using the delete key to remove it, and then typing a new name in its place.

   As you move layers around the page, especially when you want to place them on top of each other, be aware that you have two ways to reposition layers and it's easy to confuse them. First, you can change the order of a layer by dragging it to another place in the list, such as the very top to make it first. Second, you can create nested layers by dragging the name of a layer over the name of another layer and then releasing the mouse button when a box appears around the name of the first layer.

   Nesting layers is easy to do by accident when you're trying to move one layer above or below another layer. If a box appears around the name of a layer, then it will be nested within the first layer.

5. **Click to the left of the layers to turn them on or off by changing the eye icons as shown back in Figure 13-3.**

   If the eye is open, a layer is on, meaning it's visible on the screen. Click until the eye icon appears closed to turn a layer off and make it invisible.

Setting layer options

Like other HTML elements, layers come with many options, such as height and width. Dreamweaver makes these options available in the Property inspector when you select a layer (see Figure 13-4). The following list describes the layer options and what they control:

Figure 13-4:
When you
select a
layer, the
Property
inspector
reveals
these layer
options.

✔ **Name:** In the top-left corner of the Property inspector, an unmarked text box lies just under the word Layer where you can enter a name to identify the layer for scripting. Use only standard alphanumeric charac ters for a layer name (no special characters such as spaces, hyphens, slashes, or periods).

✔ **L (Left):** This value specifies the distance of the layer from the left side of the page or parent (or outer) layer. Dreamweaver automatically enters a pixel value when you create or move a layer with drag-and - drop. You can also enter a numeric value (positive or negative) to control the positioning.

✔ **T (Top):** This value specifies the distance of the layer from the top of the
page or parent (or outer) layer. Dreamweaver automatically enters a pixel value when you create or move a layer with drag-and-drop. You can also enter a numeric value (positive or negative) to control the positioning.

✔ **W (Width):** Dreamweaver automatically specifies the width when you create a layer on a page. You also have the option of entering a numeric value to specify the height. In addition, you can change the measure-ment from the default of px (pixels) to pc (picas), pt (points), in (inches), mm (millimeters), cm (centimeters), or % (percentage of the parent's value). Don't put any spaces between the number and the measurement abbreviation.

✔ **H (Height):** Dreamweaver automatically specifies the width when you create a layer on a page. You also have the option of entering a numeric value to specify the height. In addition, you can change the measure-ment from the default of px (pixels) to pc (picas), pt (points), in (inches), mm (millimeters), cm (centimeters), or % (percentage of the parent's value). Don't put any spaces between the number and the measurement abbreviation.

✔ **Z-Index:** This option determines the position of a layer in relation to other layers when layers are stacked. Higher-numbered layers appear on top of lower-numbered layers, and values can be positive or negative.

Changing the stacking order of layers is easier using the Layers palette than entering specific Z-index values. For more on using the Layers palette, see "Stacking layers and changing visibility" earlier in the chapter.

✔ **Vis:** The visibility setting controls whether a layer is visible or invisible. You can use this setting with a scripting language, such as JavaScript, to dynamically change the display of layers.

The visibility options are

- *Default:* The default option in most browsers is the same visibility property as the parent's value.

- *Inherit:* This option always uses the visibility property of the layer's parent.

- *Visible:* This option always displays the layer, regardless of the parent's value.

- *Hidden:* This option always makes the layer transparent (invisible), regardless of the parent's value. Hidden layers take up the same space as visible layers.

You can dynamically control visibility by using the JavaScript behaviors covered in "Attaching behaviors" later in this chapter.

✔ **Bg Image:** Here, you link a background image to a layer. Click the folder icon to select an image or enter the name and path in the text box.

✔ **Bg Color:** Use this option to fill the background of a layer with a solid color. Click the color square to open a color palette, from which you can select a color. If you want the layer background to be transparent, leave it blank.

✔ **Tag:** This enables you to choose between using CSS layers or Netscape layers. As a general rule, you should use CSS layers. To find out more about the difference, see the sidebar "Netscape layers versus CSS layers."

✔ **Overflow:** These options determine how the contents of a layer display if they exceed the size of the layer. (Note that this option only applies to CSS layers.)

Overflow options are

- *Visible:* This forces the layer size to increase so that all its contents are visible. The layer expands down and to the right.

- *Hidden:* This clips off the edges of content that doesn't fit within the specified size of a layer. Be careful with this option; it doesn't provide any scroll bars.

- *Scroll:* This adds scroll bars to the sides of a layer regardless of whether the contents exceed the layer's size or not. The advantage of this option is that scroll bars don't appear and disappear in a dynamic environment.

- *Auto:* Scroll bars appear only if the layer's contents don't fit within the layer's boundaries.

- ✔ **Clip:** This controls what section of the contents of a layer are cropped if the layer isn't large enough to display all the contents. You should specify the distance from the L (Left), T (Top), R (Right), and B (Bottom). You can enter values in px (pixels), pc (picas), pt (points), in (inches), mm (millimeters), cm (centimeters), or % (a percentage of the parent's value). Don't add any spaces between the number and the measurement abbreviation.

The following options apply only to Netscape layers and appear only if you select LAYER or ILAYER from the Tag option. To find out more about the difference between Netscape layers and CSS layers, see the sidebar "Netscape layers versus CSS layers."

- ✔ **Top, Left or PageX, PageY:** Use these for positioning the layer.

- ✔ **Source:** This enables you to display another HTML document within a layer. Type the path of the document or click the folder icon to browse and select the document. Note that Dreamweaver doesn't display this property in the Document window.

- ✔ **A/B:** This specifies the position of layers on the Z index, which controls the stacking of layers.

Netscape layers versus CSS layers

Netscape was the first to bring layers to the Web. However, they pushed the limits on their own and didn't wait for a standard. Unfortunately for them (and for those of us sorting out DHTML), the result is that today you have two different ways to create layers — the Netscape layer tag, which consists of the <LAYER> and <ILAYER> tags, and the CSS-P option, which uses the <DIV> and <SPAN> tags.

I recommend (and so do many others, including Macromedia) that you avoid Netscape's <LAYER> and <ILAYER> tags because the W3C and Microsoft Internet Explorer don't support them. Fortunately, Netscape did agree to adopt the standard proposed in the HTML 4.0 specification from the W3C, so some semblance of a standard is now emerging. If you use the <DIV> and <SPAN> tags, you can reach a broader audience because both Navigator 4.0 and Internet Explorer 4.0 (and probably future versions of these and other browsers) support these tags. If you use Dreamweaver, you don't have to worry about this. The <DIV> tag is the default, although you can change it in the preferences.

If, for some reason, you choose to use the <LAYER> tag, you see additional options in the lower-right corner of the Property inspector when you select the layer.

Working with Behaviors

Some of the coolest features used on the Web today can be created using Dreamweaver behaviors (which are written in JavaScript). You can apply behaviors to any element on an HTML page, and even to the entire page. Writing JavaScript is more complex than writing HTML code, but not as hard as writing in a programming language like C, C++, or Java. (No, Java and JavaScript are not the same. Read Chapter 14 for more on Java applets and how they differ from JavaScript.)

In this section, I show you how surprisingly easy Dreamweaver makes it to apply a whole range of behaviors that you can use to create dynamic effects. Using the behaviors options, you can make images swap when viewers pass their cursors over them, and create animations that start when a visitor clicks on an image or other element on a page. Combining the power of behaviors with layers opens up a range of tricks that look great on a page and load very fast. Add to that the power of the timeline, described later in this chapter, and you can make this happen automatically. The timeline enables you to trigger behaviors after a specified amount of time and set one behavior to happen before another.

If you're thinking that using a timeline and controlling layers sound like a lot to juggle, relax. This is where the fun starts. This section walks you through the steps to apply behaviors. You find out more about timelines in "Using the Timeline" later in the chapter.

Attaching behaviors

If you've always wanted to add cool interactive features, like making something flash or pop up when users move their cursors over an image or click a link, you're going to love the *behavior* feature in Dreamweaver. To fully appreciate what Dreamweaver can do for you, you may want to open the HTML Source window (available under the Window menu) just to see the complex code needed to create behaviors. If you don't like what you see, don't worry; you can close the HTML Source window and just let Dreamweaver take care of the code for you.

When you use behaviors in Dreamweaver, you don't have to write any code at all. Instead, you use a couple of dialog boxes, and with a few clicks of your mouse, you get interactive effects. You can attach behaviors to a page, a link, an image, or almost any other element on a page simply by selecting the element, specifying the action or event that triggers the behavior, and then choosing the behavior from the Behavior inspector.

Adding new behaviors to Dreamweaver

If you know how to write JavaScript, you can add your own behaviors to the list of choices in Dreamweaver by using the Action menu in the Behavior inspector. You can find instructions for creating new actions in the Dreamweaver Developers Center at www.dreamweaver.com. You can also find new behaviors created by Macromedia, as well as other developers, that you can download free of charge and then add to Dreamweaver.

To apply a behavior to an element on a page, such as an image, follow these steps:

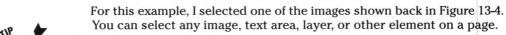

1. **Select an element on a page.**

   For this example, I selected one of the images shown back in Figure 13-4. You can select any image, text area, layer, or other element on a page.

   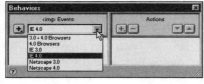

   To attach a behavior to the entire page, click the <BODY> tag in the tag selector at the bottom-left of the Document window.

2. **Choose Window⇨Behaviors to open the Behaviors inspector.**

   You can also click the Behavior button on the Launcher.

3. **Select the target browser you want from the pop-up menu to the right of Events in the Behaviors inspector (see Figure 13-5).**

   See the sidebar "Choosing a target browser" for more on this option. I've chosen Internet Explorer 4.0 because it supports the largest number of behaviors.

Figure 13-5:
Use the Behaviors inspector to select the target browser.

4. From the left side of the Behaviors inspector, click the plus sign and choose an event from the Events pop-up menu that triggers the behavior.

I chose OnClick, which causes the behavior to be triggered when a user clicks on the image. You can choose any event to trigger a behavior.

5. From the right side of the Behaviors inspector, choose an action from the Actions pop-up menu.

This is the action that's triggered by the event. As you can see in Figure 13-6, I chose Open Browser Window as the action.

If an action is grayed out on the list in the Behaviors inspector, it means that the action won't work with the file or element you selected. The Control Shockwave Action, for example, works only if you select a Shockwave file.

6. In the dialog box associated with the action, specify the parameter options to control how you want the behavior to work.

In Figure 13-6, I set the Open Browser Window so that the display area will only be 150 pixels wide by 350 pixels high when it opens. The result, shown in Figure 13-7, is that a small browser window opens when the image is clicked, displaying the contents of the page I've specified in the URL field (in this case a bouncing ball). Different dialog boxes open with different options, depending on the event you choose.

7. After you have specified the parameters, click OK.

Figure 13-6:
When you select an action, such as Open Browser Window, from the Behaviors inspector, a dialog box opens where you can make choices about how the behavior works.

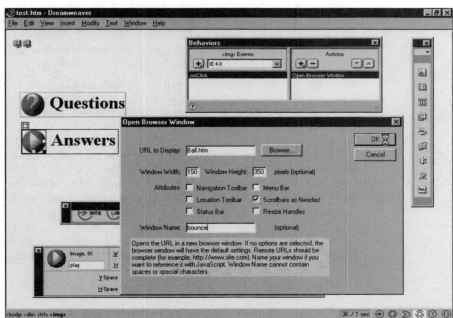

Figure 13-7:
Using
DHTML,
the small
browser
window (a
second
Internet
Explorer
window) is
opened to
display the
bouncing
ball when
the
Answers
button was
clicked.

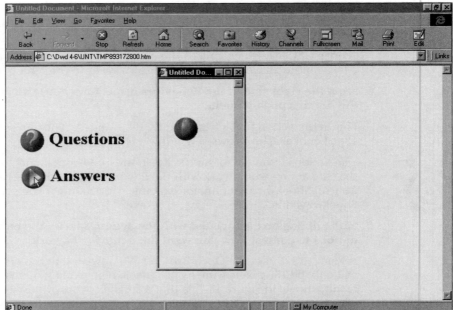

8. **To test the action, choose File⇨Preview in Browser, and then select the browser you want to test your work in.**

   This opens the page in whatever browser you choose so that you can see how it really looks in that browser. Unfortunately, most of these actions only work in Internet Explorer 4.0 or later. See the sidebar "Choosing a target browser" for more about actions and browser differences.

   If you get an error message about a filename, like the one from Internet Explorer shown in Figure 13-8, you need to go back and "name" an element in the Property inspector before the behavior can work.

Many event options, such as onmousedown, onmouseover, and onmouseout, are only available if the element is a link. Dreamweaver helps you get around this by automatically adding the link tag when you choose one of these events for an element that isn't linked. Dreamweaver doesn't link the element to anything; instead it places a pound sign in place of a filename or URL. Make sure that you don't delete the pound sign from the Property inspector or the HTML code (it looks like this `<a href="#"...`). You can replace it with a URL if you want the element to open another page. If you leave it as a pound sign, the event triggers the action, without opening a URL.

Figure 13-8:
If you apply
a behavior
to an
element
that has not
been given
a name in
the Property
inspector,
you get this
warning
message.

Attaching multiple behaviors

You can attach multiple behaviors to the same element on a page (as long as they don't conflict, of course). For example, you can attach one action that is triggered when users click on an image and another when they move their cursor over the image. You can also trigger the same action by more than one event. For example, you can play the same sound when any number of events are triggered by a user. You can't, however, attach multiple actions to one event — meaning that you can't open a browser window and play a sound when the same image is selected.

To attach additional behaviors to an element, follow the same steps in "Attaching behaviors" earlier in this chapter and then click the plus sign again and select another option from the pull-down menu to add another behavior. Repeat this as many times as you want.

Changing a behavior

You can always go back and change a behavior after you create it. You can choose a different event to trigger a behavior, choose a different action, and add and remove behaviors. You can also change the parameters that you have specified.

Follow these steps to change a behavior:

   1. Select an object with a behavior attached.

Choosing a target browser

Because behaviors are a new development on the Web, only the latest browser versions support most of the events and actions available in the Behaviors inspector. But Dreamweaver offers a couple of ways to accommodate browser differences. You can choose to limit yourself to the most basic behaviors by selecting Netscape Navigator 3.0 or Internet Explorer 3.0, or you can choose the browser with the most options (Internet Explorer 4.0). These choices ensure that your pages work in the browsers you've chosen. (If you choose one of the most advanced browsers, such as Internet Explorer 4.0, your pages may not work at all in other browsers.)

Dreamweaver provides an alternative that strives to give you the best of both worlds. To take advantage of it, design your pages for Internet Explorer 4.0 and then convert them to a copy that works in 3.0 browsers when you're done. You then have two pages to which you can direct viewers. Dreamweaver 1.2 or later can convert your pages for you and includes a script that can automatically direct viewers to the correct page based on the browser they use. You can find more on converting pages in "Ensuring That Your Pages Work in Older Browsers" at the end of this chapter.

   2. **Choose Window⇨Behaviors to open the Behavior inspector.**

   You can also click the Behaviors button in the Launcher.

   Here are some options to choose from:

   - To add a new event, choose one from the Events pop-up menu.

   - To remove an action, click to select the event that triggers the action in the Event pane on the left of the Behaviors inspector. Then, click to select the name of the action in the Actions pane on the right of the Behaviors inspector, and click the minus sign located at the top of the pane. The action disappears.

   - To delete an event or remove a behavior from a tag, select an event and then delete all the associated actions.

   - To change parameters for an action, select the event that triggers the action, double-click the action, change the parameters you want to affect in the Parameters dialog box, and then click Apply.

   - To change the order of actions, select the event that triggers the actions, select an action, and then click the Up or Down buttons.

Using the Timeline

As the name implies, a *timeline* enables you to control actions over time, making it possible to create animations and automatically trigger behaviors. If you're familiar with other animation programs, such as Macromedia Flash or Director, you can figure out the timeline feature in Dreamweaver without much trouble. If you're completely new to timelines, you may find this a bit confusing at first — but hang in there, it's not that tough.

The steps in this section introduce you to the timeline options and explain the features that you can create. Only Dynamic HTML provides the functionality that makes a timeline necessary, so you can use timelines only if you're designing DHTML features. That means the animations and effects you create with the timeline only work in 4.0 or later browsers.

Timelines work by defining a series of frames that change over time. The elements in the frames (such as images or layers) can change in a variety of ways, from moving to a new location to being replaced by another layer or image. Thus, you can use timelines to create animations or to trigger other actions, such as starting a behavior when a page loads or after a series of other actions occur. You create timelines with the Timeline inspector (see Figure 13-9).

Figure 13-9:
The
Timeline
inspector.

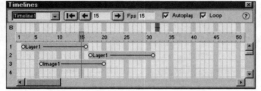

Understanding the Timeline inspector options

Before you get into using the timeline, take a few minutes to review the Timeline inspector options. Starting at the top and going from left to right, the Timeline inspector features these options:

- ✔ **Timeline pop-up menu:** You can have multiple timelines on one page. The timeline pop-up menu enables you to select which of the timelines appear in the Timeline inspector.

- ✔ **Rewind:** Represented by a left-pointing arrow that's pointing to a line, this button returns the playback to the first frame in the timeline.

- ✔ **Back:** Represented by a left-pointing arrow, this button moves the playback to the left one frame at a time. You can click and hold the Back button to play the frames backward continuously.

- ✔ **Play:** Represented by a right-pointing arrow, the Play button moves the playback to the right one frame at a time. You can click and hold the Play button to play the frames forward continuously. When you reach the last frame, the play continues at the beginning of the timeline.

- ✔ **FPS:** Represents the number of frames per second (fps). The default setting of 15 frames per second is a good rate for most browsers on Windows and Macintosh systems. Browsers always play every frame, even if they can't achieve the frame rate.

- ✔ **Autoplay:** Checking this box causes a timeline to begin playing automatically when a page loads in a browser.

- ✔ **Loop:** Checking this box causes the timeline to repeat while the page displays in a browser window. When you check the Loop box, the Go To Timeline Frame action is added. If you want to control the number of loops, you need to double-click the marker that is added to the Behavior channel, opening the Behavior inspector, where you can edit the parameters to define the number of loops.

- ✔ **Behavior channel:** Just below the controls across the top of the Timeline inspector, the Behavior channel has a B to the left of it and displays behaviors that should execute at a particular frame in the timeline.

- ✔ **Frame numbers:** The numbers (listed in increments of 5) along the bar that separates the Behavior channel and the Animation channel indicate how many frames each bar occupies. The number of the current frame also displays between the Back and Play buttons at the top of the Timeline inspector.

- ✔ **Animation channels:** This area is where the animation bars appear.

- ✔ **Playback head:** Indicated by red, this marker highlights the active frame in the timeline (the one that currently displays on the page).

- ✔ **Animation bars:** These blue lines appear in the timeline when you add an object. Each bar shows the duration of an object. You can have multiple animation bars and control multiple objects in one timeline.

- ✔ **Keyframes:** Represented by a circle, keyframes are frames in an animation bar that indicate properties, such as the position or an image on a page.

One of the advantages of timelines is that they fill in the frames between keyframes by calculating intermediate values. For example, if you set a keyframe for an image positioned at the top of a page and then set a second keyframe for the same image positioned lower on the page, the timeline draws the image moving from one place to the other automatically. For instructions on setting keyframes and an example of how this works, try the steps that follow.

You can use the HTML Source window to view the JavaScript code that Dreamweaver creates when you use a timeline. You can find the code in the MM_initTimelines function, inside a `<SCRIPT>` tag in the `<HEAD>` of the document. If you choose to edit the HTML source of a document that uses timelines, be careful not to change anything controlled by the timeline.

Creating timelines

The following steps walk you through using a timeline. Here, I use a timeline to cause two layers to automatically move into position when a page loads.

1. **Click anywhere in the layer to select it and then click the layer marker (the small box in the top-left corner of the layer) and drag it to the location on your page where you want to begin the animation sequence.**

   Make sure that you select the right layer and don't just place your cursor inside it. Use the layer marker (the little square at the top-left of the layer), or use the Layer palette to select a layer. If you want to change the position of other layers on the page, you can get them into their starting position as well.

   If you want to position a layer off the visible page, you can enter a negative number in the text boxes marked L (for left) or T (for top) in the Property inspector. This is a great trick when you want to have a layer start off-screen and then slide into position as part of the animation sequence. Controlling the position of a layer by changing these numbers, rather than using the drag-and-drop technique, also provides greater control over precise positioning.

2. **Choose Window⇨Timelines.**

   The Timeline inspector opens.

3. **Click the layer marker to select the layer that you want to add to the timeline.**

4. **Choose Modify⇨Add Object to Timeline.**

   You can also just click and drag the layer (or any other selected object) into the Timeline inspector to create a new animation bar.

   A bar appears in the first channel of the timeline. The name of the layer or image appears in the bar (like the bar that says Layer1 back in Figure 13-9).

5. **Click to select the blue dot that represents the keyframe at the right end of the animation bar.**

   Your goal in selecting this second keyframe is to create an end point for the animation that starts with the layer at the location where you placed it in Step 1. In the next step, you get to move that same layer somewhere else on your page and use this second keyframe to assign a new location for it. When triggered, the timeline automatically causes the layer to move across the page from the location associated with the first keyframe to the location now associated with this second keyframe.

6. **With the keyframe selected, move your mouse so that you can click again on the layer marker in the layer you're working with.**

7. **While holding down the mouse, drag this same layer to any place on the page where you would like it to move when the timeline is triggered.**

8. **To increase the duration of the animation, click the keyframe circle and drag it farther to the right in the Timelines inspector, or drag it to the left to shorten it.**

   This lengthens and shortens the animation bar and controls the amount of time that elapses while the timeline moves the element from the first keyframe and the second.

9. **If you want to add a bend or curve to the animation motion, click a frame in the middle of the animation bar and choose Modify⇨ Timeline⇨Add Keyframe.**

   You can add as many keyframes as you like and use them to control the location or other features of the element.

10. **With the new keyframe circle selected, move the layer on the page to the position that you want it to be in at that point in the animation sequence.**

    For example, if you wanted a layer to move across the page on a curved path instead of a straight one, you could add a keyframe like the one in Step 8 and then position it, as shown in Step 9, in a place on the page that would cause the motion of the layer to move to a third location as it progresses from the first keyframe to the last one.

11. **To preview the animation, click and hold down the Play button.**

12. **When you're finished, choose Window⇨Timelines to close the Timelines inspector.**

By following these same steps, you can add additional layers to the timeline causing simultaneous actions. You can also click and drag the animation bars to stagger frame sequences. In Figure 13-10, you see two layers, each represented by a different animation bar in the timeline. Notice that the two animation bars are staggered and that, as the layers move across the page, one progresses ahead of the other. Because both animation bars finish on the same point, they both stop at the same location on the page.

You can also add behaviors to keyframes and use behaviors to trigger actions that use timelines. In "Creating behaviors" earlier in this chapter, I assigned a behavior to a button that, when clicked, opened another browser window. That window contained a bouncing ball that animated because of the use of a timeline. You can see how that looked displayed in Internet Explorer back in Figure 13-7. I used the preceding steps to create that bouncing ball animation.

Figure 13-10:
You can control multiple layers by creating multiple animation bars in the Timeline inspector.

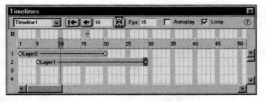

To make this animation more realistic, you may want to make it look like the ball gets a little squished at the top and bottom when it bounces. You can do that by *swapping* the round ball image with a second image that shows the same ball with a little squish on each side. You can create similar effects by swapping any images at any point in a timeline sequence. Here's how you swap images:

1. **Click to select the image (select only the image, not the layer, by carefully clicking the image itself) and drag the image into the Timeline inspector to create a second animation bar like the one you see in Figure 13-11.**

   This animation bar is labeled with the word *Image* instead of *Layer*.

2. **Create a new keyframe at the point where you want the images to swap.**

Figure 13-11:
By creating a second animation bar for the image, I swapped images and made this animation more realistic by making the ball appear to squish with each bounce.

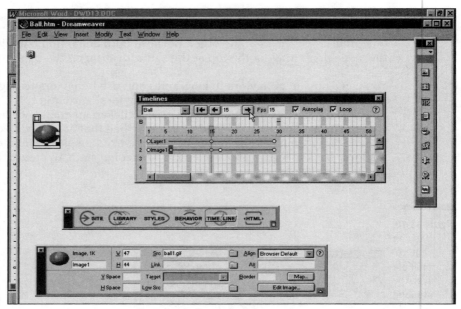

To do so, click anywhere in the image animation bar and choose Modify⇔Timeline⇔Add Keyframe. Notice where I've placed the keyframes back in Figure 13-11. Their positions, just before each end of the animation bar, are in the right place to cause the image to change just after appearing to bounce at each end of the animation bar.

3. **With a keyframe circle selected in the image animation bar, use the Property inspector to change the image source.**

   You can type in the name of another image, or click the folder icon to browse for an image. In my sample, I changed the round ball to an image of a squished ball.

4. **Select the next keyframe and change the image source again.**

   In this case, I changed it back to the round ball image.

5. **Repeat Steps 2 and 3 to change the image at any keyframe.**

6. **To preview the animation, click and hold down the Play button.**

7. **When you're finished, choose** <u>W</u>indow⇔<u>T</u>imelines **to close the Timeline inspector.**

Don't overestimate your viewer's browser

Too many Web designers overestimate their audiences. Most of us who build Web sites are quick to upgrade, downloading new browser versions and installing plug-ins as soon as they're released. But many people on the Web don't know how to upgrade their browsers, or they just can't or don't bother. Employees at big corporations are usually on networks, on which upgrading a browser means upgrading the entire system, and technical support staff are often slow to do that (usually because they're so busy with so many other upgrades these days). Home users are often intimidated by the prospect of downloading anything off the Internet, so they're likely to stick with whatever browser they got when they first set up their connection to the Net.

Slowly, things are improving. Users are getting more sophisticated and software is getting easier to use. But for now, if you want to reach the broad audience on the Web, you need to design a Web site that works in a variety of browsers. Fortunately, Macromedia understood that problem when it developed Dreamweaver and included a number of features to help make it easier to design your site so that it takes advantage of high-end browsers, while still being accessible to older browsers. Make sure that you take advantage of these features, such as the Target Browser options, Browser Check features, and the 3.0 Conversion features that enable you to easily create a second page that works in older browsers. You can find out more about all of these options in "Ensuring That Your Pages Work in Older Browsers" in this chapter.

Ensuring That Your Pages Work in Older Browsers

I love all the Dreamweaver features described in this chapter because they make creating dynamic, interactive elements for my Web pages easy. Unfortunately, most of these features can only be viewed by the latest browsers and many people on the Internet still use older browsers.

So that you can easily compensate for browser differences as you design your Web pages in Dreamweaver, the folks at Macromedia included features for targeting browsers. When you choose a target browser in the Behaviors inspector, you get a list of behavior options that work only in the browser that you select.

You can also use the Check Browser option in the Action list of the Behaviors inspector. Applying this feature to your entire page causes a browser-detect action to determine the type of browser your visitor uses, and then directs them to a URL based on that detection. You can send all visitors using Netscape 3.0 or lower to one page in your site and users of Internet Explorer 4.0 to another page. The only problem with this solution is that you have to create a dual site, one for older browsers and one for newer browsers, and that can turn into twice as much work.

So Macromedia added another feature when they developed Dreamweaver 1.2. The Convert to 3.0 Browser Compatible option automates creating a second page that can display in older browsers. Here's how it works: You create a page using all the latest features you want, such as layers and Cascading Style Sheets, and then run the conversion option. Dreamweaver automatically creates a page that works in 3.0 browsers.

This isn't a perfect solution, but it's a great step toward making maintenance of dual sites easier. The problem is that you can't have the same features in the 3.0 version that work in the 4.0 and later version, and advanced features don't all convert down to less advanced features gracefully. For example, if you have an animated timeline that moves your buttons across the page, you lose the animation in the 3.0 conversion, but at least you can see your buttons. Still, you may have to "tweak" the converted page a little to get the buttons to the best location on a static page.

The 3.0-conversion process does the best job it can and works well for most CSS options because it converts applied styles back to individual formatting options. For example, if you have applied a headline style that is Helvetica, bold, and centered, Dreamweaver changes the formatting from the headline style to the individual tags for those three formatting options. Dreamweaver also includes a Tables to Layer option that automates the process of converting a 3.0-compatible file that uses tables to a 4.0-compatible file with the positioning and animation possibilities offered by layers and DHTML.

Converting a file to 3.0 browser-compatible

When you convert a file to 3.0-compatible, Dreamweaver creates a copy of the original file and changes the code, often altering the design. Here are some of the changes you can expect:

- ✔ Layers change to tables in an effort to preserve positioning. The table displays the layers in their original locations.
- ✔ HTML character styles replace CSS markup.
- ✔ Any CSS markup that can't be converted to HTML is removed.
- ✔ Timeline code that animates layers is removed.

✔ Timeline code that doesn't use layers, such as behaviors or changes to the image source, is preserved.

✔ The timeline is automatically rewound to Frame 1 and all elements are placed in a static position on the page in the location specified in the first frame of the timeline.

You may have to reposition some of your elements after this conversion to ensure that they look good on a static page.

The Convert to 3.0 Browser Compatible option was not available in Dreamweaver 1.0. If you don't have this option in your version of the program, you can download an upgrade from www.dreamweaver.com.

To convert a file that you designed with 4.0 browser options to 3.0 browser-compatible, follow these steps:

1. Choose File➪Convert➪3.0 Browser Compatible.

2. Choose the conversions options that you want.

You can convert layers to tables or CSS styles to HTML markup. I recommend that you do both.

3. Click Continue.

Dreamweaver opens the converted file in a new, untitled window.

4. Choose File➪Save and save the page with a new name.

I like to keep all of these pages in their own folder so that I can easily keep track of them and they don't clutter the rest of my Web site structure.

If you maintain a site with two sets of pages (one for 4.0 browsers and another for 3.0 and older), don't forget that you have to update both sets every time you make a change.

Designing for multiple browsers is a key element to good Web design. Dreamweaver makes it easy to create lots of features that don't work in older browsers. Make sure that you also take advantage of the features that can help you ensure that your pages reach as broad an audience as possible.

Chapter 14

Showing Off with Multimedia

• •

• •

*T*hose who live in this multimedia world, spoiled by CD-ROMs and music videos, are still far from satisfied with flat, text-based Web sites. Most Web designers want the rich, interactive features that they know are possible, even with the limits of bandwidth. They want animation, sound, video — the features that bring life to other media. But HTML, even with the addition of Dynamic HTML features, just doesn't fulfill those desires.

That's where plug-ins come in.

Plug-ins are small programs that work in cooperation with a Web browser to play sound, video, and animation. Some plug-ins have become so popular that browser makers Netscape and Microsoft have built them into their latest browsers. Plug-ins that aren't so well known require viewers to download and install them on their computers to run with the browsers.

Well-known multimedia and plug-in technologies include Macromedia's Shockwave for Flash and Director (shown in action on *The Simpsons* Web site in Figure 14-1), RealAudio and RealVideo, and Apple's QuickTime. In this chapter, I tell you about the various types of multimedia technologies and how to use Dreamweaver to link these files to your Web pages. I also give you tips about making your pages work best in multiple browsers and how Dreamweaver makes that easy for you.

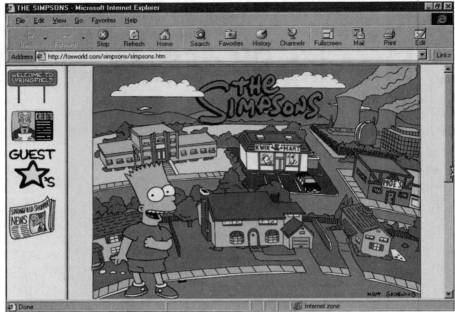

Figure 14-1:
The official
Simpsons
Web site
features
Macromedia
Flash
technology.

Creating Multimedia for Different Browsers and Platforms

When Macromedia developed Dreamweaver, they made sure that the program creates HTML code that's universally accepted by as many Web browsers as possible. The differences between Netscape Navigator and Microsoft Internet Explorer mean that you sometimes have to use two tags to do what one should handle. For example, when you link plug-in files to a Web page, you must use both the Embed and Object tags because each browser company best supports a different one. Fortunately, you don't have to worry about learning how to write the code for the Object and Embed tags, or even how they work together. Dreamweaver generates these tags for you. If you want to know how this works, read the sidebar "Using the Object and Embed tags together." If you don't really care about the difference, skip the sidebar and keep reading to find out how to use the WYSIWYG editor in Dreamweaver to link plug-in technologies and set their parameters.

Macromedia's Flash Central, as shown in Figure 14-2, is an example of a site that works well in both Netscape Navigator and Internet Explorer. Check out the site at www.flashcentral.com for more information about using and creating Flash files.

Figure 14-2:
Check out
Macromedia's
Flash
Central site
for tips on
creating
Flash files.

Working with Macromedia Shockwave

Macromedia lumps all its player plug-in technologies under the name
Shockwave, but Shockwave plug-ins exist for five different Macromedia
programs: Director, Flash, Freehand, Extreme 3D, and Authorware. Each
plug-in handles the kind of files created by its corresponding program. For
example, you can use Shockwave Freehand to display images created in the
illustration program Freehand. The advantage is that if viewers use the plug-
in, you don't have to convert your images to GIF or JPEG format; you can
keep them in the richer, more versatile Freehand file type. Viewers can
download each of these plug-ins separately or get them all in one large plug-
in package. The software that plays Shockwave for Director and Flash is
available as both a Netscape plug-in and an ActiveX control for Internet
Explorer.

Dreamweaver can handle both Shockwave for Director and Shockwave for
Flash (I describe both in more detail later). Treat the other file types as you
would any other technology not specifically described in this chapter. You
can find more on that in "Working with Other Plug-in Technologies."

Using the Object and Embed tags together

When you insert plug-in file formats, such as Macromedia's Shockwave or Flash, you can use the Object or Embed tag. If you're designing Web pages for the broader audience of the World Wide Web, your best option is to use both, because, unfortunately, Netscape and Microsoft have never agreed on a standard. You see, some time ago, the two largest browser makers went off in different directions, with Netscape creating the Embed tag and Microsoft introducing the Object tag. Today, the best way to handle the situation is to use both tags to link plug-in files.

You can use these HTML tags together because browsers ignore HTML tags that they don't recognize. That means that because Navigator doesn't support the Object tag, Navigator doesn't display any file that is embedded using that tag. If there's nothing else in the code that the browser does support, it may just display ugly gray squares in place of the plug-in file — and nobody wants ugly gray squares on a Web page. By using both the Object and Embed tags together, you can achieve the best designs for the most browsers. For example, you can use the Embed tag options to link an alternate GIF or JPEG image that displays in place of the plug-in file if the browser doesn't support plug-ins.

If you're writing the code yourself and want to design for optimal results in both browsers, make sure that you nest the Embed tag within the Object tag. You should write the tags in this order because browsers that support the Object tag, such as Internet Explorer, also support the Embed tag and need to see the Object tag first. Browsers that don't support the Object tag, such as Navigator, ignore it and read the Embed tag. Here's an example of what the HTML code looks like when you use both tags in combination to embed a Macromedia Flash file:

```
<OBJECT
    classid="clsid:D27CDB6E-
    AE6D-11cf-96B8-
    444553540000"
    codebase="http://
    active.macromedia.com/
    flash2/cabs/
    swflash.cab#version=2,0,0,0"
    width=100 height=80> <PARAM
    name="Movie"
    value="filename.swf">

<EMBED src="filename.swf"
    width=100 height=80
    pluginspage="http://
    www.macromedia.com/
    shockwave/download/
    index.cgi?P1_Prod_Version=
    ShockwaveFlash"> </EMBED>

<NOEMBED> <IMG
    src="imagename.gif"
    width=100 height=80>
    </NOEMBED>

</OBJECT>
```

Before you get too worried about how complex that code is, let me reassure you: Dreamweaver creates all this for you. Just follow the steps in the rest of this chapter and Dreamweaver takes care of the rest.

What is Shockwave for Director?

Macromedia Shockwave for Director enables you to use files created in Director on a Web page. Director is the most popular program around for creating CD-ROM multimedia titles, which means that the program already has a large following and many people know how to use it. This is one of the best formats available for creating complex multimedia files, such as games, that include animation, sound, video, and other interactive features, like the ability to hit a target or drive a car.

Shockwave for Director has become one of the most popular plug-ins on the Web. The problem is bandwidth. Most files created for CD-ROMs are huge by Web standards, and consumers are spoiled by the quality and speed of CD-ROMs. Because of the bandwidth limitations of the Web, developers who create Shockwave for Director files face many limitations. Some developers stick to small, simple files that download quickly; others create large, complex Shockwave files and hope that their users have the bandwidth, or patience, to enjoy them. For more information on creating Shockwave for Director files, visit www.macromedia.com.

What is Shockwave for Flash?

Recently, Macromedia announced Flash 3.0, which moves Flash into the realm of serious Web development tools. With features that make it possible to use Flash in dynamic sites, such as database-driven sites, Flash has become an even more attractive option for many Web developers.

Flash continues to win acclaim because you can use it to create animations that download really fast. You can also produce scalable, interactive animations with synchronized sound. All that, and you still get smaller file sizes than with any other animation technology on the Web. For more on why Flash files download more quickly than other file types, see the sidebar "Download Flash files in a flash."

Download Flash files in a flash

Flash files are dramatically faster to download because Flash images are vector-based. *Vector-based* means that the images are made up of coded instructions to draw specific geometric shapes, filled with specific colors. This takes far less space than the data needed for *raster* images, such as those used in animated GIFs. As a result, Flash files can be significantly smaller than other types of images and animation files. An animated GIF that's 200K and takes a couple of minutes to download on a 14.4 modem may only be 20K when re-created as a Flash animation. You can find lots more information about creating Flash files at www.macromedia.com/software/flash.

Inserting Shockwave for Director and Shockwave for Flash files

To link a Shockwave for Director or Shockwave for Flash file to a Web page using Dreamweaver, follow these steps:

1. **Click to insert the cursor where you want the Shockwave file to display on your Web page.**

2. **From the Object palette, click the button for either Shockwave Director or Shockwave Flash.**

   You can also choose Insert⇨Shockwave Director or Insert⇨ Shockwave Flash. The appropriate dialog box appears.

3. **Use the Browse button to locate the Shockwave file that you want linked to the page.**

4. **Click to highlight the filename, click the Select button, and then click OK to close the dialog box.**

   You can also type in the name and path to the file in the text box under Movie Source. The Shockwave Director or Flash file automatically links to the page.

   Dreamweaver doesn't display Shockwave files in the editor. Instead, you see a small icon that represents the Shockwave file. To view the Shockwave file, preview the page in a browser, such as Netscape Navigator 4.0 or Internet Explorer 4.0, with the correct Shockwave plug-in.

5. **Double-click the Shockwave icon to open the Property inspector.**

   If the Property inspector is already open, you can single click the Shockwave icon to display the options.

6. **Specify the width and height of the file in the text boxes next to W and H.**

   You can set many options in the Property inspector, but only the width and height are required. If you want to know more about the other options, check out "Setting parameters and other options for Shockwave" in the next section.

Setting parameters and other options for Shockwave

Like most HTML tags, the tags that link Shockwave and other plug-in files to Web pages have *attributes* (they're called *parameters* when used with the Object tag). These parameters are even more important for plug-in files because you must set some of them — such as the height and width — for the file to work properly in a browser. Dreamweaver takes care of setting the height and width, but you may want to change some of the other settings. This section provides a list of attributes and parameters that you can change in the Property inspector and what those attributes affect.

Don't worry about making sure that you specify property settings for both the Embed and Object tags. When you change options in the Property inspector for either Shockwave Director or Flash, Dreamweaver automatically applies those changes to both the Embed and Object tags.

If you don't see all the options in Property inspector, click the expander arrow in the bottom-right corner to display the more advanced options.

Here are the Shockwave options in the Property inspector, shown in Figure 14-3:

Figure 14-3:
The Property inspector enables you to specify options for how Shockwave files display.

- ✔ **Name:** In the top-left corner of the inspector, just to the right of the Shockwave icon and below the file size (which automatically appears), you can type a name. You can leave this blank or name it whatever you want. This name only identifies the file for scripting.

- ✔ **Width (W):** This specifies the width of the file. You can change the measurement to pc (picas), pt (points), in (inches), mm (millimeters), cm (centimeters), or % (percentage of the original file's value). Don't put any spaces between the number and the measurement abbreviation.

- ✔ **Height (H):** This specifies the height of the file. You can change the measurement to pc (picas), pt (points), in (inches), mm (millimeters), cm (centimeters), or % (percentage of the original file's value). Don't put any spaces between the number and the measurement abbreviation.

- ✔ **File:** The name and path to the file appear in the File text box. You can change this by typing in a new name or path, or by clicking the folder icon to browse for a file.

- **Tag:** This specifies whether the file links by using either the Object tag or the Embed tag, or both. Unless you're designing your pages for just one browser type, you should leave this at the default setting for both the Object and Embed tags. For more on these tags, see the sidebar "Using the Object and Embed tags together."

- **Align:** This controls the alignment of the file on the page. This setting works the same for plug-in files as for images.

- **BgColor:** This sets a background color that fills the area of the file. This color displays if the specified height and width are larger than the file and while the movie doesn't play, either because it's loading or it has finished playing.

- **ID:** This optional parameter specifies the ActiveX ID. This parameter is used to pass information between ActiveX controls.

- **Border:** This sets the width of the border around the file.

- **V Space (Vertical Space):** If you want blank space above or below the file, enter the number of pixels that you want.

- **H Space (Horizontal Space):** If you want blank space on either side of the file, enter the number of pixels that you want.

- **Alt Image:** Enter the name and path to any image file (GIF or JPEG) that you want displayed if the user's browser can't use the plug-in or ActiveX control to display the Shockwave file.

- **Parameters:** This button provides access to a dialog box where you can enter additional parameters for the Shockwave movie.

The following settings are unique to Flash; you can't use them with Director files.

- **Quality:** This enables you to prioritize the antialiasing options of your images versus the speed of playback.

  Antialiasing, which makes your files appear smoother, can slow down the rendering of each frame because the computer must first smooth the edges. The Quality parameter enables you to choose how much slower by setting priorities based on the importance of appearance versus playback speed.

  Quality options are

  - **Low:** With this option, antialiasing is never used. Playback speed has priority over appearance.

  - **High:** With this option, antialiasing is always used. Appearance has priority over playback speed.

- **Autohigh:** A somewhat more sophisticated option, Autohigh sets playback to begin with antialiasing turned on. However, if the actual frame rate supported by the user's computer drops below your specified frame rate, antialiasing automatically turns off to improve playback speed. This option emphasizes playback speed and appearance equally at first but sacrifices appearance for the sake of playback speed, if necessary.

- **Autolow:** With this option, playback begins with antialiasing turned off. If the Flash player detects that the processor can handle it, antialiasing is turned on. Use this option to emphasize speed at first but improve appearance whenever possible.

✔ **Scale:** You should specify this option only if you use percentages for the Height and Width parameter. The Scale parameter enables you to define how the Flash movie displays within the boundaries of the area specified in the browser window.

Flash movies are scaleable. With the Scale option, you can specify the original dimensions in pixels or in percentages of a browser window. This enables you to control how the Flash file displays if a browser window is a different size from your original design. For example, if you always want your Flash movie to take up a quarter of the screen (no matter how large the screen is) set it to 25%; if you want it to always fill the screen, set it to 100%.

Because using a percentage can lead to undesired effects (such as cropping or distorting a file to make it fit), the following options enable you to set preferences about how the Flash movie displays within the window:

- **Showall:** This option enables the entire movie to display in the specified area. The width and height proportions of the original movie are maintained and no distortion occurs, but borders may appear on two sides of the movie to fill the space.

- **Noborder:** This option enables you to scale a Flash movie to fill a specified area. Again, the original width and height proportions are maintained and no distortion occurs, but portions of the movie may be cropped.

- **Exactfit:** Using this option, the entire movie is visible in the specified area. However, the Flash movie may be distorted because the width and height proportions may be stretched or shrunk in order to fit the movie in the specified area.

✔ **Autoplay:** This controls the Play parameter, enabling you to determine whether a Flash movie starts as soon as it downloads to the viewer's computer or whether a user must click a button or take another action to start the Flash movie. A check in this box causes the movie to automatically start to play as soon as the page finishes loading. If you don't check this box, whatever option you've set in the Flash file (such as onmouseover or onmousedown) is required to start the movie.

✔ **Loop:** Checking this box causes the Flash file to repeat (or loop). If you don't check this box, the Flash movie stops after it reaches the last frame.

Working with Java

Java is a programming language, like C or C++ (from which Java was derived), that you can use to create executable files. What makes Java special is that it can run on any computer system. Usually, if you create a program in a language, you have to create one version for the Macintosh, another for the PC, and a third for UNIX. But Java, created by Sun Microsystems, is platform-independent so that developers can use it to create almost any kind of program — even complex programs like word processors or spreadsheets — that work on any type of computer. You can embed Java applets in Web pages, you can use Java to generate entire Web pages, or you can run Java applications separately after they download.

To find out more about Java, check out *Java For Dummies*, 2nd Edition, by Aaron E. Walsh (published by IDG Books Worldwide, Inc.).

Inserting Java applets

To link a Java applet to your Web page, follow these steps:

1. **Click to insert the cursor where you want the applet to display on your Web page.**

2. **From the Object palette, click the button for Java applets (it looks like a little coffee cup).**

   You can also choose Insert➪Applet. The Insert Applet dialog box appears.

3. **Use the Browse button to locate the file that you want linked to the page.**

4. **Click to highlight the filename, click the Select button, and then click OK to close the dialog box.**

   You can also type in the name and path to the file in the text box under Java Class Source. The applet automatically links to the page.

Dreamweaver doesn't display applets in the editor. Instead, you see a small icon that represents the applet (it looks like the coffee cup icon you see in the Object palette). To view the applet on your Web page, preview the page in a browser, such as Navigator 4.0, that supports applets.

5. Double-click the Applet icon to open the Property inspector.

You can set many options in the Property inspector. If you want to know more about the these options, see the next section.

Setting Java parameters and other options

Like other file formats that require plug-ins or advanced browser support, applets come with the following options, as shown in Figure 14-4:

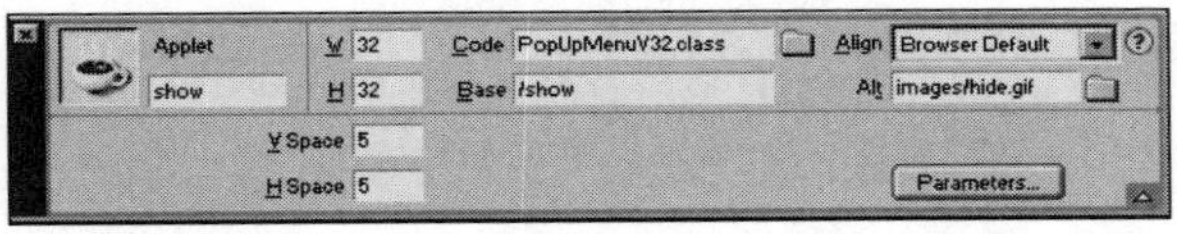

Figure 14-4:
The Property inspector enables you to specify options for Java applets.

	Applet	W 32	Code PopUpMenuV32.class	Align Browser Default	?
	show	H 32	Base /show	Alt images/hide.gif	
		V Space 5			
		H Space 5		Parameters...	

✔ **Name:** In the top-left corner, you can enter any name that you want in the text box under Applet. This name identifies the applet for scripting.

✔ **Width (W):** This specifies the width of the applet. You can change the measurement to pc (picas), pt (points), in (inches), mm (millimeters), cm (centimeters), or % (percentage of the original file's value). Don't put any spaces between the number and the measurement abbreviation.

✔ **Height (H):** This specifies the height of the applet. You can change the measurement to pc (picas), pt (points), in (inches), mm (millimeters), cm (centimeters), or % (percentage of the original file's value). Don't put any spaces between the number and the measurement abbreviation.

✔ **Code:** Dreamweaver automatically enters the Code when you link the file. Code specifies the content file of the applet. You may type in your own filename or click the folder icon to choose a file.

✔ **Base:** Automatically entered when you link the file, Base identifies the folder that contains the applet. You may type in your own filename.

✔ **Align:** This determines how the object aligns on the page.

✔ **Alt:** This enables you to specify an alternate file, such as an image, that displays if the viewer's browser doesn't support Java. If you type text into this field, Dreamweaver writes it into the code using the Alt attribute of the Applet tag. If you use the folder icon to select an image, Dreamweaver automatically inserts an Image tag within the open and close tags of the applet.

✔ **V Space (Vertical Space):** If you want blank space above or below the applet, enter the number of pixels that you want.

✔ **H Space (Horizontal Space):** If you want blank space on either side of the applet, enter the number of pixels that you want.

✔ **Parameters:** Click this button to access a dialog box where you can enter additional parameters for the applet.

Using alternative attributes with Java applets and images

If you want to provide content for as many browsers as possible, use an image as the alternate option and then include alternative text within the image tag. Dreamweaver doesn't do this automatically, so you have to use the HTML inspector or another text editor to insert the Alt attribute within the Image tag. The code generated by Dreamweaver for the image should look something like this:

```
<IMG SRC="images/hide.gif"
    WIDTH="32" HEIGHT="32"
    VSPACE="5" HSPACE="5">
```

To add alternative text, add the following with your own message:

```
ALT="Enter your alternate text
    here"
```

The final image source code remains between the Applet tags and would look something like this:

```
<IMG SRC="images/hide.gif"
    WIDTH="32" HEIGHT="32"
    VSPACE="5" HSPACE="5"
    ALT="enter your alternate
    text here">
```

JavaScript is not Java

JavaScript is a subset of Java that Netscape created. You can embed JavaScript into HTML pages to create interactive features, but you can't use it to create standalone applications. You won't get the complex functionality of Java, but JavaScript is a lot easier to use and doesn't require a plug-in.

JavaScript is often used in combination with other multimedia features, such as images or sound files, to add greater levels of interactivity. Dynamic HTML, which I cover in Chapter 13, explains how to use Dreamweaver to apply behaviors and other features created by using JavaScript with HTML.

You can find lots more on JavaScript in *JavaScript For Dummies,* 2nd edition, by Emily A. Vander Veer (published by IDG Books Worldwide, Inc.).

Using ActiveX Objects and Controls

Microsoft created ActiveX, but it hasn't been widely accepted on the Web. As a result, no clear standard for identifying ActiveX objects and controls exists. Dreamweaver provides some flexibility so that you can set the parameters for the ActiveX control that you use. Here are the settings of the ActiveX Property inspector (see Figure 14-5):

Figure 14-5:
The Property inspector enables you to specify options for ActiveX objects and controls.

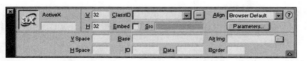

✔ **Name:** In the top-left corner of the inspector, just to the right of the ActiveX icon and below the file size (which automatically appears) is a space in which you can type a name. You can leave this blank or name it whatever you want. This name identifies the ActiveX object only for scripting purposes.

- ✔ **Width (W):** You can specify the measurement of an ActiveX object in pc (picas), pt (points), in (inches), mm (millimeters), cm (centimeters), or % (percentage of the original file's value). Don't put any spaces between the number and the measurement abbreviation.

- ✔ **Height (H):** You can specify the measurement of an ActiveX object in pc (picas), pt (points), in (inches), mm (millimeters), cm (centimeters), or % (percentage of the original file's value). Don't put any spaces between the number and the measurement abbreviation.

- ✔ **ClassID:** The browser uses the ClassID to identify the ActiveX control. You can enter any value or choose any of these options from the pop-up menu: RealPlayer, Shockwave for Director, and Shockwave for Flash.

- ✔ **Embed:** Checking this box tells Dreamweaver to add an Embed tag within the Object tag. The Embed tag activates a Netscape plug-in equivalent, if available, and makes your pages more accessible to Navigator users. Dreamweaver automatically sets the values that you've entered for ActiveX properties to the Embed tag for any equivalent Netscape plug-in.

- ✔ **Source (Src):** This identifies the file to be associated with the Embed tag and used by a Netscape plug-in.

- ✔ **Align:** This specifies how the object aligns on the page.

- ✔ **Parameters:** Click this button to access a dialog box in which you can enter additional parameters for the ActiveX controls.

- ✔ **V Space (Vertical Space):** If you want blank space above or below the object, enter the number of pixels that you want.

- ✔ **H Space (Horizontal Space):** If you want blank space on either side of the object, enter the number of pixels that you want.

- ✔ **Base:** This enables you to specify a URL for the ActiveX control so that Internet Explorer can automatically download the control if it's not installed in the user's system.

- ✔ **ID:** This identifies an optional ActiveX ID parameter.

- ✔ **Data:** This specifies a data file for the ActiveX control to load.

- ✔ **Alt Img:** This enables you to link an image that displays if the browser doesn't support the Object tag.

- ✔ **Border:** This enables you to specify the width of the border around an object.

Working with Other Plug-In Technologies

So many plug-ins, so little bandwidth. You can find literally hundreds of plug-ins available for Web pages. Some of them give you fabulous results, such as sound, video, a variety of image formats, and even three-dimensional worlds and animations. But with plug-ins — perhaps more than with any other technology on the Web — you have to be very careful. Web page visitors aren't usually excited about having to download a new plug-in. Indeed, some are scared off by the idea and others are just plain annoyed. Don't risk doing that to your viewers unless you have a compelling reason.

If I visited your site, I wouldn't be happy if you sent me off to get a plug-in just so I could see your logo spinning around in all its three-dimensional splendor. On the other hand, if your site features interactive games or a three-dimensional environment with chat capability, I might be quite happy to get a plug-in that enables me to experience something as interesting as a multiuser game or interactive environment. Make sure that you let your users know what they're in for before you send them off on a plug-in adventure. You're also wise to stick to the better known plug-in technologies — such as RealAudio, RealVideo, and the Shockwave suite — because users are more likely to already have them or appreciate the benefit of getting them because they know that they can use them on other sites.

Inserting Netscape plug-ins

To use Dreamweaver to link a Netscape plug-in file to your Web page, follow these steps:

1. **Click to insert the cursor where you want the file to display on your Web page.**

2. **From the Object palette, click the button for Netscape Plug-Ins (it looks like a puzzle piece).**

   You can also choose Insert⇨Plug-in. The Insert Plug-in dialog box appears.

3. **Use the Browse button to locate the file that you want linked to the page.**

4. **Click to highlight the filename, click the Select button, and then click OK to close the dialog box.**

   You can also type in the name and path to the file in the text box under Plug-in Source. The file automatically links to the page.

Dreamweaver doesn't display plug-ins in the editor. Instead, you see a small icon that represents the file (it looks like the puzzle piece icon in the Object palette). To view the plug-in file on your Web page, preview the page in a browser, such as Navigator 4.0, with the corresponding plug-in installed.

5. **Double-click the Plug-in icon to open the Property inspector.**

You can set many options in the Property inspector. If you want to know more about the these options, see the next section.

Setting Netscape plug-in parameters and other options

You can specify the following settings in the Plug-In Property inspector (see Figure 14-6):

Figure 14-6:
The Property inspector enables you to specify options for Netscape plug-ins.

✔ **Name:** In the top-left corner of the inspector, just to the right of the plug-in icon and below the file size (which automatically appears) is a space in which you can type a name. You can leave this blank or provide any name you want. This name identifies the file only for scripting purposes.

✔ **Width (W):** You can specify the measurement of any Netscape plug-in in pc (picas), pt (points), in (inches), mm (millimeters), cm (centimeters), or % (percentage of the original file's value). Don't put any spaces between the number and the measurement abbreviation.

✔ **Height (H):** You can specify the measurement of any Netscape plug-in in pc (picas), pt (points), in (inches), mm (millimeters), cm (centimeters), or % (percentage of the original file's value). Don't put any spaces between the number and the measurement abbreviation.

For most plug-ins, the height and width tags are required. However, in some cases, such as sound files that don't display on a page, you can't specify height and width.

- ✔ **Source (Src):** This specifies the name and path to the plug-in file. You can type in a filename, or click the folder icon to browse for the file.

- ✔ **Plg URL:** This enables you to provide a URL where viewers can download a plug-in if they don't already have it.

- ✔ **Align:** This specifies how the element aligns on the page.

- ✔ **Alt:** Here, you can provide alternate content that displays if the viewer's browser doesn't support the Embed tag. You can link an image as an alternate or simply enter text that displays in place of the plug-in file.

- ✔ **V Space (Vertical Space):** If you want blank space above and below the plug-in, enter the number of pixels that you want.

- ✔ **H Space (Horizontal Space):** If you want blank space on either side of the plug-in, enter the number of pixels that you want.

- ✔ **Border:** This specifies the width of the border around the file.

- ✔ **Parameters:** Click this button to access a dialog box in which you can enter additional parameters for the plug-in file.

Chapter 15

Forms Follow Function

● ●

In This Chapter

▶ Discovering what forms can do

▶ Creating forms

▶ Making forms work

▶ Finding and using scripts

● ●

*T*he most interactive features on a Web site require HTML forms. Whether you want to create a simple guest book or a complicated online shopping cart system, you need to know how to set up the text areas, radio buttons, and pull-down menus that make up an HTML form. Fortunately, Dreamweaver makes creating forms easy by including a special toolbar on the Object palette to provide easy access to common form elements.

In this chapter, I introduce you to the kinds of forms commonly used on the Web and show you how to use Dreamweaver to create them. I also explain the CGI (Common Gateway Interface) scripts required to process forms, how they work, and where you can get scripts for your Web site.

Appreciating What HTML Forms Can Do for You

Forms follows function, to paraphrase the old saying. On the Web, forms are an integral part of the function of many interactive features. By using forms, Web designers can collect information about users — information that they can then use in a variety of ways. Here are a few of the forms that you can create for your Web site.

Signing in: Guest books

The most common form on the Web is the simple *guest book*. Guest books usually include a few fields to collect basic contact information, such as name, e-mail address, and comments or feedback about the Web site. The information collected goes via e-mail to the Web site administrator or anyone else who wants to collect it. The CGI script that makes a guest book work is usually a basic e-mail script, meaning the script collects the data and e-mails the data to a specified address. More complex guest book systems post user comments on an automatically created Web page, generating a long list of messages from viewers.

Inquiring with surveys and feedback forms

Using the same kind of CGI scripts as guest books, *feedback forms* and *surveys* collect information from users. Feedback forms and surveys differ from guest books in that they generally include a list of questions designed to gather specific information, rather than just a text area for general comments. A survey may ask such questions as where you purchased a product, what you like or dislike about a product or service, and any other questions that the designers (or their clients) want to ask.

Shopping-cart systems

Most sophisticated commerce sites that sell products include an online shopping system, often called a *shopping-cart system* because it's like a shopping cart at a grocery store. Shopping systems can be as simple as an order form that lists products and quantities and then tabulates the total purchase price, or as complex as a system that enables users to collect products in a shopping cart as they navigate through a Web site, and then pay for all the products when they're done shopping. The collected items show up on an order form that shoppers can use when they complete their purchases. Although the engine that drives a shopping system is complex, the order forms and other pages are basic HTML forms, which you can create in Dreamweaver.

Setting up secure commerce systems

Many shopping-cart systems link to *secure commerce systems*. By using encryption technology, secure commerce systems encode data (such as credit card numbers and customer addresses) that's entered into a form, making it difficult for anyone to steal the information as it travels over the

Internet. These systems often connect to financial systems, such as Cybercash and Checkfree, which can process orders online and immediately approve or deny a credit card and credit the appropriate bank account for the amount of the transaction.

Conversing in discussion areas and chat rooms

Online discussion areas and chat rooms enable users to post comments that others can read, creating ongoing, typed "conversations" that take place on a Web site. Also called conferencing systems, *discussion areas* enable users to post comments that other users can read. These comments are archived so that users can review the messages, and conversations can take place over time. *Chat rooms,* also known as Internet Relay Chat (IRC), enable users to contribute comments that are immediately posted to a Web site, enabling conversations to take place in real time. These conversations are generally not archived, so users must be logged on to the site to read comments.

Finding information with search engines

Whenever you type a keyword into a search text field, you enter information into a simple HTML form. The text box and the search button, which is really a submit button, are both form elements that you can easily add to a Web page with Dreamweaver. In a *search engine,* a CGI script compares the information entered (usually keywords) with a collection of information, such as all the text on the rest of the Web site, and then produces a list of results that match.

Generating database-driven Web pages

Connecting a database to a Web site enables Web developers to create the most dynamic systems. Database systems serve many purposes, such as enabling sales people in the field to search through products in a database and get up-to-the-minute pricing and availability. The most complex database systems collect information about users, such as buying habits and preferences, and then use the information to automatically create Web pages specific to each user when they visit the site.

Understanding how CGI scripts work

Think of CGI scripts as the engine behind an HTML form and many other automated features on a Web site. CGI (or Common Gateway Interface) scripts are programs that are usually written in a programming language, such as Perl, Java, C, or C++. These scripts are much more complex to create than HTML pages, and these languages take much longer to learn. CGI scripts reside and run on the server and are usually triggered by an action that a user makes, such as clicking the Submit button in an HTML form.

A common scenario with a script may go like this:

1. The user loads a page, such as a guest book, fills out the HTML form, and clicks the Submit button.

2. That action triggers the CGI script on the server to gather the data entered into the form, format it, place it in an e-mail message, and send it to a specified e-mail address.

In Dreamweaver, you can easily create the HTML forms and the Submit buttons that go with them, but you have to provide your own CGI scripts. If you know a programming language, writing most simple CGI scripts isn't that hard. But if you don't know a programming language, you're probably better off hiring someone else to do it for you or downloading ready-made scripts from the Web. If you search the Web for CGI scripts, you can find that many programmers write them and then give them away for free. Be aware, however, that you still have to install those scripts on your server and almost always have to alter the programming code at least a little to tailor them to work with your unique system. You may also need to contact your Internet service provider (ISP) to help you place the script on the server.

Many ISPs make basic CGI scripts (such as guest-book forms and simple shopping-cart systems) available to their customers as part of membership. This is an easy way to get scripts for your Web site and may even be worth changing ISPs if your current ISP doesn't offer scripts. Most ISPs that offer CGI scripts provide instructions for using them on their Web sites. These instructions include the location of the script on the server. You must include this information in your HTML form so that the Submit button triggers the proper script. You can find more information about setting your HTML form to work with a script in the section "Creating HTML Forms."

Creating HTML Forms

The basic elements of HTML forms, such as radio buttons, check boxes, and text areas, are easy to create with Dreamweaver, as I demonstrate in the sections that follow. But remember, your form won't work unless it links to a CGI script. Although Dreamweaver doesn't provide any scripts, it does make it easy to link your HTML forms to a CGI script (for more on scripts, see the sidebar "Understanding how CGI scripts work"). You need to know where the script resides on the server to set this link. The name and location of the script depend on your server, but for the purposes of showing you how to link to a script with Dreamweaver, assume that the script you need to link to is called guestbook.pl (the .pl indicates the script was written in Perl), and that the script is located in a folder on the server called cgi-bin (a common name for the folder that holds scripts).

The following numbered steps walk you through linking any form to this sample script. To use these steps with a different script, simply change the name of the script and the name of the directory location to reflect your system. Start with an open page, either a new page or one you want to add a form to.

1. **Select Insert⇨Form.**

   You can also select the Insert Form icon of the Object palette, as shown in Figure 15-1. This handy option reveals all of the form elements that you may want to add as you create your form.

   A blank form in Dreamweaver shows up as a rectangle outlined by a red dotted line, like the one you see in Figure 15-2.

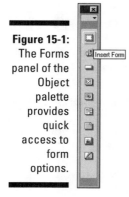

Figure 15-1: The Forms panel of the Object palette provides quick access to form options.

2. **Click the red outline to select the form and display the form options in the Property inspector.**

3. **Enter a name in the text box under Form.**

   You can choose any name for this field. This name is used by scripting languages, such as JavaScript or VBScript, to control the form.

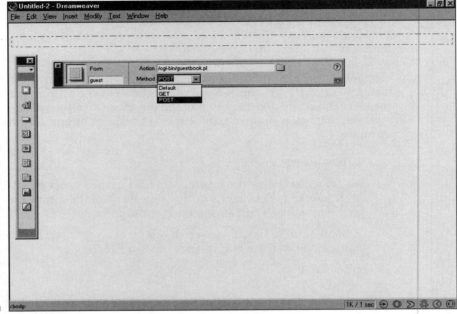

Figure 15-2:
Set form
properties,
such as the
name and
link to a
script,
in the
Property
inspector.

4. Enter the directory name and the name of the script in the text area next to Action.

Using the sample script described earlier, type **/cgi-bin/guestbook.pl** to specify the path to the Perl script in the cgi-bin directory. You can only use the folder icon in the Property inspector to set this link if you have a copy of the script on your computer in the same relative location in which it resides on the server. Usually, you have to enter this by typing the directory and filename into the text box. Make sure that you specify the entire path (you should get this information from your system administrator or Internet service provider).

5. In the Property inspector, use the Method pull-down menu to choose Default, Get, or Post.

The Get and Post options control how the form works in relation to the CGI script on the server. This depends on the script that you use. You should get this information from your system administrator, programmer, or Internet service provider.

These are just the preliminary steps that you need to take to create a form. When you established the boundaries of a form, as represented by the dotted red line that appeared after Step 1, Dreamweaver created the code that goes in the background of your form and enables it to interact with a script on your server. The rest of this chapter shows you how to add various form elements, such as text boxes, radio buttons, and pull-down menus.

Comparing radio buttons and check boxes

Radio buttons and check boxes make forms easier for users by limiting the action required. Instead of making users type in a word, such as *yes* or *no,* you can provide radio buttons and check boxes that make it easier for users to choose.

What's the difference between radio buttons and check boxes? Radio buttons enable users to make one choice because you can only make one radio button active. Thus, radio buttons are good for yes/no options or options in which you want users to make only one choice. Check boxes enable users to make multiple choices, so they're good for "choose all that apply" situations when users may make multiple choices.

Creating radio buttons

Here's how to create radio buttons on a form:

1. **Click your form to select it.**

   If you haven't yet created a form, go back to the numbered steps in the section "Creating HTML Forms."

2. **Click the Insert Radio Button icon from the Forms panel of the Object palette.**

   You can also select Insert⇨Form Object⇨Radio Button. Either way, a radio button appears inside the form's perimeter.

3. **Repeat Step 2 until you have the number of radio buttons that you want.**

4. **Select one of the radio buttons to reveal the radio button properties in the Property inspector, as shown in Figure 15-3.**

5. **Enter a name in the text area under RadioButton.**

   All radio buttons in a group should have the same name to enable the script to identify the response and limit selections to one button.

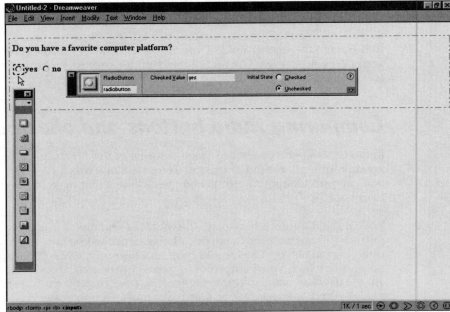

Figure 15-3:
Set radio
button
properties,
such as the
Checked or
Unchecked,
in the
Property
inspector.

6. **Enter a name in the text area next to Checked Value.**

   Each radio button in a group should have a different Checked Value name so that the CGI script can distinguish them. Naming them the same thing they represent is usually best — "yes" when the choice is yes and "no" when it's no. This name is usually included in the data you get back when the contents of the form are processed and returned to you (often in an e-mail message). If you're looking at the data later, it's easier to interpret if the name means something that makes sense to you.

7. **Choose Checked or Unchecked next to Initial State.**

   This determines whether the radio button appears already selected when the Web page loads. Use this feature if you want to preselect a choice. A user can always override this preselection by choosing another radio button.

8. **Select the other radio buttons one by one and repeat Steps 5 through 7 to set their properties in the Property inspector for each one.**

Creating check boxes

Here's how to create check boxes in a form:

1. **Click your form to select it.**

   If you haven't yet created a form, go back to the numbered steps in the section "Creating HTML Forms."

2. **Click the Insert Check Box icon from the Forms panel of the Object palette.**

   You can also select Insert⇨Form Object⇨Check Box.

3. **Repeat Step 2 to place as many check boxes as you want.**

4. **Select one of the check boxes to reveal the check box properties in the Property inspector, as shown in Figure 15-4.**

5. **Enter a name in the text area under Check Box.**

   You can use the same or distinct names for check boxes.

6. **Enter a name in the text area next to Checked Value.**

   Each check box in a group should have a different Checked Value name so that the CGI script can distinguish them. Naming them the same thing they represent is usually best. In Figure 15-4, you see that I named the Macintosh option Mac, the Windows option Windows, and so on. This name is usually included in the data you get back when the contents of the form are processed and returned to you (often in an e-mail message). If you're looking at the data later, it's easier to interpret if the name means something that makes sense to you.

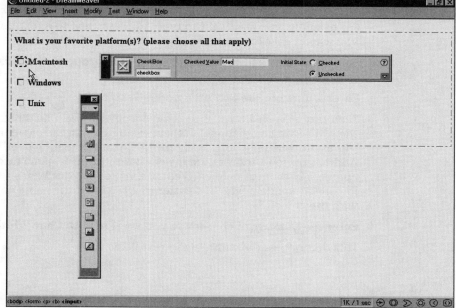

Figure 15-4:
Set
check box
properties,
such as the
Checked
Value,
in the
Property
inspector.

7. **Choose Checked or Unchecked next to Initial State.**

   This determines whether the check box appears already selected when the Web page loads. Use this feature if you want to preselect a choice. A user can always override this preselection by clicking the text box again to deselect it.

8. **Select the other check boxes one by one and repeat Steps 5 through 7 to set the properties in the Property inspector for each one.**

Adding text fields

When you want users to enter text, such as a name, e-mail address, or comment, use a text field. Here's how to insert text fields using Dreamweaver:

1. **Click your form to select it.**

   If you haven't yet created a form, go back to the numbered steps in the section "Creating HTML Forms."

2. **Click the Insert Text Field icon from the Forms panel of the Object palette.**

   You can also select Insert⇨Form Object⇨Text Field. A text field box appears.

3. **Click to place your cursor next to the Text Field and enter a question or other text prompt.**

   For example, you may want to type **Address:** next to a text box where you want a user to enter an address.

4. **Select the text field to reveal the text field properties in the Property inspector, as shown in Figure 15-5.**

5. **Enter a name in the text area under TextField.**

   Each text area on a form should have a different text field name so that the CGI script can distinguish them. Naming them the same thing they represent is usually best. In Figure 15-5, you see that I named the Address option "Address." Many scripts return this name next to the contents of the text field entered by a visitor to your Web site. If you're looking at the data later, it's easier to interpret if the name corresponds with the choice.

6. **Enter the number of characters you want next to Char Width.**

   This determines the width of the text field.

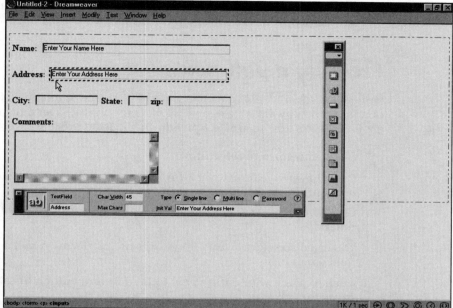

Figure 15-5:
Set text
field
properties,
such as the
Name,
in the
Property
inspector.

7. Enter the maximum number of characters that you want to allow next to Max Chars.

If you leave this field blank, the user can enter as many characters as they choose. I usually only limit the number of characters if I want to maintain consistency in the data. For example, I like to limit the State field to a two-character abbreviation.

8. Next to Type, choose <u>S</u>ingle Line, <u>M</u>ulti Line, or <u>P</u>assword.

Choose Single Line if you want to create a one-line text box, such as the kind I created for the Name and Address fields back in Figure 15-5.

Choose Multi Line if you want to give users space to enter text, such as the box I created for Comments back in Figure 15-5. (Note that if you choose Multi Line, you also need to specify the number of lines that you want the text area to cover by typing a number in the Num Lines field.)

Choose Password if this is a text line in which you ask a user to enter data that you don't want displayed on the screen. This causes entered data to appear as asterisks.

9. Next to <u>I</u>nit Val, enter any text you want displayed in this area when the form loads.

For example, back in Figure 15-5, the words *Enter Your Address Here* appear in the Init Val field and display in the text field next to Address in the form.

10. **Select the other text areas one by one and repeat Steps 5 through 9 to set the properties in the Property inspector for each one.**

Creating a pull-down list

Pull-down lists are ideal when you want to give users a multiple choice option but don't want to take up a lot of space on the page to display the choices. Here's how to create a pull-down list using Dreamweaver:

1. **Click your form to select it.**

   If you haven't yet created a form, go back to the numbered steps in the section "Creating HTML Forms."

2. **Choose the Insert List/Menu icon from the Forms panel of the Object palette.**

   You can also select Insert➪Form Object➪List/Menu. A pull-down list field appears.

3. **Click to place your cursor next to the List and enter a question or other text prompt.**

   In Figure 15-6, I use the example, "What type of music do you prefer?"

Figure 15-6: When you create a pull-down list, you must enter the options you want in the Initial List Values dialog box available from the Property inspector.

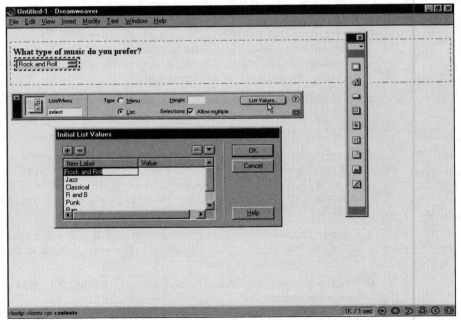

4. **Select the List to reveal the List/Menu properties in the Property inspector, as shown back in Figure 15-6.**

5. **Enter a name in the text area under List/Menu.**

   Each list or menu on a form should have a different name so that you can differentiate the lists when you sort out the data.

6. **Next to Type, choose Menu or List.**

   This determines if this form element is a pull-down menu or a scrollable list. If you choose List, you can specify the height and control how many items show at once. You can also specify if a user can select more than one item. If you choose Menu, these options aren't available.

7. **Click the List Values button from the top-right corner of the Property inspector.**

   A dialog box like the one back in Figure 15-6 opens and you can enter the choices that you want to make available. Select the plus sign to add an Item Label and then type the text you want in the text box that appears in the dialog box. Item Labels display in the menu or list on the Web page in the order that you enter them. Use the minus sign to delete a selected option. Click the Value button if you want to enter a value. Values are sent to the server. If you don't enter a value, the label is sent instead. Click OK to close the dialog box.

Finishing off your form with Submit and Clear buttons

In order for your users to send their completed forms to you, you need to create a Submit button, which, when clicked, tells the user's browser to send the form to the CGI script that processes the form. You may also want to add a Cancel or Clear button, which enable users to either not send the form at all or erase any information they've entered if they want to start over.

These buttons are easy to create in Dreamweaver. Follow these steps:

1. **Click your form to select it.**

   If you haven't yet created a form, go back to the numbered steps in the section "Creating HTML Forms."

2. **Click the Insert Button icon from the Forms panel of the Object palette.**

   A button appears, and the Form Property inspector changes to reveal button properties.

3. **Select the button you just added to display the button properties in the Property inspector, as shown in Figure 15-7.**

4. **Click either the Submit Form, Reset Form, or None button next to Action.**

   When you choose one of these options, Dreamweaver enters a corresponding name, Submit or Reset, in the text area under Button.

5. **In the text area next to Label, enter the text you want to display on the button.**

   You can enter any text you want for the Label, such as Search, Go, Clear, or Delete.

So, there you have it! Now that you know how to use Dreamweaver to create the basic elements of HTML forms, you can go on and develop more intricate forms for your Web site. Check out *HTML 4 For Dummies* and *MORE HTML For Dummies,* 2nd Edition, both by Ed Tittel and Stephen N. James (published by IDG Books Worldwide, Inc.) for more detailed info on creating and using HTML forms.

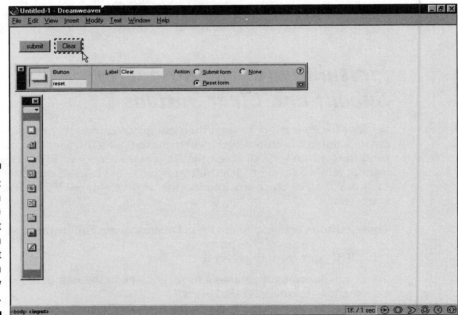

Figure 15-7:
You can change the text that displays on the Submit button in the Property inspector.

Part VI
The Part of Tens

"Finally - a Web publishing program with enough patterns and colors to handle our line of clothing on the Web."

In this part . . .

The Part of Tens features ten Web sites created with Dreamweaver, ten great design ideas you should keep in mind as you build your pages, and ten timesaving tips that can make your work with Dreamweaver easier and more productive.

Chapter 16

Ten Great Sites Designed with Dreamweaver

*A*s the popularity of Dreamweaver spreads, more and more sophisticated Web sites are built with this great tool. Checking out sites created with Dreamweaver is fun because so many of these sites take advantage of the latest Web technologies, such as Dynamic HTML, Shockwave for Flash and Director, and more. The sites listed in this chapter provide an excellent overview of what you can do with Dreamweaver. Spend time at each site and you're sure to pick up some good ideas for your own Web site.

Discovery Online

www.discovery.com

Dreamweaver helped Discovery Online integrate Dynamic HTML into its award-winning design. In Figures 16-1 and 16-2, you see the effect of an onmouseover event, which provides additional information about a linked section before a user clicks it. Simply running the mouse over the images in the navigation bar changes the image below it.

Figure 16-1:
The
Discovery
Channel
uses
Dynamic
HTML to
make the
site
interactive.
Notice the
difference
between
this figure
and Figure
16-2.

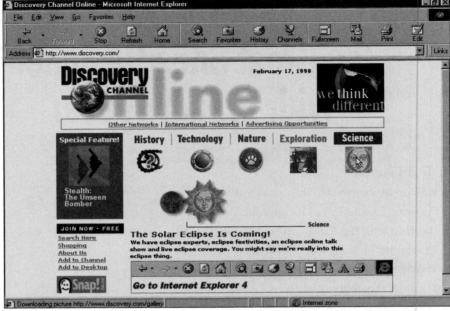

Figure 16-2:
Compare
this figure
with Figure
16-1 and
you see the
effect of an
onmouseover
event that
provides
additional
information
about a link
when a
user moves
a cursor
over an
image.

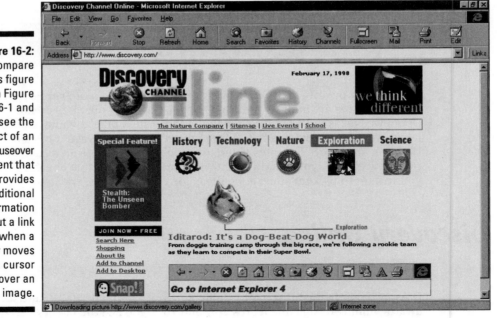

The Discovery Channel built this site exclusively for Internet Explorer 4.0, so the designers didn't worry about limiting the effects. If you visit the Discovery site with Netscape 4.0 or any earlier version of any browser, you get a completely different site that doesn't use Dynamic HTML. Discovery's programmers set up a special program on the server that detects the browser that you use and directs you automatically to the appropriate page. Dreamweaver includes a feature called Browser Detect in its Behaviors inspector that makes it easy for you to do the same thing at your Web site. Read Chapter 13 to find out how to apply behaviors such as this one.

The X-Files

www.thex-files.com

You can hear the eerie sounds of *The X-Files* in the form of Shockwave files on the site (see Figure 16-3). Dreamweaver makes it easy for designers to integrate plug-in technologies, such as Shockwave, to provide a rich, multimedia experience. *The X-Files* designers also appreciated the drag-and-drop table-building features that make these complex designs simpler to create. If you're an *X-Files* fan, you'll love this site for its episode updates, show schedules, bios, and sound bytes.

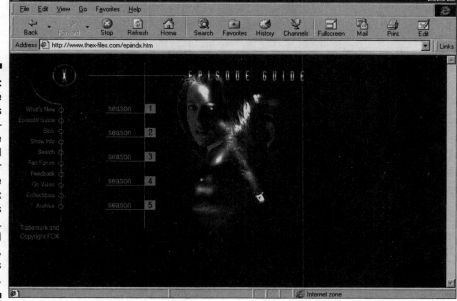

Figure 16-3:
The developers of *The X-Files* site used Dreamweaver to create complex designs using HTML tables and plug-ins, such as Shockwave.

The San Francisco Ballet

www.sfballet.org

The San Francisco Ballet (see Figure 16-4) didn't need a cutting-edge Web site to show off 65 years of traditional dance in the Bay Area. These designers used Dreamweaver to create a site that works well in both Netscape Navigator and Internet Explorer, ensuring that all potential viewers can access the site. The site used the Library feature to repeat the same images and links throughout the site and create an easy and intuitive navigation system.

Figure 16-4: The developers of the San Francisco Ballet site used Dreamweaver to create a site that works well on both Netscape Navigator and Internet Explorer.

The Wild World of Wonka

www.wonka.com

Based on the movie *Willy Wonka and the Chocolate Factory*, this site was created by 2-Lane Media (www.21m.com) for the Nestlé Corporation. The Wild World of Wonka takes for granted the short attention spans of today's kids. 2-Lane created complex designs using the drag-and-drop table design features that make Dreamweaver so useful. As shown in Figure 16-5, 2-Lane also used Dreamweaver to build in a variety of Shockwave files throughout the site, providing a sophisticated range of interactive games and other features.

Figure 16-5:
The Wild World of Wonka was designed by 2-Lane Media to captivate young minds.

signal2noise

www.hotwired.com/rgb/signal2noise/

This uncommon and highly entertaining storytelling site is featured at HotWired. Using sophisticated design techniques, signal2noise completely takes over your screen, blocking out every part of the browser and the operating system (see Figure 16-6). Don't panic when you lose all the buttons on your browser; you can always get them back by closing the browser window or using the site's Quit button.

This artistic site combines sound with black-and-white etchings to tell stories that automatically unfold on the screen in front of you. A small icon at the bottom-right of the screen enables visitors to retell the story or move on to another. In the bottom-left is a Quit button, making this site feel much more like a CD-ROM than a page on the World Wide Web.

Figure 16-6:
signal2noise takes over your monitor, blocking out any trace of the browser or operating system while it tells stories using images and sound.

Deep Rising

www.deeprising.com

In addition to Dreamweaver, this interactive Web site also uses Macromedia Shockwave to show off the features of the Hollywood thriller, *Deep Rising*. A deep pulsing sound accompanies the game Creature Hunt (see Figure 16-7). If you stumble into the wrong area, the creature gets you and the game ends with the words "You're dead." In addition to offering the game for players online using Shockwave, the designers of the Deep Rising Web page also enable visitors to download Macintosh or Windows versions of the game to play offline. Many movie sites take advantage of the power of Dreamweaver to add similar features, using Shockwave movie clips and sound files to create a multimedia experience.

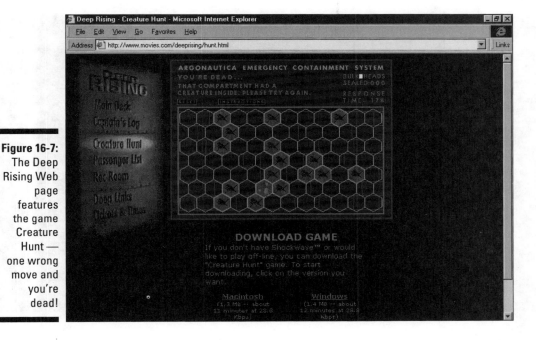

Figure 16-7:
The Deep
Rising Web
page
features
the game
Creature
Hunt —
one wrong
move and
you're
dead!

The Replacement Killers

www.spe.sony.com/movies/replacementkillers

This movie Web site, created by Akimbo Design (www.akimbodesign.com),
features lots of animation, sound files, and great interactivity. In Figure 16-8,
you see the target effect that the designers created using layers. The target
moves across the face of the characters as if someone is trying to fix a scope
on them to shoot. It's a simple, yet effective, technique that fits the theme of
the movie. The designers at Akimbo used Dreamweaver to build most of the
site, using drag-and-drop layer positioning and timeline features to create
these animation sequences. They also took advantage of the ability to
ensure that the site works on both of the most popular browsers.

Figure 16-8:
This site
features
previews
of the
movie, *The
Replacement
Killers*, with
animations
created
using
Dynamic
HTML
layers.

Fabric8

www.fabric8.com

The online boutique at Fabric8 uses three-dimensional mannequins to show off high-end designer fashions. In Figure 16-9, you see the front page of the site where the mannequin's head turns when you move your cursor over it and an explanation appears to the right of the mannequin when you pass your cursor over link options. Olivia Ongpin, this site's talented creator, achieved this by using Dreamweaver to create Dynamic HTML layers.

Macromedia

www.macromedia.com

The Macromedia Web site, shown in Figure 16-10, provides a rich multimedia experience that showcases the many Macromedia technologies from Shockwave for Flash and Director to Dreamweaver. You also find a developer's section with great design and development tips and a forum where you can share information with other Dreamweaver users.

Figure 16-9:
This fashion
site
features
three-
dimensional
mannequins
and lots of
interactive
techniques.

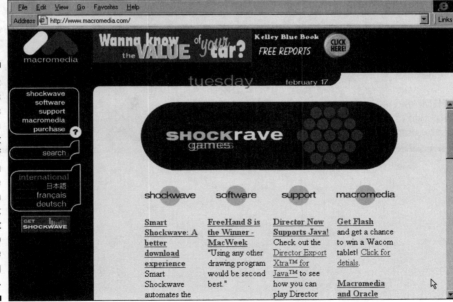

Figure 16-10:
Macromedia's
Web site is
not only a
great
example of
what you
can create
with
Dreamweaver;
it's a great
place to
learn more
about using
the program.

Elixir

www.macromedia.com/software/dreamweaver/elixir/

Created to highlight the features of Dreamweaver, this movie trailer is fake, but its cutting-edge design features are real. The site, see Figure 16-11, is an excellent example of the range of techniques made possible by Dreamweaver. Akimbo Design (www.akimbodesign.com) created the Elixir site and the Macromedia site hosts it. Visit this site and you see rollover effects, animations, timelines, and layers used in combination to present the movie and its characters in a dynamic and interactive display.

Figure 16-11: Akimbo Design created the Elixir site to showcase Dynamic HTML and the power of Dreamweaver.

Chapter 17

Ten Web Site Ideas You Can Use

● ●

In This Chapter

▶ Making your Web site easy to read

▶ Designing for your audience

▶ Pulling it all together

▶ Following the rules

● ●

*A*ll good Web sites grow and evolve. If you start with a strong design, paying close attention to some basic rules about interface, navigation, and style, you have a better foundation to build on. The following design ideas can help you create a compelling Web site that can grow gracefully.

Make It Easy

Creating a clear and intuitive navigational system is one of the most important elements in creating a Web site. Nothing is likely to frustrate your visitors more than not being able to find what they're looking for. Make sure visitors can easily get to all the main sections of your site from every page in the site. You can best do this by creating a row of links to each of the main sections and placing it at the top, bottom, or side of every page. I call this a *navigation row* or *navigation bar,* and it's a common feature on most well-designed sites. If the pages are very long, then you should make sure that these links are at the top of the page, and you may want to include them at the bottom as well. A set of graphic icons can make this navigational element an attractive part of your design. Your goal is to make sure that viewers don't have to use the Back button in their browsers to move around your site. Using the Back button wastes your user's time, and believe it or not, some browsers don't even have a Back button. You can find more tips about creating an intuitive navigation system in Chapter 5.

White Space Is Not Wasted Space

Often, one of the best design features you can add to a page is nothing at all (also known as *white space*). Understand that *white space*, in this case, is not always white; it's simply the space where you don't have text or images, and is the color or pattern of your background. White space gives the eye a rest, and readers need more breaks when looking at a computer monitor than when reading print. You can use white space to separate one type of information from another and to focus the viewer's attention where you want it most. Some of the most beautiful and compelling designs on the Web use only a few well-thought-out elements against lots of white space. HotWired's signal2noise site, featured in Chapter 16, is a good example of this design technique.

Design for Your Audience

No matter how technically sophisticated a Web site is or how great the writing, most people notice the design first. Make sure that you leave plenty of time and budget to develop an appropriate and attractive design for your Web site. The right design is one that best suits your audience — that may or may not mean lots of fancy graphics and animations.

Think about who you want to attract to your Web site before you develop the design. A gaming Web site geared toward teenagers should look very different from a Web site with gardening tips or an online banking site. Review other sites designed for your target market. Consider your audience's time constraints and attention span, and most importantly, consider your audience's goals. If you design your site to provide information to busy business people, you want fast-loading pages with few graphics and little or no animation. If you design your site for entertainment, then your audience may be willing to wait a little longer for animation and other interactive features.

Pull It Together

As you lay out your Web page, keep related items physically close to one another. You want your viewers to understand instantly which pieces of information are related. You should give elements of similar importance the same weight on a page. Distinguish different kinds of information by their design, location, and prominence. This kind of organization makes following information visually much easier for your viewers. You can find many other design tips in Chapters 5 and 6.

Be Consistent

Make sure that all similar elements follow the same design parameters, such as type style, banner size, and page background color. If you use too many different elements on a page or within the same Web site, you quickly have a very "busy" design, and you may confuse your viewers. Defining a set of colors, shapes, or other elements that you use throughout the site is a good way to ensure a consistent style. Choose two or three fonts for your Web site and use those consistently as well. Using too many fonts makes your pages less appealing and harder to read.

Late-Breaking News

The sites on the Internet that report the most hits are those that change most frequently, thereby keeping visitors coming back for new content. Even small changes can make a big difference, especially if viewers know to look for them. Keep your site fresh and dynamic, and let viewers know when to come back for more. If you can always make changes at the same time (every Friday morning, for example), viewers have a specific date to look forward to and are more likely to come back on a regular basis. Dynamic sites grow quickly, however, and generally require even more planning than static sites. In Chapter 4, you can find suggestions and strategies for building a site that can easily accommodate growth and regular updates.

Small and Fast

The biggest problem on the Internet is still speed. Making sure your pages download quickly makes your viewers more likely to keep clicking. You may create the best design ever to grace the Web, but if it takes too long to appear on your viewer's screen, no one will wait around long enough to compliment your design talents. You can find tips about creating and linking fast-loading graphics in Chapter 6.

Accessible Designs

As you design your site, keep in mind that viewers come to your pages with a variety of computers, operating systems, and monitors. Ensure that your site is accessible to all your potential viewers by testing your pages on a variety of systems. If you want to attract a large audience to your site, you need to ensure that it looks good on a broad range of systems. A design that looks great in Navigator 4.0 may be unreadable in Internet Explorer 2.0, and many people still use old browsers because they haven't bothered — or don't know how — to download new versions.

Accessible design on the Web also means pages that can be read (actually, converted to synthesized speech) by special browsers used by the blind. Using the Alternative Text attribute in your image tags is a simple way to ensure that all of your visitors can get the information they need. The Alternative Text attribute specifies a text alternative that displays if the image doesn't appear.

Follow the Three Clicks Rule

The Three Clicks Rule states that no important piece of information should ever be more than three clicks away from anywhere else on your Web site. The most important information should be even closer at hand. Some information, such as contact information, should never be more than one click away. Make it easy for viewers to find information by creating a site map (as I explain in the next section) and a navigation bar — a set of links to all the main sections on your site.

Map It Out

As your site gets larger, providing easy access to all the information on your Web site may get harder and harder. A great solution is to provide a *site map,* which is a page that includes links to almost every other page in the site. The site map can become a busy page and usually appears best in outline form. This page should be highly functional — it doesn't matter if it looks pretty. Don't put lots of graphics on this page; it should load quickly and provide easy access to anything that your visitors need.

Chapter 18

Ten Timesaving Dreamweaver Tips

In This Chapter

▶ Making the most of Dreamweaver

▶ Saving time with shortcuts

▶ Designing for all Web browsers

▶ Extending features by adding behaviors

*E*ven the best programs get better when you know how to make the most of them. As I put this book together, I collected tips and tricks and gathered them into this handy list. Take a moment to check out these tips and save tons of time in developing your Web site. Most of these tips apply to both Macintosh and Windows users, but I wrote this book on a PC, so I couldn't help but include more tips for the Windows version than the Mac version. To help make up for that, I include a couple of bonus tips at the end of this list especially for Macintosh users.

Finding Functional Fonts

Designers get so excited when they find out that they can use any font on a Web page. But, in reality, your viewers must still have the font on their computers for it to display. That means common fonts are most likely to display the way you intend them. If you want to try for a more unusual font, go for it — just make sure to include alternatives. The Dreamweaver Font List already includes collections of common fonts, and you can always create your own Font List by choosing Text⇨Font⇨Edit Font List.

And here's another tip: To ensure the best results when your pages display in Internet Explorer 3.0, list a Windows font first.

Differentiating DHTML for All Browsers

If you like pushing the technical limits of what works on the Web, don't overlook one of the most valuable features of Dreamweaver: the Evolve/Devolve option. Available in Dreamweaver 1.2 and later, Devolve automatically converts your complex page designs that work only in 4.0 and later browsers into alternate pages that display in 3.0 browsers. The feature works by converting CSS and DHTML tags into regular HTML 3.2 tags. To devolve CSS and other features on a page, choose File⇨Convert⇨3.0 Browser Compatible. To convert layers to tables, choose File⇨Convert⇨ Tables to Layers.

Directing Your Viewers

Creating multiple sites is the most fail-safe solution for making sure that all your viewers are happy when you use cutting-edge page designs filled with DHTML and CSS. That means you create two or more sets of pages: one that uses the latest features and one that uses older, more universally supported HTML tags. But then how do you ensure that viewers get to the right pages? Use the new Check Browser behavior. Available in Dreamweaver 1.2 or higher (and from Macromedia's Web site), the Check Browser behavior is a JavaScript that determines the browser type of each viewer that lands on your site and directs them to the page design best suited to their browser version.

Solving Problems in Applying Styles

Cascading Style Sheets offer timesaving design capabilities that can help you maintain a consistent style across your entire site. But if you're applying styles to text or other elements that are already formatted with HTML tags, you may run into problems. If you're having trouble achieving consistent style control with a style sheet, you may have already applied conflicting formatting (such as bold or italics) to the element. To solve this problem, make sure that you take out any other formatting before you apply a style sheet.

Finding Style Sheet Shortcuts

Style sheets can save time, enabling you to specify multiple formatting options with the application of just one style. The next step to speed and efficiency is finding a shortcut that can get you to the style sheets options faster. To save even more time, use the Style Sheet Shortcut menu; it's just a right-click away if you use Windows, or a Ctrl+click away on the Mac. The shortcut menu includes Edit, Duplicate, Remove, and Apply commands.

Appreciating DHTML Differences

One of the most dramatic differences between Internet Explorer 4.0 and Netscape Navigator 4.0 when it comes to DHTML has to do with style properties. In Internet Explorer 4.0, you can change style properties of elements after a page has loaded. In Navigator 4.0, you can't. That means that, in Explorer, you can create DHTML effects, such as making text change color (by changing the font color attribute) or change size (by changing the font size attribute). You can't do these things in Navigator. Fortunately, both browsers support changes to positioning properties, which allow animations and other tricks created by moving layers over time.

Using the Best Layers

Netscape deserves some credit for being the first to support layers in HTML. Unfortunately, their <LAYER> and <ILAYER> tags didn't catch on. Instead, positioned elements created with the <DIV> and <SPAN> tags are the standard. Commonly referred to as "CSS layers" or "CSS-P elements," the <DIV> and <SPAN> tags are defined by the World Wide Web Consortium's Cascading Style Sheets Positioning Specification (CSS-P). That makes them the closest thing to a standard as you can get on the Web these days. It also means that both Microsoft and Netscape support CSS layers in their 4.0 browsers, but only Netscape Navigator 4.0 supports positioned elements created with the <LAYER> and <ILAYER> tags. Stick with the standards; use the <DIV> and <SPAN> options.

Adding Behaviors

When your Web pages get out of line, you may find that you need new behaviors. I don't mean manners and following the rules; I mean JavaScript behaviors that can add interactivity and animation. Macromedia showed great foresight when it made Dreamweaver extensible. Not only can you download new behaviors from the Macromedia site and add them to the program, but you can also create your own. This is an excellent, timesaving solution when you have a team of people working on a site, because your most experienced staffers can create new behaviors and even your most novice team members can apply them. You can find additional objects and behavior actions at www.macromedia.com/support/dreamweaver/ upndown/objects/. Visit the site regularly; they're always adding more.

Creating Prototypes and Templates

Because Dreamweaver is a visual tool that's quick and easy to use, it's great for prototyping a Web site, even if you use other programs for some or all of the final development. Dreamweaver is also ideal for creating templates, which less experienced developers can then use to update and maintain a site. Consider getting a copy of Dreamweaver for your clients to ensure that any changes they make have clean, accurate code behind them.

Controlling Palettes

Dreamweaver features many tool palettes, providing easy access to a variety of options and HTML tags. But keeping them all open at once can be confusing and can clutter your work area. Close all palettes you're not using so that you can focus your attention on your designs. Remember that you can always open up the palettes again when you need them by choosing the palette, such as Object, Properties, or Launcher, from the Window menu. Also notice that you can get quick access to some HTML tags from the lower-left part of the frame of your page window. In the lower-right section, you find icons that provide shortcuts to all the options in the Launcher palette.

Addressing All Mac Users: Bonus Tips

The previous tips apply to both Macintosh and Windows users, but these last tips address a couple of unique issues only Mac users are likely to experience.

> ✔ **Allot as much memory to Dreamweaver as you can spare.** On the Mac, you do that by selecting the program icon in the Finder, choosing File⇨Get Info, and increasing the Minimum and Preferred size options to 20MB or higher, if you can spare it. If you don't have a lot of RAM, you may run into trouble, especially if you're also running a RAM-hungry browser, such as Netscape Navigator and Internet Explorer. If you have to, preview your pages in one browser first, and then quit the first browser and preview in the second browser.

✔ **Switch back to Dreamweaver from BBEdit to save changes.** The BBEdit version that comes with Dreamweaver sometimes runs into trouble when working with very large pages in BBEdit. One problem I've found is that it can take a long time to save your changes in BBEdit when you have both it and Dreamweaver open. Switching back to Dreamweaver to save changes makes saving your documents much faster. Here's another tip: BBEdit works better if you close the HTML source palette in Dreamweaver.

✔ **If you upgrade to Dreamweaver 1.2 and can't get Dreamweaver to work properly on your Macintosh, check for conflicting extensions.** A likely culprit is the Visual C++ 4.0b package: Microsoft C Runtime Library. Turning this extension off in the Extensions Manager should solve the problem.

Appendix A

Glossary

● ●

absolute link (URL): An HTML hyperlink that uses the complete URL, starting with the machine name or domain name on which the file resides. For example: `<A HREF="http://www.domain_name.com/directory/filename.html">`. See also *relative link.*

absolute positioning: Refers to the HTML feature that enables you to precisely specify the location of an element in relation to the window.

Acrobat: Adobe System's software suite for creating portable electronic documents. The suite includes Acrobat Exchange, Acrobat Distiller, Acrobat Catalog, and the new Capture plug-in.

ActiveX: A set of technologies created by Microsoft that enables software components to interact with one another in a networked environment, regardless of the computer language in which they were created.

add-on: An accessory or utility program that extends the capabilities of an application program. See also *plug-in.*

alignment: Horizontal arrangement of lines of text, graphics, or other elements on a page with respect to the left and right margins.

anchor: The start or destination of a hyperlink. See also *absolute link* and *relative link.*

animated GIFs: Part of the GIF89a specification that allows you to store multiple still frames in the same file, which, upon loading, display in a specified sequence to create movie-like motion. Created by programs such as GIFBuilder (which is included on the CD-ROM that accompanies this book). See also *animation.*

animation: Series of images created in successive positions that, when displayed one after the other, creates the effect of movement.

antialiasing: The process that gives the illusion of smoothing the pixelated (or jagged) edges in a graphic image by intermixing pixels of the adjoining colors along the edges of the graphic.

applet: A small application created with the Java programming language that you can embed in an HTML page to execute animations or interactive applications.

application: A program (such as a word processor, spreadsheet, database, presentation program, or desktop publishing program) that performs functions for a user. The words *application* and *program* are generally used interchangeably.

ASCII (American Standard Code for Information Interchange): Pronounced *ask-ee.* The original 128-character set, or a file containing only those characters and no special formatting.

attribute: A part of the HTML specification that modifies the behavior of the tag as well as the text, graphic, or other element that it describes.

AVI (Audio/Video/Interactive): The Microsoft file format for Video for Windows movies.

background: A solid color, image, or textured pattern linked in the <BODY> tag so that it displays behind the text and graphics on a Web page.

bandwidth: A measure of the carrying capacity of the Internet. Some kinds of information, such as graphics, take up more bandwidth than others, such as text.

banner: An advertisement on a Web page. Usually a commercial advertisement that links to the advertiser's Web site or to another page dedicated to the product being advertised. Banners are almost always composed of bitmapped GIF graphics and sometimes with animated GIFs.

batch processing: Performing the same function on many files or documents at the same time.

baud: Measure of the speed at which data is transmitted. Baud rate indicates the number of bits of data transmitted in one second. One baud is one bit per second. Common modems today have baud rates of 14,400, 28,800, 33,600, or 56,000.

BBS (Bulletin Board System): An electronic messaging system, such as an online discussion area, that you dial into directly to access and contribute messages.

beta version: The name for the last stages of development for a computer program before it is ready and sold to the public. In this stage, the program is released to a select group of users for testing.

BinHex: A file-encoding system used mostly on Macintosh computers.

bit: Binary digit — the smallest piece of information used by a computer. Bits can be turned on or off and used in various combinations to represent different kinds of information. Eight bits form a *byte*.

bitmapped image: A black-and-white or color graphic image formed by an array of dots (pixels) on a screen.

bookmark: Means of saving the URL of a Web site in the browser for easy access later.

bps (bits per second): A measure of how fast data is transmitted. Often used to describe modem speed. See also *baud*.

browse: To look over a collection of information casually, especially in an effort to find something of interest, as in browsing through folders (directories) or browsing the Internet. See also *browser*.

browser: A program, such as Netscape Navigator or Microsoft Internet Explorer, used through an Internet connection to view pages on the World Wide Web.

bullets: Simple-shaped graphics that call attention to something. Usually, they look like tiny buttons without words and are used to set apart items in an unnumbered list.

byte: Measurement of computer storage. Usually eight bits.

C or C++: Programming languages preferred by many professional programmers.

cache: Pronounced *cash*. Special section of RAM or disk memory set aside to store frequently accessed information.

Cascading Style Sheets (CSS): Part of the HTML 4.0 specification that enables you to define style properties (such as font, color, and spacing) and use them to control the appearance of elements. Cascading Style Sheets enable you to make global formatting changes by redefining and applying styles.

CGI (Common Gateway Interface) script: Format and syntax for passing information from browsers to servers via forms or queries in HTML. Generally written in Perl, C, or C++.

chat: Real-time discussions that take place on the Internet.

clear GIF: A completely invisible GIF. It can be any size but is usually only a single pixel. Used to create white space on a Web page for better placement of text by changing the height and width attributes of the image tag.

client: The Internet is a client/server arrangement. The client is the end-user side (often the browser), which resides on a remote computer and communicates with a server. See also *server.*

client-side image map: Image map that is interpreted by the browser. See also *image map* and *server-side image map.*

close-tag: An HMTL tag that designates the end of a formatting section, usually the same as the opening tag with a forward slash mark. For example, the close `<CENTER>` tag is `</CENTER>`. See also *end-tag.*

compressed file: Data file that has been modified to consume less space than it did before modification. Prior to use, a compressed file must be decompressed.

computerese (or computereze): Slang to describe the jargon and special terminology related to computers.

container: Refers to a Cascading Style Sheet positioning element that you can use to position elements relative to their parent element.

cookie: Information that is stored on your hard drive by a program on a Web site you visit. This information can be used to track your preferences and activities as you use the site and if you return to it later. Cookie technology allows a Web site to greet you by name, remember your password, and provide custom-made information. Cookies have become very controversial because some people view them as an invasion of privacy. Most of the latest browsers enable you to prevent cookies from being stored on your computer.

cross-platform: A computer program with versions for more than one operating system, such as UNIX, Macintosh, and Windows 98. Can also mean applications, such as those created in Java, that run across multiple, incompatible computer systems with little or no modification.

CSS property: An attribute or value that is used to configure styles for a given selector.

CSS value: Also called a CSS attribute, specifies the parameter for a CSS property.

cyberspace: Refers to the entire world of online information and services. Coined by William Gibson in his science fiction novel *Neuromancer.*

data binding: Refers to the process of automatically placing or connecting data into an HTML element from a data source.

database program: Enables the collection of data in an organized format, permitting manipulation of the data in a variety of ways. Examples include FileMaker Pro, Access, Foxpro, and dBase.

default: Condition set automatically in a program when no selection has been made explicitly. In HTML, the value assigned to an attribute when none is supplied.

desktop: In a graphical environment, a representation of your day-to-day work as though you're looking at an actual desk littered with folders full of work to do.

desktop publishing program: Application programs, such as Adobe PageMaker and QuarkXPress, used for typesetting publications, such as newsletters and magazines.

dialog box: On-screen message box that conveys or requests information.

digital format: The form of something, such as an image or sound, when stored as computer data.

Director movie: An animation, presentation, or interactive file created in Macromedia Director, the most widely used program for creating multimedia.

directory (subdirectory): List of computer files contained on a disk or drive. May be nested to facilitate organization of data on the disk or drive. Called *folders* on Macintosh or Windows 98 systems.

dithering: Method employed to simulate natural shading in images with a limited color range. Shades are represented with combinations of different colored dots (pixels) on the screen in various patterns. Often used to give the appearance of smoother transitions between shades of color.

document source: The HTML code behind a page displayed on the World Wide Web. You can view this information for almost every page on the Web.

domain name: A unique identifier that assigns a name to a specific IP address. Translates computer names (IP addresses) into physical addresses. Domain names in the United States are read from right to left. The right-most part is the zone and tells what type of institution the name is related to: .com (commercial), .edu (educational), .net (network operations), .gov (U.S. government), or .mil (U.S. military). Most countries also have a country code: .us (United States), .uk (United Kingdom), and .au (Australia), for example.

DOS (Disk Operating System): Underlying control system for many personal computers. Usually refers to MS-DOS, the operating system for IBM-compatible computers.

download: Process of moving information from a remote computer to your computer.

dpi (dots per inch): Measure of image resolution that counts the dots in a linear inch. The higher the dpi, the better the resolution. A 600-dpi printer gives you much better quality printouts than a 300-dpi printer, but it costs a lot more.

drag and drop: Method for moving text or graphics to other locations. Highlight the item with the cursor, place the cursor over it, hold down the mouse button, and then drag the item to its new location. Release the mouse button to "drop" the item in its new location. You can also launch applications this way. Many HTML editors also set links to images and graphics using drag and drop.

dynamic: Marked by continuous activity or change.

Dynamic HTML (DHTML): This part of the HTML specification adds the ability to change style or positioning properties with a scripting language. DHTML includes Cascading Styles Sheets, layers, timelines, and behaviors.

dynamic styles: Refers to the ability to change the style attributes or values of any element at the time a page is loaded or the action is otherwise triggered.

8.3 rule: In DOS and older versions of Windows (those prior to Windows 95), filenames should not have more than eight characters, and the extensions should not have more than three.

element: Component of a hierarchical structure (for example, in a Web site). Also used to mean any shape that can be individually manipulated in a graphic. In this usage, the term *element* is synonymous with the term *object*.

e-mail (electronic mail): The system that enables one computer user to send a message to another computer user over a network.

e-mail address: Domain-based address used for sending electronic mail (e-mail) to a specified destination. Within company systems and commercial service providers, such as America Online, the e-mail address is often just the name that the person has chosen as an address. On the greater Internet, e-mail addresses must include an @ sign and extension, such as .com or .org. For example: janine@visiontec.com.

embed: Command placed directly in a program. Also an HTML tag used to link objects and elements that require plug-ins for viewing.

end-tag: In HTML programming, identifies the end of an element, also called the close tag. Usually the same as the opening tag, but with a forward slash mark. For example, the close tag for bold font is </B>. See also *close-tag*.

environment: Hardware and/or operating system for application programs (DOS, Macintosh, Windows).

event: User-initiated happening, such as clicking a mouse. Programs are often designed to respond to such an event.

event binding: Connecting an event to an event handler.

event handler: An action or function that is connected to an event by an event binding that responds to the event.

extension (or filename extension): 1. Tags or attributes that are introduced by a browser company such as Netscape or Microsoft, but aren't part of the current HTML specification and are usually only supported by that browser. 2. The latter portion of a filename on a DOS or UNIX machine, such as .doc for document, .gif for Graphics Interchange Format. Macintosh filenames don't require extensions. However, all files that are to be displayed by a browser must include an extension.

external style sheet: A Cascading Style Sheet file that is a separate text file containing style definitions and can be linked to any of the HTML files in a Web site.

FAQ (Frequently Asked Questions): A list of questions and answers with basic information about a Web site or other Internet resource.

Fetch: The most popular Macintosh program for file transfer between client and server.

filename: The name of any document (or file) on a computer, such as word processing documents, graphics, and so on.

first-generation browsers: Early versions of browsers that predate the ability to recognize plug-ins, tables, animated GIFs, background colors, or background images.

folder: List of computer files contained on a disk or drive. May be nested (in subfolders) to facilitate organization of data on the disk or drive. Called *directories* on DOS or UNIX systems and *subdirectories* when nested.

font: One complete collection of letters, punctuation marks, numbers, and special characters with a consistent and identifiable typeface, weight, posture, and font size. Sometimes used to refer to typefaces or font families.

font family: Set of fonts in several sizes and weights that share the same typeface.

frames: A Netscape HTML extension, now also supported by Microsoft Internet Explorer, that enables more than one HTML document to be displayed on a Web page. Creates distinct sections of a page that can be individually scrollable and contain links that alter the contents of other sections, or frames, on the same Web page.

FTP (File Transfer Protocol): Used for copying files to and from servers elsewhere on a network, such as the Internet.

GIF (Graphics Interchange Format): A bit-mapped image format that uses compression to reduce file sizes. The format was pioneered by CompuServe for storing and transmitting graphics over remote networks. It's currently the most universally accepted graphics file format on the World Wide Web.

GIF87a and GIF89a: GIF87a is the original specification for the Graphics Interchange Format standard. GIF89a is an enhanced specification that gives this format the ability to display any specific color as transparent and the ability to store and display multiple files as an animation. See also ***animated GIF***.

global: Of, relating to, or applying to a whole (such as a computer program or Web site).

graphic: Representation of an object on a two-dimensional surface.

graphical environment: An environment that includes the use of graphics instead of only text.

GUI (Graphical User Interface): Used to describe an interface that uses graphic metaphors to operate a computer program or operating system. These graphical interfaces replaced text-based systems, such as the DOS operating system.

hits: Visits to a Web site. Hits can be very misleading because they're counted in varying ways. The most traditional systems for counting hits on a Web page count all the graphics and external links as hits when one user views a page. For example, a page with three graphics and two external links counts as five hits when one user views the page.

home page: The first page seen when someone accesses a Web site. Also called the *title page* or *front page*. On a small site (for example, a personal site), this may be the only page. On a larger site (business or organization, for example), it's the first and main page and includes links to other pages within the site.

host: A computer that enables users to communicate with other hosts by using application programs such as electronic mail, Telnet, and FTP. Any computer capable of connecting to others on the Internet is a host. This term generally refers to Web servers, but hosts aren't always servers.

HTML (Hypertext Markup Language): A hypertext-based, distributed information system created in 1991 by a group of physicists in Switzerland so they could trade images of their scientific research, as well as the words they had been sending back and forth for years. Later adopted by graphic designers for use on the World Wide Web, HTML is a subset of SGML (Standard Generalized Markup Language).

HTML authoring tools: Programs designed to edit or convert HTML documents.

HTML converters: Programs that convert (or change) documents from various programs into HTML documents.

HTML editors: Programs that you can use to alter or create HTML pages. HTML editors can be text or WYSIWYG (What You See Is What You Get) editors.

HTTP (Hypertext Transfer Protocol): A fixed set of messages and replies between a World Wide Web browser and a World Wide Web server.

hyperlink (or link): Programmed connection between locations in the same file (Web site) or between different files. See also *hypertext.*

hypermedia: Links between pictures, sounds, and text in the same or related files or Web sites.

hypertext: Word or series of words with related HTML programming linking the words to other locations. Users who click these words can skip from one document

to the next or from one area of a document to another area in the same document.

icon: Small, "high concept" images meant to give the reader a message that takes less time to read and is more universally understood than if the same message were spelled out in words.

ID: Refers to a CSS property that is used to assign a name to an element.

image maps: GIF or JPEG images that have a corresponding set of coordinates to designate distinct areas of the image using square, circular, or polygon shapes. Those areas can be linked to any URL so that a user reaches different destinations by selecting different sections of the image. See also *client-side image maps* and *server-side image maps.*

inline images: Images that can be given a specific location on a Web page, in context with text and other multimedia elements. Inline images can be viewed by the browser and don't require a plug-in or separate window for viewing.

interface: The place where independent and often unrelated systems meet and act on or communicate with one another. Also, the design of the computer screen's graphical command layout in reference to the clarity and convenient placement of such application control elements as menu bars, toolbars, status bars, and so on. This type of interface is most often referred to as the *user interface* or *GUI (Graphical User Interface).*

interlacing: Enables an image to load in several stages of resolution. Creates the illusion that graphics (and, therefore, whole pages) load more quickly, and gives the reader a chance to see a fuzzy recognizable image quickly enough to know whether to wait or move on.

Internet Assistants: Microsoft Office add-ons that convert existing Word, Excel, and PowerPoint documents into HTML.

Internet: Note the capital I. While an *internet* is a network, *Internet* refers to an international collection of interconnected networks. The Internet is the largest internet in the world.

InterNIC Information Services: Nonprofit organization located in Reston, Virginia, that registers domain names and addresses so that no two sites use the same name or number. Their Web address is www.internic.net.

intranet: The term used for a private Web site and other Internet communications that are set up and maintained within a corporation.

IP (Internet Protocol): Allows information to be passed from one network (set of computers) to another by using a unique string of numbers (addresses) for each network.

ISDN (Integrated Services Digital Network) connections or ISDN lines: Digital technology for Internet connections and other telecommunications that offers higher bandwidth and better signal quality than telephone lines.

ISP (Internet service provider): A national or local company that sells access to the Internet. Well-known examples in the United States include CompuServe, America Online, Prodigy, Netcom, and The Well.

Java: Programming language invented at Sun Microsystems that executes on any computer platform. This makes it possible to place applications on remote computers that run on any computer connected to that remote computer. Small Java applications, called *applets,* are used on

many Web pages to perform operations that can't normally be accomplished in HTML code.

JPEG or JPG (Joint Photographic Experts Group): File format in which to save graphics for use on the Web if they're full-color, continuous-tone images (such as photographs) and larger than approximately 150 pixels square.

JScript: What Microsoft calls its implementation of JavaScript in Internet Explorer.

Kbps (kilobits per second): Measurement of communication speed (of modems, for example).

kilobyte (K): 1,024 bytes of data.

link (hyperlink): A connection between locations in the same file (Web site) or between different files created by the HTML anchor or link tag. See also *hypertext.*

local links: Links that go to HTML documents or other files within your Web site. The path in a local link doesn't require the domain name or name of the host computer.

logical styles: HTML markup tags that provide emphasis or indicate a particular kind of device or action. See also *physical styles.*

Lynx: Character-mode World Wide Web browser that displays only text. Believe it or not, some people can still only view text on the Web because they're limited to using the Lynx browser.

macro: Stored list of commands to perform tedious and often-repeated tasks.

markup language: Special characters embedded within a text file to instruct a computer program how to handle or display the contents of the file itself. HTML is a markup language.

megabyte (MB): 1,024 kilobytes, or 1,048,576 bytes.

menu: A list of options presented to a user by a program or Web site.

menu bar: In graphical programs, the menu may appear as a bar that represents many of the common functions of the program. In a Web site, the menu bar is often an image map of the site that enables the user to click a menu item and jump to the linked page automatically.

metacharacter: Specific character within a text file that signals the need for special handling. In HTML, metacharacters are angle brackets (< >), ampersands (&), pound signs (#), and semicolons (;).

Microsoft Internet Explorer: One of the two most widely used graphical World Wide Web browsers. See also *browser*.

Microsoft Office viewers: Enable users to view Word, Excel, and PowerPoint documents over the Internet in their native form without converting them to HTML. Can be used in conjunction with a browser. Especially useful on intranets.

MIDI (Musical Instrument Device Interface): Pronounced *middy*. Protocol for the exchange of information between computers and musical synthesizers. After being placed into computer-represented form, all the aspects of the digitized sound can be edited and altered.

MIME (Multipurpose Internet Mail Extensions): Extension to Internet e-mail that enables the transfer of nontextual data, such as graphics, audio, and video.

modem: Acronym for MOdulator-DEModulator. Device that converts (or modulates) electrical pulses from a computer to signals suitable for transmission over a telephone line.

Mosaic: The first graphical World Wide Web browser created for the Internet.

Mozilla: Early name coined for Netscape products that derives from "Mosaic meets Godzilla." The word and associated image often appear in Netscape products or in references to them.

multimedia: Presentation of information on a computer by using video sequences, animation, sound (either as background or synchronized to a video or animation), and vector illustrations.

navigational icons: In this case, navigation refers to the use of hyperlinks to move through a Web site. Navigational icons show the user where to find information. These icons often move viewers through sequential pages and back again.

NCSA (National Center for Supercomputing Applications): Department at the University of Illinois where the Mosaic Web browser, the first browser ever created, was developed.

nested: When one structure occurs within another, it is said to be *nested*. HTML tags are often nested.

Netscape Navigator: One of the two most widely used graphical World Wide Web browsers. See also *browser*.

network administrator: The person responsible for maintaining a network. See *system administrator*.

Object Model: The breaking down of functionality into unique elements, or objects, that can be accessed and manipulated by a scripting language.

palette: An array showing each color in an indexed image. Netscape and Microsoft have created palettes that best use colors for cross-platform display. Copies of both palettes are included on the CD-ROM that accompanies this book.

PDF (Portable Document Format): File that carries all font and layout specifications with it, regardless of the platform on which it displays. The best solution for putting print documents on the Web when those print documents must be as close as possible to their paper counterparts. Generally requires a viewer such as Adobe Acrobat.

Perl (Practical Extraction and Reporting Language): First developed by Larry Wall for UNIX systems, this language is frequently used for writing CGI scripts.

physical styles: HTML markup tags that specifically control character styles, such as bold <B> or italic <I>. Contrast with *logical styles.*

PICT: Probably the most common Macintosh graphics format. Enables use of JPEG compression when saving a file on a Macintosh. However, neither a Web browser nor any other program recognizes a PICT file as a JPEG file.

pixel: Pronounced *picks-el*. Abbreviated word standing for Picture Element. Smallest element (dot) that a computer can display on-screen. Images created for the Web are most commonly measured in pixels. Spacing attributes in HTML tags are also commonly measured in pixels. A pixel measured on a screen is the equivalent of a dot (as in dots per inch) on a printed page.

plain text: Text format that doesn't include formatting codes that maintain layout and appearance of text.

platform: Computer hardware standard, such as IBM PC-compatible or Macintosh personal computers.

plug-in: Accessory or utility program that extends the capabilities of an application program, such as the RealAudio player.

PNG: Pronounced *ping*. Bitmapped file format, designed especially for network graphics. PNG is a new format meant to be a patent-free replacement for GIF, but it's not yet widely readable by browsers.

program: An application (such as a word processor, spreadsheet, database, or desktop publishing program) that performs functions for a user. The words *application* and *program* are generally used to mean the same thing.

progressive JPEG: Like interlaced GIF, progressive JPEG enables an image to load in stages of increasingly higher resolution.

properties: Characteristics of an object defining its state, appearance, or value.

query: A method by which data is requested from a server.

QuickTime: Created by Apple Computer, QuickTime is the industry standard multimedia architecture used by software tool vendors and content creators to store, edit, and play synchronized graphics, sound, video, text, and music. QuickTime is the most common system for storing and playing multimedia content delivered on CD-ROM and the Internet. Includes QuickTime Movies and QuickTime VR (virtual reality).

RAM (Random Access Memory): Computer memory that stores ongoing work or any operating systems and applications actually running at the moment.

raster image: The horizontal pattern of lines, made up of pixels, that form an image on a computer screen or monitor. See also *bitmapped image.*

raw code: Refers to the HTML code behind a Web page.

RealAudio: A sound technology developed by Progressive Networks to enable streaming sound play on Web pages.

relative link (URL): Link set using the path within a Web site directory structure that doesn't include the domain name. For example: `<A HREF="file_name.html">` or `<A HREF="/resources/ file_name.html">`. Contrast with *absolute link.*

relative positioning: The process of placing an element in relation to its parent elements.

render: Used when working with three-dimensional images, rendering is the process of converting an outline of an image into a detailed version.

resolution: The number of picture elements per unit in an image. Resolution on a printer is described by dots per inch (dpi). Resolution on a monitor is described by pixels horizontally and lines vertically.

ROM (Read-Only Memory): Storage capacity that can be read but not deleted or altered. For example, you can't save data to or delete information from a CD-ROM; you can only read or copy information off of it.

Roundtrip HTML: Macromedia coined this term and defines it this way: "Roundtrip HTML editing is a unique feature of Dreamweaver that lets you move your documents between Dreamweaver and a text-based HTML editor with little or no impact on the content and structure of the document's HTML source code." More simply put: Dreamweaver doesn't goof around with the code you create in other HTML editors.

RTF (Rich Text Format): Special plain-text format that retains formatting code and can be interpreted by a variety of text-editing programs.

sans serif: Sans serif fonts have no cross strokes.

scripting language: A computer language, such as JavaScript or VBScript, that can run within a Web browser.

scrolling: Moving the window horizontally or vertically to make visible the information that extends beyond the viewing area.

search engine: 1. Web sites that contain searchable databases or search programs capable of retrieving other Web pages based on user queries. 2. A program created to search the contents of a particular Web site for information related to a specific topic or keyword supplied by a user.

serif: Serif fonts have cross strokes across the ends of the main strokes of characters.

server (Web server): A computer connected to the Internet that "serves" files by sending them to another computer. The Internet is a client/server arrangement. The *server* is on a remote computer and responds to requests from the *client.* See also *client.*

server-side image map: Image map that requires a CGI script on the server. See also *image map* and *client-side image map.*

SGML (Standard Generalized Markup Language): Sequence of characters organized physically as a set of entities and logically into a hierarchy of elements. Document definition, specification, and creation mechanism that makes platform and display differences across multiple computers irrelevant to the delivery and rendering of documents. HTML is a subset of SGML.

shareware: Copyrighted software that can be freely shared with others, provided certain restrictions regarding distribution are followed, as specified by the author. Often involves payment of a fee to the author for continued use.

Shockwave: Macromedia products for viewing Director files, Flash movies, and Freehand files. Shockwave plug-ins exist for both Director 4.0 and 5.0 and for both Mac and PC.

special characters: Typed characters such as ~ or &. On Web pages, these characters must be created as HTML entities or by using special character tags. With the exception of the underline (or underscore) character, these characters should not be used in filenames.

splash screen: The opening screen that appears when you start a program. Usually includes information about the manufacturer.

spreadsheet: Program that simulates an accountant's worksheet on-screen and enables the embedding of hidden formulas to perform calculations on data. (Examples include Lotus 1-2-3, Microsoft Excel, and Paradox.)

sprite: Used to describe an individual element in an animation or multimedia file.

start-tag: In HTML programming, identifies the start of an HTML element. Can include attributes. See also *end-tag.*

still graphics: Representations of objects without animation.

streaming: *Streaming* technology starts playing sound, video, or other data as soon as enough material has downloaded so that the rest downloads before the movie or sound file finishes playing.

string: Series of related text or formatting characters.

structural element: Element that determines how your document looks. For example, a heading is a structural element, but paragraph text is not.

subdirectory: A directory (also known as a folder) that resides inside another directory or folder. See also *directory.*

surfing: Used to describe the action of moving from one place to another on the World Wide Web with no apparent plan or pattern — following any "wave" that looks like a good one.

synchronize: To arrange events so that they happen at the same time.

syntax: Connected or orderly system; rules that govern the use of HTML code.

system administrator: Also known as network administrator. Person or group responsible for configuring and maintaining a network or Web server.

T1 line: High-speed, dedicated connection to the Internet. Transmits a digital signal at 1.544 megabits per second.

T3 line: Very high-speed, dedicated connection to the Internet. Transmits a digital signal at 44.746 megabits per second.

tables: HTML table tags organize text and/or graphics in relation to one another on a Web page.

tags: Formal name for an element of HTML markup, usually enclosed in angle brackets (< >).

TCP/IP (Transmission Control Protocol/Internet Protocol): Suite of protocols and services used to manage network communications and applications over the Internet.

third-party (programs, plug-ins): Developed by a company other than the company who developed the program that they function with.

tools: 1. Icons or palette items in a graphical program that perform specific functions when selected. 2. Useful software programs.

transparent GIF (tGIF): Generally means a GIF that appears as a graphic that "floats" over the background because the image's background is transparent. Transparency can be set to any single color section.

typeface: The distinctive design of a set of type. Grouped into two categories: serif and sans serif.

UNIX operating system: Pronounced *u-nicks.* Operating system written in the C programming language for a variety of computers from PCs to mainframes.

upload: Process of moving information from your computer to a remote computer, as in uploading Web site files to a server.

URL (Uniform Resource Locator): Pronounced U-R-L or *earl.* Server and path information that locates a document on the Internet. For example: www.domain_name.com.

user: Person who visits a Web site. See also *viewer.*

vector graphics: Images whose shapes are described by geometric formulae. Vector files are resolution independent, meaning that they're always drawn at the best possible resolution of the device generating them. Because even a fairly complex geometric shape can be described in a few lines of text as a formula, vector images tend to be much smaller than a typical equivalent bitmapped image, which has to be described using several bits of data for each pixel in the image.

viewer: 1. Special program launched by a browser to display elements such as sound files or video that can't be displayed by the browser. 2. Person who visits a Web site. See also *user.*

viewing window: A defined area of the screen through which portions of text or other information can be seen. See *windows.*

virtual reality: An artificial environment experienced through sensory stimuli (as sights and sounds) provided by a computer and in which one's actions partially determine what happens in the environment.

Visual Basic Scripting Edition (VB Script): The Microsoft scripting language designed to compete with JavaScript. It's basically a stripped down version of Visual Basic, a program used to create Windows applications.

VRML (Virtual Reality Modeling Language): Enables the creation of three-dimensional models and walk-through spaces that provide a more real-life experience. Graphics can be mapped to the surfaces of three-dimensional models, and links can be attached to surfaces. Links can display a media type, take users to another model or another part of the current model, or perform any of the functions of any Web hyperlink.

Web designer: Anyone, professional or hobbyist, who creates Web pages. Also called Web developers.

Web page: One file in a collection of files that make up a Web site. Usually used to describe the first page that appears in a Web site. See also *home page.*

Web site: A specific location on the Internet, housed on a Web server and accessible through a URL. Consists of one or more Web pages.

Webmaster: One of many titles used to describe people who design or manage Web sites. (I've always preferred Electronic Goddess.)

windows: A frame on a computer screen that displays information, such as a document or application.

Windows: Commonly used to refer to Microsoft's operating system (Windows versions 3.1, 95, 98, and NT).

wizard: Program sequence within software products that lead you step-by-step through a task.

World Wide Web (WWW): All Web servers available on the Internet.

World Wide Web Consortium (W3C): An industry consortium that seeks to promote standards for the evolution of the Web and interoperability between World Wide Web products by producing specifications and reference software. The international group is jointly hosted by the MIT Laboratory for Computer Science in the United States and by INRIA in Europe.

WYSIWYG (What You See Is What You Get): Pronounced *wizzy-wig.* Describes HTML authoring tools and other programs that attempt to show on-screen what the final document looks like.

x coordinates: Controls the horizontal placement of elements on a page.

y coordinates: Controls the vertical placement of elements on a page.

z coordinates: Controls the way elements are layered on a page.

zip: Compression method used on Windows and DOS computers. Uses the .zip file extension.

zipped archive: A file that consists of compressed files.

Appendix B
Web Design Resources You Can Find Online

● ●

The best place to keep up with the latest developments in Web design is the Internet itself. Whenever I do research on new Web technologies and features, I visit a few of my favorite Web sites to see what they have to say. Visit these sites regularly to gain insight into the evolving HTML 4.0 specification and the implementation of Dynamic HTML, as well as many other aspects of Web design.

Adobe Systems, Inc.

www.adobe.com

Adobe is not only a great resource for graphics and other products, but its Web site features an impressive collection of design tips and strategies for creating graphics for the Web, as well as well-designed HTML pages.

Art and the Zen of Web Sites

www.tlc-systems.com/webtips.shtml

As the name implies, this site shows you the way to simplistic, yet powerful, Web design.

BrowserWatch

`browserwatch.internet.com`

This site keeps you up-to-date on the latest in the browser wars and helps you appreciate the quantity and diversity of Web browsers used on the Internet. If you want to design your pages for the broader Web audience, especially if you want to use advanced features, you need to keep an eye on this site and download a few browsers that you can use when testing your work.

CGI Overview

`www.w3.org/hypertext/WWW/CGI`

The World Wide Web Consortium offers a great guide to writing CGI (Common Gateway Interface) scripts. If you already have some programming experience and want to write your own scripts, this is an ideal resource. If you've never done any programming before, this site can introduce you to what CGI scripts are all about.

CNET

`www.cnet.com`

CNET gives you hot news about all aspects of the Web, as well as in-depth reports on new technologies and other news affecting Web designers. CNET also has extensive software libraries for both Windows and Macintosh platforms.

Communication Arts Interactive

`www.commarts.com`

Need some design guidance or a few tips on how to create the best graphics for your site? Point your browser in the direction of Communication Arts Interactive.

David Siegel's Site

dsiegel.com

Famous for popularizing the clear GIF trick and many other ways to "break the rules" of HTML, Siegel's site features loads of design tips.

DHTML Zone

www.dhtmlzone.com

Macromedia created this site to help developers learn about Dynamic HTML. You can find tons of information here about how to create your own DHTML features, what DHTML really is, and how to design features to work for the broadest audience.

The Directory

www.thedirectory.org/

Looking for an Internet service provider? Look no further. The Directory is the most comprehensive guide to ISPs on the Net, featuring a searchable database of more than 10,000 ISPs worldwide.

The GrafX Design Site

www.grafx-design.com/index.shtml

A comprehensive design reference full of materials about how to create Web graphics.

The HTML Writers Guild

www.hwg.org

An international organization of World Wide Web designers and Internet publishing professionals. Its Web site includes a variety of HTML resources, as well as Web business mailing lists, information repositories, and a chance to interact with peers.

IDG Books Worldwide, Inc.

www.idgbooks.com

IDG Books Worldwide, Inc., offers a wide range of books on Web design (including this one!) and features links to a wide range of great magazines and other resources for Web designers.

International Data Group (IDG)

www.idg.com

IDG is the parent company of IDG Books. Visit the main IDG site to find links to all its research and publication services, including magazines like *Publish*, *InfoWorld*, *MacWorld*, and *PCWorld*.

Lynda's Homegurrl Page

www.lynda.com

My favorite Web graphics expert, Lynda Weinman, shows off her books and insights into creating fast-loading, beautiful images.

Macromedia's Designers and Developers Center

www.macromedia.com/support/

Macromedia's official help center is filled with tutorials, samples, and other assets designed to keep developers up-to-date, especially if you use its programs, such as Dreamweaver, Freehand, and Flash.

Microsoft

www.microsoft.com

Watch the Microsoft site for updates to Internet Explorer, as well as information on how it plans to support DHTML and other advanced HTML tags.

Netscape

www.netscape.com

Keep your eye on the Netscape site for updates to Navigator, as well as the latest on how it plans to support DHTML and other advanced HTML tags.

Project Cool

www.projectcool.com

One of my all-time favorite Web sites, Project Cool is dedicated to helping anyone become a better Web designer. The creators of this site make Web design easy to understand and accessible to anyone who visits the site. They do a great job of keeping up with the latest developments, such as DHTML and Cascading Style Sheets. You can also find a great list of award-winning sites that make great examples of what works on the Web. Their newest feature, devSearch, enables you to search through Web development resources across the Web.

Weblint

www.weblint.com

Can't figure out why a site won't work properly? Run the URL through Weblint and pinpoint any errors, as well as HTML code that may not work in some browsers.

WebMonkey

www.webmonkey.com

Tune up your browser and make sure your Web site is up to snuff at HotWired's WebMonkey site. You can use its online diagnostic tools to test your browser and find out about plug-ins and other Web development tools. You can also find HTML tutorials and other Web design references.

Web Reference

www.webreference.com

As the name implies, you can find a long list of reference materials at this site to answer almost any question a Web designer could have.

The World Wide Web Artists Consortium

www.wwwac.org

Better known as the WWWAC, this nonprofit, member-supported organization of Web designers keeps you up-to-date on current Web design issues when you subscribe to its e-mail list. But, as with any mailing list, make sure that you read a few week's worth of messages before you post one of your own. More than 1,000 people share their ideas on the WWWAC list, including some of the most respected designers on the Web.

World Wide Web Consortium

www.w3c.net

The official source for HTML updates, the W3C sets the standards for HTML code. At this site, you find all the published HTML specifications, as well as a wide range of resources for Web developers.

ZDNET

www.zdnet.com

Constantly updated, this site provides a large collection of Web design resources, as well as links to more than 30 online magazines published by Ziff-Davis, such as *Yahoo! Internet Life, Inter@ctive, PC Week, MacWeek,* and many others. While you're at it, check out www.zdtv.com. Ziff-Davis' latest endeavor, ZDTV is a new cable channel with programming about computers, technology, and the Internet.

Appendix C

About the CD

● ●

*T*he CD-ROM that accompanies this book contains the following goodies:

- Dreamweaver, a fully functional, 30-day version of the program
- Debabelizer Pro and Toolbox for all your image manipulation needs
- BeyondPress and HTML Transit, converters that can save you hours
- GIFMation and GIF Animator for creating sophisticated animated GIFs

System Requirements

Make sure that your computer meets the minimum system requirements listed here. If your computer doesn't match up to most of these requirements, you may have problems using the contents of the CD.

- A PC with a 486 or faster processor, or a Mac OS computer with a 68030 or faster processor.
- Microsoft Windows 95 or later, or Mac OS system software 7.5 or later.
- At least 8MB of total RAM installed on your computer. For best performance, I recommend that Windows 95- or 98-equipped PCs and Mac OS computers with PowerPC or G3 processors have at least 16MB of RAM installed.
- At least 111MB of hard drive space available to install all the software from this CD. (You need less space if you don't install every program.)
- A CD-ROM drive — double-speed (2x) or faster.
- A sound card for PCs. (Mac OS computers have built-in sound support.)
- A monitor capable of displaying at least 256 colors or grayscale.
- A modem with a speed of at least 14,400 bps.

If you need more information on the basics, check out *PCs For Dummies,* 4th Edition, by Dan Gookin; *Macs For Dummies,* 4th Edition, by David Pogue; or *Windows 98 For Dummies* and *Windows 95 For Dummies* by Andy Rathbone (all published by IDG Books Worldwide, Inc.).

Using the CD with Microsoft Windows

To install the items from the CD to your hard drive, follow these steps:

1. **Insert the CD into your computer's CD-ROM drive.**

2. **Click Start⇨Run.**

3. **In the dialog box that appears, type** D:\SETUP.EXE.

   Replace *D* with the proper drive letter if your CD-ROM drive uses a different letter. (If you don't know the letter, see how your CD-ROM drive is listed under My Computer in Windows 95 or 98.)

4. **Click OK.**

   A license agreement window appears.

5. **Read through the license agreement, nod your head, and then click the Agree button if you want to use the CD — after you click Agree, you'll never be bothered by the License Agreement window again.**

   The CD interface Welcome screen appears. The interface is a little program that shows you what's on the CD and coordinates installing the programs and running the demos. The interface basically enables you to click a button or two to make things happen.

6. **Click anywhere on the Welcome screen to enter the interface.**

   Now you're getting to the action. This next screen lists categories for the software on the CD.

7. **To view the items within a category, just click the category's name.**

   A list of programs in the category appears.

8. **For more information about a program, click the program's name.**

   Be sure to read the information that appears. Sometimes a program has its own system requirements or requires you to do a few tricks on your computer before you can install or run the program, and this screen tells you what you may need to do, if necessary.

9. **If you don't want to install the program, click the Go Back button to return to the previous screen.**

   You can always return to the previous screen by clicking the Go Back button. This feature enables you to browse the different categories and products and decide what you want to install.

10. **To install a program, click the appropriate Install button.**

    The CD interface drops to the background while the CD installs the program you chose.

11. **To install other items, repeat Steps 7 through 10.**

12. **When you finish installing programs, click the Quit button to close the interface.**

    You can eject the CD now. Carefully place it back in the plastic jacket of the book for safekeeping.

Using the CD with Mac OS

To install the items from the CD to your hard drive, follow these steps:

1. **Insert the CD into your computer's CD-ROM drive.**

   In a moment, an icon representing the CD that you just inserted appears on your Mac desktop. Chances are, the icon looks like a CD-ROM.

2. **Double-click the CD icon to show the CD's contents.**

3. **Double-click the Read Me First icon.**

   The Read Me First text file contains information about the CD's programs and any last-minute instructions that you may need to correctly install them.

4. **To install most programs, just drag the program's folder from the CD window and drop it on your hard drive icon.**

5. **Other programs come with installer programs — with these, you simply open the program's folder on the CD, and then double-click the icon with the words "Install" or "Installer."**

   Sometimes the installers are actually *self-extracting archives,* which just means that the program files have been bundled up into an archive, and this self-extractor unbundles the files and places them on your hard drive. This kind of program is often called an .sea. Double-click anything with .sea in the title, and it runs just like an installer.

   After you've installed the programs that you want, you can eject the CD. Carefully place it back in the plastic jacket of the book for safekeeping.

What You'll Find

Here's a summary of the software on this CD, arranged by category. If you use Windows, the CD interface helps you install software easily. (If you have no idea what I'm talking about when I say "CD interface," flip back a page or two to find the section, "Using the CD with Microsoft Windows.")

If you use a Mac OS computer, you can take advantage of the easy Mac interface to quickly install the programs.

Graphics programs

Debabelizer Pro 4.5, from Equilibrium

For Windows 95, 98, NT. Demo version. This graphics processor from Equilibrium enables you to convert images into GIFs or JPEGs automatically. Check out the demo version on the CD to see how it handles many other graphics tasks as well. Check out www.equilibrium.com for a more detailed description.

Debabelizer 1.6.5, from Equilibrium

For Mac OS. Demo version. This graphics processor from Equilibrium enables you to convert many images into GIFs or JPEGs automatically. Check out the demo version on the CD to see how it handles many other graphics tasks as well. Check out www.equilibrium.com for a more detailed description.

Debabelizer Toolbox 1.1.3 Lite LE, from Equilibrium

For Mac OS. Lite version. This version of Equilibrium's graphics processor handles some of the image conversion of the Toolbox version. Check out www.equilibrium.com for a more detailed description.

GIF Animator, from Ulead

For Windows. The trial version of GIF Animator from Ulead enables you to combine GIF images into animations that you can use on your Web pages. Visit www.ulead.com for a more detailed description.

GIFMation 2.1, from BoxTop Software

For Mac OS and Windows. GIFMation by BoxTop Software enables you to combine a series of GIF images into an animated sequence. This is one of the best tools on the market for creating animated GIFs. Visit www.boxtopsoft.com for a more detailed description.

Illustrator 7.0, from Adobe

For Mac OS and Windows 95 and 98. Tryout version. Adobe's advanced vector drawing program enables you to create complex images with powerful precision. To learn more, check out the Adobe Web site at www.adobe.com.

Photoshop 4.0.1, from Adobe

For Mac OS and Windows 95 and 98. Tryout version. The most popular and best respected photo manipulation program available, Photoshop is a must-have for any serious graphic designer and a great tool for developing Web graphics. To learn more, check out the Adobe Web site at www.adobe.com.

HTML converters and editors

BBEdit 4.5, from Bare Bones Software

For Mac OS. Demo version. This demo introduces you to the power of BBEdit as an HTML text editor. The full version of Dreamweaver includes BBEdit and provides fully integrated editing so that you can move easily between the two programs. For more on BBEdit, visit www.barebones.com.

BBEdit 4.0, from Bare Bones Software

For Mac OS. Lite version. This lite version enables you to test out the power of BBEdit as an HTML text editor. For more on BBEdit, visit www.barebones.com.

BeyondPress, from Astrobyte

Mac OS. Evaluation version. The best conversion program available for QuarkXPress files, this Xtension plugs into XPress and provides lots of room for tailoring your conversions. Check out the evaluation version on the CD and visit their Web site at www.astrobyte.com to find out more.

Dreamweaver, from Macromedia

For Windows and Mac OS. Thirty-day trial version. Including this trial version of Dreamweaver on the CD means that you have everything you need to get started when you buy this book. This fully functional version of the program gets you on your way to developing Web sites and makes it easy for you to test out the product before you buy it. Visit the Macromedia Web site at www.macromedia.com for purchase information and updates.

HomeSite 3.0, by Allaire

For Windows. Shareware. This HTML text editor for Windows enables you to work in the raw HTML code with a little help. The full version of Dreamweaver includes HomeSite and provides fully integrated editing so that you can move easily between the two programs. For more information about HomeSite, visit www.allaire.com.

HTML Transit 3.0, from InfoAccess

For Windows. Trial version. The most powerful HTML conversion tool available for word-processing files, HTML Transit can turn hundreds, and even thousands, of pages into beautifully formatted HTML in minutes. You can even set background images, headers, and footers, and you can automatically create a linked table of contents. For more about the product, visit their Web site at www.infoaccess.com.

Web browsers and plug-ins

Internet Explorer 4.0, from Microsoft

For Mac and Windows. Free. Microsoft Internet Explorer 4.0 provides the best support to date for Dynamic HTML and CSS. Use this program to test your work when you take advantage of the most powerful features in Dreamweaver. Keep an eye on the Microsoft Web site at `www.microsoft.com`. This program is updated frequently!

Note: This software, if run under Windows NT 4.0, needs Service Pack 3 to run. If you don't have Service Pack 3, visit the Microsoft Web site to download it. If you do have it, or after you install it, continue the installation and follow the prompts on your screen to install the NT version of Internet Explorer.

Navigator 4.0, from Netscape

For Mac and Windows. Free. Netscape Navigator 4.0 provides some support for Dynamic HTML and CSS. You should always test your work in this browser, as well as in Internet Explorer, to ensure that your pages look good to viewers using either program. Keep an eye on the Netscape Web site at `home.netscape.com`. This program is updated frequently!

Shockwave, from Macromedia

For Mac and Windows. Free. Use the plug-ins to view Director and Flash files. Visit the Macromedia Web site at `www.macromedia.com` for more information and program updates.

If You've Got Problems (Of the CD Kind)

I tried my best to compile programs that work on most computers with the minimum system requirements. Alas, your computer may differ, and some programs may not work properly for some reason.

The two likeliest problems are that you don't have enough memory (RAM) for the programs you want to use, or you have other programs running that are affecting installation or running of a program. If you get error messages like `Not enough memory` or `Setup cannot continue`, try one or more of these methods and then try using the software again:

✔ **Turn off any antivirus software that you have on your computer.** Installers sometimes mimic virus activity and may make your computer incorrectly believe that it's being infected by a virus.

✔ **Close all running programs.** The more programs you're running, the less memory is available to other programs. Installers also typically update files and programs; if you keep other programs running, installation may not work properly.

✔ **In Windows, close the CD interface and run demos or installations directly from Windows Explorer.** The interface itself can tie up system memory or even conflict with certain kinds of interactive demos. Use Windows Explorer to browse the files on the CD and launch installers or demos.

✔ **Have your local computer store add more RAM to your computer.** This is, admittedly, a drastic and somewhat expensive step. However, if you have a Windows 95 or 98 PC or a Mac OS computer with a PowerPC or G3 chip, adding more memory can really help the speed of your computer and enable more programs to run at the same time.

If you still have trouble installing the items from the CD, please call the IDG Books Worldwide Customer Service phone number: 800-762-2974 (outside the U.S.: 317-596-5430).

Index

• Q •

• *X* •

• *Z* •

Notes

Notes

Notes

Notes

Notes

IDG Books Worldwide, Inc., End-User License Agreement

READ THIS. You should carefully read these terms and conditions before opening the software packet(s) included with this book ("Book"). This is a license agreement ("Agreement") between you and IDG Books Worldwide, Inc. ("IDGB"). By opening the accompanying software packet(s), you acknowledge that you have read and accept the following terms and conditions. If you do not agree and do not want to be bound by such terms and conditions, promptly return the Book and the unopened software packet(s) to the place you obtained them for a full refund.

1. **License Grant.** IDGB grants to you (either an individual or entity) a nonexclusive license to use one copy of the enclosed software program(s) (collectively, the "Software") solely for your own personal or business purposes on a single computer (whether a standard computer or a workstation component of a multiuser network). The Software is in use on a computer when it is loaded into temporary memory (RAM) or installed into permanent memory (hard disk, CD-ROM, or other storage device). IDGB reserves all rights not expressly granted herein.

2. **Ownership.** IDGB is the owner of all right, title, and interest, including copyright, in and to the compilation of the Software recorded on the CD-ROM ("Software Media"). Copyright to the individual programs recorded on the Software Media is owned by the author or other authorized copyright owner of each program. Ownership of the Software and all proprietary rights relating thereto remain with IDGB and its licensers.

3. **Restrictions on Use and Transfer.**

   (a) You may only (i) make one copy of the Software for backup or archival purposes, or (ii) transfer the Software to a single hard disk, provided that you keep the original for backup or archival purposes. You may not (i) rent or lease the Software, (ii) copy or reproduce the Software through a LAN or other network system or through any computer subscriber system or bulletin-board system, or (iii) modify, adapt, or create derivative works based on the Software.

   (b) You may not reverse engineer, decompile, or disassemble the Software. You may transfer the Software and user documentation on a permanent basis, provided that the transferee agrees to accept the terms and conditions of this Agreement and you retain no copies. If the Software is an update or has been updated, any transfer must include the most recent update and all prior versions.

4. **Restrictions on Use of Individual Programs.** You must follow the individual requirements and restrictions detailed for each individual program in Appendix C of this Book. These limitations are also contained in the individual license agreements recorded on the Software Media. These limitations may include a requirement that after using the program for a specified period of time, the user must pay a registration fee or discontinue use. By opening the Software packet(s), you will be agreeing to abide by the licenses and restrictions for these individual programs that are detailed in Appendix C and on the Software Media. None of the material on this Software Media or listed in this Book may ever be redistributed, in original or modified form, for commercial purposes.

5. Limited Warranty.

(a) IDGB warrants that the Software and Software Media are free from defects in materials and workmanship under normal use for a period of sixty (60) days from the date of purchase of this Book. If IDGB receives notification within the warranty period of defects in materials or workmanship, IDGB will replace the defective Software Media.

(b) IDGB AND THE AUTHOR OF THE BOOK DISCLAIM ALL OTHER WARRANTIES, EXPRESS OR IMPLIED, INCLUDING WITHOUT LIMITATION IMPLIED WARRANTIES OF MERCHANTABILITY AND FITNESS FOR A PARTICULAR PURPOSE, WITH RESPECT TO THE SOFTWARE, THE PROGRAMS, THE SOURCE CODE CONTAINED THEREIN, AND/OR THE TECHNIQUES DESCRIBED IN THIS BOOK. IDGB DOES NOT WARRANT THAT THE FUNCTIONS CONTAINED IN THE SOFTWARE WILL MEET YOUR REQUIREMENTS OR THAT THE OPERATION OF THE SOFTWARE WILL BE ERROR FREE.

(c) This limited warranty gives you specific legal rights, and you may have other rights that vary from jurisdiction to jurisdiction.

6. Remedies.

(a) IDGB's entire liability and your exclusive remedy for defects in materials and workmanship shall be limited to replacement of the Software Media, which may be returned to IDGB with a copy of your receipt at the following address: Software Media Fulfillment Department, Attn.: *Dreamweaver For Dummies,* IDG Books Worldwide, Inc., 7260 Shadeland Station, Ste. 100, Indianapolis, IN 46256, or call 800-762-2974. Please allow three to four weeks for delivery. This Limited Warranty is void if failure of the Software Media has resulted from accident, abuse, or misapplication. Any replacement Software Media will be warranted for the remainder of the original warranty period or thirty (30) days, whichever is longer.

(b) In no event shall IDGB or the author be liable for any damages whatsoever (including without limitation damages for loss of business profits, business interruption, loss of business information, or any other pecuniary loss) arising from the use of or inability to use the Book or the Software, even if IDGB has been advised of the possibility of such damages.

(c) Because some jurisdictions do not allow the exclusion or limitation of liability for consequential or incidental damages, the above limitation or exclusion may not apply to you.

7. U.S. Government Restricted Rights. Use, duplication, or disclosure of the Software by the U.S. Government is subject to restrictions stated in paragraph (c)(1)(ii) of the Rights in Technical Data and Computer Software clause of DFARS 252.227-7013, and in subparagraphs (a) through (d) of the Commercial Computer–Restricted Rights clause at FAR 52.227-19, and in similar clauses in the NASA FAR supplement, when applicable.

8. General. This Agreement constitutes the entire understanding of the parties and revokes and supersedes all prior agreements, oral or written, between them and may not be modified or amended except in a writing signed by both parties hereto that specifically refers to this Agreement. This Agreement shall take precedence over any other documents that may be in conflict herewith. If any one or more provisions contained in this Agreement are held by any court or tribunal to be invalid, illegal, or otherwise unenforceable, each and every other provision shall remain in full force and effect.

Installation Instructions

For Microsoft Windows users

1. Insert the CD into your computer's CD-ROM drive.
2. Click Start⇨Run.
3. In the dialog box that appears, type D:\SETUP.EXE.
4. Click OK.
5. Read through the license agreement, nod your head, and then click the Agree button if you want to use the CD — after you click Agree, you'll never be bothered by the License Agreement window again.
6. Click anywhere on the Welcome screen to enter the interface.

    This next screen lists categories for the software on the CD.
7. To view the items within a category, just click the category's name.

    A list of programs in the category appears.
8. For more information about a program, click the program's name.
9. To install a program, click the appropriate Install button.

For Mac OS users

1. Insert the CD into your computer's CD-ROM drive.
2. Double-click the CD icon to show the CD's contents.
3. Double-click the Read Me First icon.
4. To install most programs, just drag the program's folder from the CD window and drop it on your hard drive icon.
5. Other programs come with installer programs — with these, you simply open the program's folder on the CD, and then double-click the icon with the words "Install" or "Installer."

Discover Dummies™ Online!

The *Dummies* Web Site is your fun and friendly online resource for the latest information about *...For Dummies*® books on all your favorite topics. From cars to computers, wine to Windows, and investing to the Internet, we've got a shelf full of *...For Dummies* books waiting for you!

Ten Fun and Useful Things You Can Do at www.dummies.com

1. Register this book and win!
2. Find and buy the *...For Dummies* books you want online.
3. Get ten great *Dummies Tips*™ every week.
4. Chat with your favorite *...For Dummies* authors.
5. Subscribe free to *The Dummies Dispatch*™ newsletter.
6. Enter our sweepstakes and win cool stuff.
7. Send a free cartoon postcard to a friend.
8. Download free software.
9. Sample a book before you buy.
10. Talk to us. Make comments, ask questions, and get answers!

Jump online to these ten fun and useful things at
http://www.dummies.com/10useful

For other technology titles from IDG Books Worldwide, go to
www.idgbooks.com

Not online yet? It's easy to get started with *The Internet For Dummies*, 5th Edition, or *Dummies 101*®: *The Internet For Windows*® *98*, available at local retailers everywhere.

Find other *...For Dummies* books on these topics:
Business • Careers • Databases • Food & Beverages • Games • Gardening • Graphics • Hardware
Health & Fitness • Internet and the World Wide Web • Networking • Office Suites
Operating Systems • Personal Finance • Pets • Programming • Recreation • Sports
Spreadsheets • Teacher Resources • Test Prep • Word Processing

IDG BOOKS WORLDWIDE BOOK REGISTRATION

We want to hear from you!

Register This Book and Win!

Visit **http://my2cents.dummies.com** to register this book and tell us how you liked it!

- Get entered in our monthly prize giveaway.
- Give us feedback about this book — tell us what you like best, what you like least, or maybe what you'd like to ask the author and us to change!
- Let us know any other ...*For Dummies*® topics that interest you.

Your feedback helps us determine what books to publish, tells us what coverage to add as we revise our books, and lets us know whether we're meeting your needs as a ...*For Dummies* reader. You're our most valuable resource, and what you have to say is important to us!

Not on the Web yet? It's easy to get started with *Dummies 101*®: *The Internet For Windows*® *98* or *The Internet For Dummies*®, 5th Edition, at local retailers everywhere.

Or let us know what you think by sending us a letter at the following address:

...*For Dummies* Book Registration
Dummies Press
7260 Shadeland Station, Suite 100
Indianapolis, IN 46256-3917
Fax 317-596-5498

...FOR DUMMIES™

BESTSELLING BOOK SERIES